A COMMON MAN'S GUI...
MARKET

A COMMON MAN'S GUIDE TO THE COMMON MARKET

SECOND EDITION

Hugh Arbuthnott
and
Geoffrey Edwards

MACMILLAN

First edition 1979
Reprinted 1980, 1981, 1985
Second edition 1989

Published by
THE MACMILLAN PRESS LTD
Houndmills, Basingstoke, Hampshire RG21 2XS
and London
Companies and representatives
throughout the world

Printed in Hong Kong

British Library Cataloguing in Publication Data
A Common man's guide to the Common Market. —
2nd ed.
1. European Community
I. Arbuthnott, Hugh   II. Edwards, Geoffrey,
1945–
341.24'22
ISBN 0–333–40913–2 (hardcover)
ISBN 0–333–40914–0 (paperback)

Contents

Preface

When the first edition of *A Common Man's Guide to the Common Market* was published in 1979, its aim was to describe 'as impartially as possible, the primary objectives of the European Community and the mechanisms and policies which have been adopted to achieve those objectives.' That remains our aim in this second edition. There remains a considerable need, we believe, for a work which 'stands back from the major controversies in order to examine how and why the Community exists as it does.'

A great deal has happened in the Community since 1979. In some instances policies are barely recognisable, others are only too observably the same. However, whereas in 1979 we approached a number of experts to provide basic material on which we could work, in this edition, we have been presumptuous enough to provide the additional information ourselves. The original contributions were invaluable; for much the greater part they continue to form the basic foundation of each chapter, and we have merely built on them. We continue therefore to owe the original contributors a considerable debt. They were as follows:

David Allen, Loughborough University of Technology
Doreen Collins, University of Leeds
Geoffrey Denton, Federal Trust for Education & Research
Nigel Lucas, Imperial College, London
Malcolm MacLennan, University of Glasgow
Neville March Hunnings, *Common Market Law Reports*

John Marsh, University of Aberdeen
John Pinder, Policy Studies Institute
Loukas Tsoukalis, St Catherine's College, Oxford
Carole Cosgrove Twitchett, University of Surrey
Carole Webb, Institute of Science and Technology, University of
Manchester

However, while the above deserve credit for the original work, they cannot, of course, be made accountable for any errors in this current edition; that responsibility has to be borne solely by the two authors. Moreover, any opinions expressed in the book commit only the authors and no Government Department.

The first edition of the book was written under the auspices of the Federal Trust for Education and Research. The authors are grateful to the Trust for transferring copyright to them and encouraging them to prepare a second revised edition.

The bulk of this edition was written in the first half of 1987. Since then, a number of changes of some importance have occurred. While we have not been able fully to incorporate these in the period between submitting the manuscript and reading the proofs, we have attempted to indicate where the most significant changes have taken place.

HUGH ARBUTHNOTT
GEOFFREY EDWARDS

1 Introduction

In the perspective of 1945 the present European Community must be considered a remarkable achievement. It now includes twelve members, Spain and Portugal being the last to join, in January 1986. Another eight Western European countries are closely linked to it. Much of the history of the European Community appears as giant leaps into the political unknown, followed by some rapid back-pedalling as the enormity of the leaps became more fully realised. The 1980s, however, have seen a more avowedly modest approach adopted by the member states towards the construction of Europe, an approach reflected in the Single European Act signed in 1986.

There are, of course, many reasons which explain the phenomenon. The idea of a united Europe is far from new; throughout the centuries philosophers and statesmen have argued in its favour. But it was only after the devastation and suffering caused by the two world wars of this century that the idea became practical politics. The pursuit of national self-interest was seen by many to have been at the root of the failure of the League of Nations and the cause of war. For peace to be assured in Europe in the future there were many, especially from within the many Resistance groups, who echoed Winston Churchill's call for a 'kind of United States of Europe'. Others, preoccupied with the massive task of reconstruction, were convinced that the nation state was no longer able, alone and individually, to deal with all the problems involved. The increasing division among the wartime allies, particularly the two super-powers of the United States and the Soviet Union, lent an additional element of urgency to solving the problems of Western European reconstruction.

The later 1940s saw, therefore, enormous activity directed towards the creation of greater unity in Western Europe. Three main strands of thought became identifiable which are still present today. There were those who were convinced that only by taking the political initiative to create a federal system based on the United States of America, with for example federal control over foreign affairs and defence, would a form of government be established which could provide both sufficient strength and security. Others, while seeing a federal Europe as the ultimate goal, were more pragmatic in their approach, adopting what has often been called a functional or neo-functionalist approach. Common economic problems called for common responses. A sector-by-sector approach would ultimately create the conditions necessary for the creation of a United Europe. Still others, however, were reluctant to accede to such a pooling of authority or sovereignty, at least in the economic sphere, and looked to greater unity in Europe through closer cooperation among governments. This latter approach tended to characterise the position adopted by the Scandinavian countries and the UK. The UK for more than a decade after the war stood aside from purely European developments in the interests of pursuing a continued world role.

These three approaches towards Europe have persisted. Rarely has one been absent in the major decisions taken on Western Europe, even if one or another has been of greater influence at any particular time. They have been reflected in the policies of all the member states of the Community at some time or another, and indeed, the platforms of all the political parties within the Community.

In the face of the traditional and basically nineteenth-century concept of the nation state, the idea of an authority above national governments was almost revolutionary. International organisations established after the war to tackle the problems of economic chaos tended, therefore, to be inter-governmental rather than supranational. In 1947 the Organisation for European Economic Cooperation (OEEC) was established in response to the proposal put forward by the United States Secretary of State, General Marshall, to distribute US aid. The physical and economic devastation of Europe created the very clear and immediate need for a long-term and comprehensive strategy which, without US help, would have been extraordinarily difficult to accomplish. The OEEC was an intergovernmental body with control vested in the Council representing the member states. Decisions were, and continue to be, taken on the basis of unanimity and implemented by the member governments themselves. This structure continued when the OEEC became the Organization for Economic Co-operation and Development (OECD) in 1961 with a more world-wide membership.

Those who favoured a federal Europe were, however, extremely active. A series of international meetings bringing together large numbers of unofficial bodies and groups culminated in the Congress at The Hague in May 1948 and led to the creation of the European Movement. In most Western European countries strong pressure was exerted on governments to create a European Assembly which could foster closer union and political and economic cooperation. However, the result was a compromise which inevitably disappointed many. The Council of Europe, set up in 1949, consisted of an inter-governmental Committee of Ministers responsible to national governments and, attached somewhat loosely, a Consultative Assembly. The combination has been described as a continuous diplomatic conference and a debating society. Under its Statute, however, only defence issues are out-side its competence.

The opposition of the UK and the Scandinavians to any supranational element in the Council of Europe led the defeated federalists to concentrate their activities more in France, Italy, West Germany, and in the Benelux countries of Belgium, the Netherlands and Luxembourg. The latter three countries had already established the Benelux customs union in 1948. Federalism and integration appealed to many, not simply as ends in themselves, but as the means by which the historic rivalry of France and Germany could be transformed, and pressing economic problems might be resolved. Most important of these economic problems were the French and German coal and steel industries. These industries, considered basic to economic revival, were geographically contiguous but nationally separated. The conditions favourable to the establishment of the Coal and Steel Community arose from a French fear of a German resurgence if Germany regained sole control over its industries and the West German desire to achieve economic recovery and political respectability. Inspired by the proposals of Jean Monnet, then head of the French economic recovery programme, the French Foreign Minister, Robert Schuman, put forward his plan in May 1950 for pooling the coal and steel resources of Western Europe under a single authority and creating a single market. Although full participation was rejected by the British (who later became 'associated'), West Germany, Italy and the Benelux countries received the Schuman Plan with enthusiasm and negotiations were completed by April 1951. The Treaty of Paris, establishing the European Coal and Steel Community (ECSC), entered into force in July 1952.

The significance of the ECSC has been enormous. The supra-national element was strong: executive power lay in the hands of the High Authority which represented the interests of the Community as a whole and which was not dismissible by the Council of Ministers representing the member states. The Council, set up largely to overcome Benelux fears of being dominated by France and Germany, was conceived as a check to the powers of the High Authority, although to many it was considered a potential upper house comparable to the US Senate in a future United States of Europe. The successful conclusion of the ECSC negotiations gave an enormous fillip to the federalist cause, while the early success of the High Authority lent considerable weight to the functionalist approach towards integration and future union.

These successes, combined with the increasing threat posed by the Soviet Union, and particularly the outbreak of the Korean War, led to an attempt to establish more ambitious supranational organisations, a European Defence Community (EDC) and a European Political Community (EPC). Initially the fear of a revival of German aggression had led France and Britain to sign a defensive alliance under the Treaty of Dunkirk in 1947 and to extend that alliance to the Benelux countries by the Treaty of Brussels in 1948. The signing of the Brussels Treaty took place, however, against the background of the Communist coup in Czechoslovakia, Communist pressure on Greece, and the growing fear of a conflict with the Soviet Union. The Soviet blockade of West Berlin in 1948 led to the greater willingness of the United States to enter into alliance with the Brussels Treaty powers and the North Atlantic Treaty was signed in 1949.

The outbreak of the Korean War created further alarm over

Soviet intentions in Europe and proposals were made for the rearmament of West Germany. The model of the ECSC was therefore taken to create a European Defence Community, with a supranational framework in which West German forces could contribute to Western defences. Again, however, the British, while welcoming the development, determined to stand aside. This, together with continued fears of German rearmament, and a reluctance to concede a further loss of sovereignty, led the French National Assembly to reject the EDC Treaty in 1954. The result was the gradual development of the integrated military structure of NATO and the establishment of the intergovernmental body, the Western European Union (WEU) on a largely British initiative. The latter was in effect the Brussels Treaty revised and extended to include West Germany and Italy. It provided the framework within which German entry into NATO was acceptable and provided also for the maintenance of British forces on the European mainland.

The collapse of the EDC brought with it the automatic collapse of the European Political Community which was to incorporate both the EDC and the Coal and Steel Community. These setbacks reflected not only factors such as the temporary thaw in East–West relations between the death of Stalin in 1953 and the invasion of Hungary in 1956. It also reflected the resilience and strength of the traditional concept of the nation state, especially in France and Britain. Membership of NATO, while a significant pooling of control over national defence forces, remained acceptable as a more traditional and familiar alliance system (although even this proved too much for General de Gaulle, who withdrew French forces in 1966.) Such setbacks led to a re-emphasis on the more pragmatic functionalist approach to integration.

The second phase of integration in Western Europe took place, therefore, against a background of the failure of two grandiose schemes and the modest, but none the less profound, success of the Coal and Steel Community. When the governments of the Six met at Messina in June 1955 to appoint a replacement for Jean Monnet as chairman of the ECSC High Authority, several proposals had been prepared to relaunch the idea of closer unity. Jean Monnet and the Action Committee for a United States of Europe pressed hard for an atomic energy agency, regarding atomic energy as the most vital energy source of the future (see Chapter 9). The Benelux countries and West Germany put more emphasis on the need for economic unity and a customs union. The Italians wanted social policy and economic development as priorities. It was agreed at Messina, therefore, to set up a committee to look further into the possibilities for 'a fresh advance towards the building of Europe'. Paul-Henri Spaak, the Belgian Foreign Minister, was appointed the committee's chairman.

The Spaak Committee's report, presented in April 1956, provided the basic framework for the Treaty of Rome, creating the European Economic Community (EEC) and the European Atomic Energy Community (Euratom). The basic aim of the new Communities remained the establishment of an 'ever closer union of the European peoples'. In order, however, to avoid the possibility, so soon after the failure of the EDC, of fundamental differences arising among the Six, the supranational element of the new Communities was more limited than under the ECSC. The Council of Ministers was given a greater control over decision-making and over the new Executive, the Commission. (The supranational element remained, however, too strong for the British government, who had sent official representatives to several of the meetings of the Spaak Committee.) A customs union or common market with a common external tariff was agreed to, rather than a free trade area (which further alienated the UK). Agreement among the Six was based on the reconciliation of German industrial strength and a general *laissez-faire* approach to the economy on the one hand; and French agricultural protectionism and a *dirigiste* approach on the other. There was a belief that a common market would lead more effectively to the gradual integration of the economies of the member states. In order to underline both points, the Treaty of Rome went beyond the 'negative' aspects of integration, of dismantling trade barriers. It suggested, in the form of general principles rather than specific rules, 'positive' integration or common policies in various fields, most importantly in agriculture. Within this framework, the institutions themselves, especially the Council of Ministers, the Commission and the European Assembly, were given the task of formulating actual policies.

The Community represented a new form of organisation, based on different, sometimes conflicting, economic philosophies, pragmatism and political bargaining. It none the less proved strong enough almost at once to withstand first the challenge posed by the British and later that of General de Gaulle. Many, especially in France, considered Euratom to be of greater significance, particularly after the invasion of Suez had pointed to the unreliability of oil supplies. The UK, on the other hand, was much more concerned with the prospect of trade discrimination and therefore proposed linking the Six to a wider free trade area including all the members of the OECC. The discussions lasted a year before failing in November 1958 particularly on French opposition. General de Gaulle, who became President of France in 1958, disliked the European Community, but opposed even more the idea of linking it to a free trade area. Opposition centred on the fact that all the members of the free trade area would receive comparable trade benefits, including of course the UK, which would also retain its Commonwealth preferences. It left only the Six, however, committed to a common commercial policy and substantial harmonisation of economic and social policies. Many federalists were also opposed to the British Plan on the grounds that it would weaken the nascent Community and the momentum created towards further integration. The result was that Britain and the other so-called 'outer seven' countries (Austria, Denmark, Norway, Portugal, Sweden and Switzerland) created in 1960 the European Free Trade Area (EFTA). The aim of EFTA was not only to increase trade among its members but also to create a common position from which to treat the Community, until such time, that is, as a single Western European market was possible.

For much of the 1960s two highly diverse forces appeared in conflict over the future of the Community. On the one hand, all the member states benefited from the graduated reduction of tariffs and an increase in intra-Community trade. The stages of development foreseen in the Treaties, including the adoption of a common agricultural policy, were for the most part successfully achieved, some even before the suggested deadline, others, including the agricultural policy, only after marathon sessions of the Council of Ministers. On the other hand, resurgent nationalism, embodied so clearly in the person of General de Gaulle, appeared at times to be acting in a diametrically opposed manner, or at least against the institutional balance created by the Treaty of Rome.

The main thrust of the Gaullist challenge was against the supranational element of the Treaty of Rome and the role of the Commission. In 1960 de Gaulle took the initiative in suggesting a series of measures towards the creation of a political union, with a common authority over foreign policy and defence. Two French plans were put forward which were discussed in the Fouchet Committee, both of which were markedly different from those put forward in 1952. Both were based very firmly not on supranational control as in the EDC and EPC, but on inter-governmental agreement. Regular summits were to be held among the Heads of Government. Four inter-governmental committees were to be set up to deal with foreign policy, defence, economic and cultural affairs, with a permanent secretariat staffed by national officials. A revision of the arrangements would be held after three years.

Opposition among the other five members of the Community was unanimous, even if with some variations. While the Council of Ministers had begun to appear the dominant institution, the five did not wish to see such inter-governmentalism enshrined in a Treaty. Indeed, the five favoured a much more extensive use of majority voting. They were also concerned that the proposed revision would inevitably include a French proposal to review the Treaties of Paris and Rome and demote the Commission to a mere Secretariat. The defence system appeared to be conceived as operating outside the framework of NATO. And the Dutch and the Belgians were particularly concerned to avoid any union dependent largely on Franco-German accord which excluded the UK (which had applied for membership in 1961). Negotiations therefore broke down in 1962.

Britain's application to join the Community in July 1961 led to further strains between France and its partners. It also created serious differences within the UK. For the Conservative Government under Macmillan the dangers of standing aside from the Community had come to outweigh the possible risks of joining. An independent world role seemed increasingly expensive and not particularly successful, and the United States was clearly in favour of Britain joining. US support, although designed to help Britain, had the reverse effect. In 1962 the Nassau agreement between Macmillan and Kennedy, under which Britain bought American Polaris nuclear missiles, appeared to underwrite the US-UK 'special relationship'. It proved to be the final straw for de Gaulle, who vetoed Britain's application on the grounds of the UK's 'non-European' character and interests. The exclusion of Britain also meant that France avoided the dangers of a potential rival. West Germany under Chancellor Konrad Adenauer appeared to place at least as much emphasis on maintaining good relations with France as it did on the development of the Community and the 1963 Franco-German agreement underlined the point. None the less France's veto on further negotiations created a widespread distrust of French tactics.

A willingness also to go to the brink to protect French interests was shown most clearly in the 1965 crisis. The Commission put forward three related proposals: the completion of the common agricultural financing regulations; the introduction of the Community's own sources of revenue to replace contributions from the member states; and the introduction of European Parliamentary control over the Community's budget. The proposals thus combined the strengthening of the Commission and the European Parliament, with progress towards further economic integration. But, despite France's interest in settling the issue of the CAP, de Gaulle was violently opposed to the weakening of the position of the nation state in the interests of enhancing the authority of the Commission. When the French found it impossible to disentangle the three parts of the package they effectively boycotted the Community. Although the Five continued to meet to discuss largely routine business and to show a united front, the Community was paralysed.

The agreement drawn up in Luxembourg in January 1966 to settle the crisis tipped the institutional scales further against the Commission while, at the same time, ending de Gaulle's attempt to restructure the Community into a more acceptable mould. De Gaulle was led to reach a settlement after the French Presidential elections of December 1965, in which the General had been forced into a second-round ballot. The so-called Luxembourg compromise confirmed in many ways the institutional role of the Commission, but settled on an agreement to disagree on the use of majority voting in the Council of Ministers. France insisted, without support, that on issues of 'vital national importance' it would retain a veto.

The crisis and the compromise dashed hopes that the Community could move rapidly towards a supranational authority. Despite the uneasy truce which followed, in May 1966 there was sufficient common ground for the member states to agree that 1 July 1968 should be the date for the completion of the customs union and the CAP. The merger of the executives of the three Communities took place in 1967. But France remained in many ways isolated; for example, in refusing to continue negotiations with the UK when the Labour Government, under Harold Wilson, applied once again to join the Community in 1967.

It was only in 1969 with the retirement of de Gaulle that European integration appeared to regain momentum. It was again based in large measure on the coincidence of Franco-German views, of the new French President, Georges Pompidou, and the new German Chancellor, Willy Brandt. The goals agreed by the Heads of Government at the Hague in 1969 were, and remain, of enormous significance for the Community. They were summed up in the words: 'completion', 'deepening' and 'enlargement'.

The 'completion' of the Community took the form of member states finally agreeing to the arrangements for the financing of the CAP, and the financing of the Community from its own resources, two of the issues which had caused the Luxembourg crisis. Beyond completion however, and beyond the detailed provisions of the Treaty of Rome, the Heads of Government agreed on two major goals, economic and monetary union, and further steps towards political union. While the member states ran into difficulties almost immediately on how to move towards economic and monetary union, progress was quickly made on one element vital to the idea of political union. Although it was limited and cautious the so-called 'political cooperation machinery' to co-ordinate the foreign policies of the member states was established.

The third element of the Hague agreement was the enlargement of the Community. Negotiations opened in June 1970 with the UK, Denmark, Ireland and Norway and within a year agreement had been reached on most substantive issues. The Treaty of Accession was signed on 22 January 1972. On 1 January 1973 the UK, Denmark and Ireland became members of the Community, the Norwegian people having rejected membership in a referendum.

With the successful conclusion of the enlargement negotiations the Community seemed set for a new period of positive development. The Summit meeting held in Paris in 1972, in which the new members participated, went even further than the Hague summit in setting ambitious new goals. At the suggestion of the French President, they declared themselves in favour of creating a European Union by 1980. New areas for common action were suggested that went well beyond the Treaties, in part to meet the criticism that the Community was merely a commercial venture.

This 'human face' of the Community was portrayed not merely in the declaration that 'economic expansion is not an end in itself' but in suggested new movements towards social, regional and environmental policies.

The great leap forward suggested by the Heads of Government was almost immediately beset by problems. Inevitably the summit declaration itself had been the result of bargaining among the Heads of Government to get favoured policies included. Actual decisions had been left for the institutions to work out. Those institutions designed for the Six, had now to deal with three additional members with very different approaches and, indeed, interests. Certainly, a number of problems were exacerbated by the first enlargement. The problem of the Community's Budget and Britain's contribution to it which, in one form or another, was rarely missing from the Community's agenda between 1974 and 1984, forced such differences to the fore. British efforts to settle the budgetary problem also drew considerable hostility from other member governments, with the resulting conflict sometimes appearing as a substitute for the serious discussion of other issues. Many of the latter had been magnified by the general economic recession to which the oil price rises of 1973–4 and 1978–9 so seriously contributed.

The problems created by the recession and changes in the international economic system, not least the rise of the Newly Industrialising Countries (the NICs) have been persistent. They have had direct impact on the political as well as the economic development of the Community because the three major problems, of restructuring, unemployment and inflation have been tackled very largely on an individual rather than a Community-wide basis. The 1980s, therefore, began with some particularly gloomy prognoses that, with the member states intent upon retaining as much authority as possible in their efforts to counter such economic problems, the Community as such would inevitably stagnate.

Yet, limited though some policies have proved to be, there has been agreement over a wide range of issues within the Community. Direct elections to the European Parliament, for example, took place for the first time in June 1979, and, even if they, and the second elections in 1984, remained very largely 'national' elections in many ways, they none the less remain a unique expression of popular will in the international system. The European Monetary System has also proved a significant milestone, even though the international monetary system remains very largely dominated by the US dollar. European Political Cooperation might not add up to a common European foreign policy, but it has become a highly important factor in the foreign policies of all the member states.

Moreover, despite the pessimists of the late 1970s, the European Community retained enough attraction to cause other states to apply for membership and to suffer protracted negotiations before gaining entry. Thus even while some claimed that the problems of the first enlargement had still to be digested, Greece in 1981, and then Spain and Portugal in 1986, became members. The full impact of this enlargement to the south has still to be felt. Concern over potential problems obviously explains the duration of the entry negotiations and the Community's insistence on long transitional periods in some sectors (notably in agriculture) before the Spanish and Portuguese economies are fully integrated into the Community. But the position of the existing Mediterranean countries of France and Italy towards enlargement was ambivalent. Although they were concerned about the potential competition of the new members, especially, of course, from Spain, in terms of both trade and access to Community funds and resources, they were also aware of the possibilities of a Mediterranean block to counter the weight of the north. This applied particularly to Italy, despite its own internal division between its highly industrialised northern regions and the Mezzogiorno of the south, so that enlargement opened up prospects of a renewed emphasis on 'solidarity' and 'cohesion' within the Community and greater attention to the needs of the peripheral regions. A new negotiating pattern may therefore emerge especially on issues with a potential redistributional element. Even in the negotiations on the Single European Act (in which Spain and Portugal participated), it was clear that the less developed south had demanded a *quid pro quo* in terms of a commitment to cohesion within the Community, in return for the agreement to establish a genuine common market by 1992 which would benefit the north.

Because of the concern over the consequences of enlargement – or perhaps despite it – the 10 and later the 12 member states have made efforts to deepen their mutual relations. A number of initiatives were taken to counter the general gloom both by the newly-elected European Parliament and by member states, notably West Germany and Italy in the first instance. The European

Parliament, largely on the initiative of the veteran federalist, Altiero Spinelli, sought to further European unity less by a series of amendments to the Treaty of Rome than by changing the basic framework of member states' relations. In February 1984 the Parliament, by an overwhelming majority, approved a Draft Treaty establishing the European Union. The member states were not wholly hostile. West Germany and Italy, led by their Foreign Ministers, Hans-Dietrich Genscher and Emilio Colombo, had attempted to halt the general malaise by strengthening the institutional framework of the Community. Their Plan was not, however, successful. In negotiation, what had begun as a proposal for a new Treaty relationship, emerged as only a Solemn Declaration which was sufficiently anodyne that all heads of state could adhere to it without difficulty when they met at the European Council in Stuttgart in June 1983.

None the less, a momentum had begun to build up, encouraged by the work of the European Parliament, and, more importantly, by the resolution of the British budgetary problem at the Fontainebleau Council of June 1984. New opportunities thereby seemed to be opening up and in response the Council established two *ad hoc* committees, one on a Citizens' Europe, which later became known as the Andonnino Committee after its Italian chairman, and the other on Institutional Affairs, otherwise known as the Dooge Committee after its Irish chairman. The Dooge Commitee was made up of personal representatives of the heads of government (a way forward that consciously echoed past successes, not least the Spaak Committee of 1955). Its report tackled three major issues: priority policy areas, where it stressed the need for a genuine internal or common market, greater efforts in relation to technology and solidarity within the Community; decision-making within the Community, where despite major differences within the Committee, the majority sought to limit the use of the veto and introduce more majority voting, and to strengthen the role of the European Parliament; and ways in which these aims could be achieved, on which it recommended – although again with some dissent from the UK, Denmark and Greece, whose frequent reservations led them to be referred to as 'the footnote countries' – an Inter-Governmental Conference.

Desite their initial reluctance, the 'footnote countries' were finally persuaded to take part in an Inter-Governmental Conference on the basis of building on the existing policies of the

Community, the *acquis communautaire*, and improving the decision-making process. Each member state had an interest in gaining agreement on some policy areas; each also had interests to protect. The result was the Single European Act of February 1986. Under the Act, a number of policies are brought within a Treaty framework for the first time, most notably European Political Cooperation, but also regional, science and technology and environmental policies. Reference, albeit very brief, is also made to the European Monetary System. The Act contains commitments to both the establishment of an Internal Market and to cohesion within the Community. It also extends the number of issues on which majority voting is necessary in the Council of Ministers (including many within the framework of the Internal Market) and involves the European Parliament more intimately within the legislative process.

Because of delays in ratification – on the part especially of Denmark and Ireland, both of whom put the Act to referendum – it did not come fully into force until 1987. It will therefore be some time before the changes introduced by the Act become fully implemented. When the Act was signed, opinion appeared divided between those who regarded it as little more than a codification of what already existed which did little to satisfy demands for reform; to others, however, it marked a further if modest step in the construction of the European Community.

SUGGESTIONS FOR FURTHER READING

J. Barber and B. Reed (eds), *European Community: Vision and Reality* (Croom Helm, 1973)

M. Butler, *Europe: More than a Continent* (Heinemann, 1986)

M. Camps, *European Unification in the Sixties* (OUP, for the RIIA, 1967)

W. Diebold, *The Schuman plan* (Praeger, for the Council on Foreign Relations, 1959)

E. Fursdon, *The European Defence Community* (Macmillan, 1979)

A. Grosser, *The Western Alliance: European-American Relations since 1945* (Macmillan, 1980)

E. Haas, *The Uniting of Europe* (2nd edition, Stanford, 1968)

W. Lipgens, *A History of European Integration* (OUP, 1982)

J. Lodge (ed.), *European Union: the European Community in Search of a Future* (Macmillan, 1986)

R. Mayne, *The Recovery of Europe* (Weidenfeld & Nicolson, 1970)

A. S. Milward, *The Reconstruction of Western Europe 1945–51* (Methuen, 1984)

J. Monnet, *Memoirs* (Collins, 1978)

R. Pryce (ed.), *The Dynamics of European Union* (Croom Helm, 1987)

H. Simonian, *The Privileged Partnership: Franco-German Relations in the European Community 1969–1984* (Clarendon Press, Oxford, 1985)

A. Spinelli, *The European Adventure* (Charles Knight & Co, 1972)

P. Taylor, *The Limits to Integration* (Croom Helm, 1985)

L. Tsoukalis (ed.), *The European Community: Past, Present and Future* (Basil Blackwell, 1983)

C. Tugendhat, *Making Sense of Europe* (Viking, Penguin Books, 1986)

C. and K. Twitchett (eds), *Building Europe* (Europa, 1981)

H. Wallace, *Europe: the Challenge of Diversity* (RKP/RIIA, 1985)

F. Roy Willis, *France, Germany and the New Europe* (2nd edition, Stanford/OUP, 1968)

J. Young, *Britain, France and the Unity of Europe* (Leicester University Press, 1984)

2 The Institutions of the European Community

The European Community has often had a bad press. Its image is frequently unflattering: of a bloated and powerful Brussels bureaucracy; a Council of Ministers perpetually at loggerheads; and an ineffective yet highly paid, Parliament. All political institutions are difficult to project fairly and accurately. Those of the European Community have perhaps suffered more than most from comparisons made with more familiar national institutions, or seemingly less threatening and less exclusive international organisations, such as the United Nations. The location and dispersal of the headquarters of the Community institutions in Brussels, Luxembourg and Strasbourg have reinforced a sense of distance and unfamiliarity. It also remains true that involvement with the Community institutions is largely confined to a fairly narrow group of politicians, government officials and leaders of interest groups.

Yet in many ways the institutions of the Community are more straightforward, informal, and accessible than their British or other European counterparts. Their powers and functions are defined and limited by a legal document – the Treaty of Rome – as amended by subsequent treaties such as the Single European Act of 1986. Information on the various expert committees and working groups, which form an essential part of the everyday working life of the European Commission and the Council of Ministers, is widely available. It is not clothed in the kind of secrecy which surrounds the committee structure of the British cabinet, even if

Council proceedings do take place behind closed doors. This does not mean that the official and formal account of how the Community institutions work, how decisions are taken, and who exercises real power is the most accurate. Not only are the informal channels and political processes often of greater significance, but the Community institutions themselves have also developed in many ways quite differently from the intentions of the founders. Furthermore, it is misleading to think of the Community institutions as working in splendid isolation in Brussels. The essential characteristic of Community politics is that power and involvement in policy-making is shared, not only among the institutions themselves, but also much more widely with national governments and their administrations. Far from the European Community being over-centralised, a more accurate impression is that of dispersal and fragmentation of power and authority. This not only makes Community activity infinitely more complex, but also less remote and autonomous than is often assumed.

The political institutions of the Community are, nevertheless, very distinctive, if not unique. For example, the European Parliament is to some extent modelled on national parliaments, yet it lacks the most important power – the power to legislate – which is the *raison d'etre* of national parliaments. The Commission combines the functions of a non-political administration with the political responsibility of proposing Community legislation. Yet it too is incomplete in that it is denied the most significant power of actually taking decisions. This lies with the Council of Ministers, in the hands of national ministers who represent their separate governments. The Ministers of Foreign Affairs, Agriculture, Economic Affairs and Finance, etc., who make up the Council in its various forms, exercise the legislative power which is normally the province of their parliaments. Although there were many during the negotiations on the Single European Act, not least in the European Parliament and elsewhere, who pressed hard for the introduction of a more significant element of co-decision in the Community, the Council of Ministers does not need, nor does it depend on, a parliamentary majority for political authority or legitimacy.

This combination of checks and balances and blend of 'Community' with 'national' interests, reflected in the Community institutions, makes it almost impossible to attach any political identity tag to them. Taken together, they are neither wholly federal, confederal nor supranational. Rather they resemble a building in the process of conversion, but without an architectural blueprint of the final result.

The special character of the institutions stems partly from the nature of the European integration process itself, and partly from the political context in which they have had to operate. The formal Treaties setting up the Community, as well as the expectations of their signatories, envisaged European integration as a gradual process in which the participating states and, above all, their governments, would agree to pool more and more of their national resources and political authority. They saw the newly established institutions as the key to long-term success. The major and specially designated 'Community' institutions, the Commission, the Council of Ministers, the European Parliament, and the Court of Justice, were to form the hard core of a growing political community. Gradually, that is, the institutions would assume more responsibility, especially the Commission as it acquired greater authority in managing the common policies agreed by the member states. The Council of Ministers, itself the most schizophrenic of the institutions in its representation of national and Community interests, would gradually shed the safeguards of national suspicion and caution in the shape of the veto. The progression from unanimity to majority voting in the Council was to be both the symbol and concrete evidence of the establishment of a truly European Community.

Today, it is clear that political practice has fallen somewhat short of what the original signatories of the Treaty had envisaged. However, this had been increasingly evident even before the first enlargement of 1973, for France, under General de Gaulle, had made clear its antipathy towards majority voting. After 1973, Britain and Denmark became more closely identified as champions of an institutional balance that remained favourable to national governments and the Council rather than 'the Community' and the Commission and Parliament. After the electoral victory of Mr Papandreou in 1981, Greece, too, lent its weight on the side of those reluctant to envisage the institutional development of the Community. During 1984, in the Dooge committee negotiations Greece joined Britain and Denmark as 'the footnote countries' because of the number of their reservations. The Danish Government also considered it necessary to put the Single European Act, which embodies many of the reforms proposed by the Dooge

Committee, to a referendum. However, although otherwise in support, the Irish too found difficulty with the proposals on European Political Cooperation, fearing that these might undermine its neutrality – difficulties which eventually led to a delay in the implementation of the SEA. At the other end of the spectrum, the Italian government expressed its disappointment with the Act, agreeing to it only after the majority of the European Parliament had not opposed it.

Differences over the long-term institutional balance thus remain, even if temporarily quiescent. The reforms embodied in the SEA on majority voting and the involvement of the European Parliament in the legislative process entered into force on 1 July 1987. It is too early to assess their impact. Meanwhile, the full effects of the entry of Spain and Portugal are only now being felt.

THE COMMISSION

Of the four 'Community' institutions the Commission is the most original in conception and distinctive in composition. The Commissioners themselves, increased to 17 in 1986 as a result of enlargement, are appointed for four years, formally by common accord among the member governments, although in practice no government has refused the nominee of another. There must be at least one national from each member state. In fact there are two each from the five larger countries and one each from the seven smaller ones. The Commission President is also appointed by agreement among the member governments for a two-year term, with, normally the Presidency rotating in turn among the member countries. (In 1984, West Germany did not take up the opportunity to hold the Presidency and M. Delors, the former French Finance Minister, was appointed although France had held the Presidency in the person of M. Ortoli in 1974–76.) In 1976, following the recommendation of the Tindemans Report on European Union, the incoming President, Roy Jenkins, toured the national capitals in advance of the nominations of individual Commissioners in the hope of influencing the choice of governments, thereby increasing the authority of the Commission President and the overall cohesion of the Commission itself. However, since governments regard their right to nominate Commissioners as an opportunity to limit what they regard as the undesirable independence of the

Commission, neither Mr Jenkins nor his successors, including M. Delors, had any great success.

In spite of their dependence on governments for nomination (and renomination), all Commissioners, once appointed, are pledged to act in complete independence. They can neither seek nor receive instructions from any government. Their prime task is to represent and promote the Community as distinct from the national interest. This has not, of course, inhibited the appointment of Commissioners who have been closely involved with government and politics in their own countries. The three most recently in the post of President, Messrs Delors, Thorn and Jenkins, have all been important political figures in their own right. Their intimate knowledge of their national politics does not lie dormant on their taking office. Contact with, and access to, political channels of various kinds is, if anything, regarded as a necessity in helping to prevent the Commission from becoming too isolated. Moreover, the political stature of men like Mr Jenkins and M. Delors adds greater weight to the Community interest itself. National governments have not always nominated 'safe' men who could be relied on, if only in the general sense, to protect their interests.

British governments, for example, have consistently nominated one Conservative and one Labour politician; and so common is the practice that there was some surprise when the French Socialist Government appointed two former Socialist Ministers, Messrs Delors and Cheysson, to the Commission in 1984.

Once appointed the Commissioners are required by the Treaties to act as a collegiate body in spite of their widely differing national backgrounds and often marked political differences. They take decisions by simple majority and, following the analogy of national cabinets, they are, in theory, collectively responsible for all Commission activities. The Commissioners are supported in their work by a multinational administration organised into 20 separate departments or Directorates General (DGs), grouped together under the responsibility of individual Commissioners. It is usual, although not a strict rule, that Directors General are of a different nationality from the Commissioners in charge. The total number of officials working in the Commission has grown steadily over the years to some 11 000 (including the very large numbers of translators and interpreters), still far fewer than is popularly supposed and certainly far fewer than many single departments of national governments. Some Commission departments are, of course, more important than others. This is well reflected in the attempts by incoming Commissioners, backed by their nominating governments, to win the portfolios of attractive DGs, such as Agriculture or External Relations, and by the difficulties of maintaining a reasonable nationality ratio in these areas between the large and smaller member states.

The two parts of the Commission, the Commissioners and their officials, reflect the combination of functions which it is called upon to perform by the treaties. The Commission is both a quasi-political and administrative–executive institution. It has three major tasks, each of which brings it into regular contact with the other Community institutions, and with officials and political representatives of member states. As the chief representative of the Community interest, the Commission has the formal responsibility for initiating all policy, including the detailed drafting of all proposals for Community legislation. While it is denied the right and the resources to decide policy, it does at least enable member governments to begin to negotiate from a common starting-point. Because the Commission is dependent on the Council of Ministers' decision-making authority, it necessarily has to take the particular interests of the member states into account before drawing up and presenting its proposals to the Council. This demands extensive, sometimes exhaustive, prior consultations between Commission officials and all interested parties to a proposal. (See below, Chapter 3.) The difference between national and Community policy-making lies in the range of interests and views to be reconciled. The Commission's position is at the pivot of the process. In the last resort the Commission is required to protect and promote the Community interest. In practice this frequently means balancing or trading off several national interests with one another.

The second major task of the Commission is to implement Community policies once they have been agreed. It does this through executive action and, in very restricted circumstances, by minor legislation. The Commission also, in conjunction with the member states in the Technical Progress Committees, has the right in some areas to adjust legislation to new circumstances. The Commission plays a sometimes crucial role in implementing the Common Agricultural Policy through the Agricultural Management Committees. Although the Commission's staff has grown modestly over the last decade to keep pace with the growing administrative burden of Community activity, the Commission relies extensively on national administrations to carry out the work 'on the ground'. For example, national customs officials collect duties levied (at a Community-fixed rate) at national frontiers, even though the revenue is transferred to the Community, and not retained by national exchequers. Another example is the work of the agricultural intervention agencies, staffed by national officials, which manage the supply of agricultural produce to the market in accordance with the rules of the Common Agricultural Policy.

The third, and perhaps most controversial of the Commission's tasks, is also the most unfamiliar. The Commission is required by the treaties to be the watchdog, or 'conscience', of the Community in monitoring the implementation of Community policies in the member states, and making sure that Community obligations are honoured. The Commission is, therefore, empowered to take member states to the Court of Justice for disobeying or failing to carry out Community rules. When combined with the Commission's exclusive right to propose legislation (a right which remains even if the initial impetus behind a new measure may come from a member state), this policing role carries important political connotations, in that the Commission acts as a 'motor' of the Community. By pushing forward with the Treaty objectives and cajoling member states into agreeing to new areas of common action, the Commission can quicken the pace of European integration. On the other hand, a less than dynamic or effective Commission removes the lubricant from the political process and increases the chances of stagnation.

THE COUNCIL OF MINISTERS

If the Commission can be described as one half of the policy-making tandem, the other, and certainly the more powerful, half is the Council of Ministers. All decisions of any importance are taken by the representatives of the 12 governments in the Council of Ministers. The Commission takes part in the discussions only on a non-voting basis. Although the Treaties refer to a single Council of Ministers, it has several different compositions. The meetings of Ministers of Agriculture, Finance, Social Affairs and so on are called 'Technical' or 'Specialist' Councils because of their limited responsibility for specific sectors. Foreign Ministers are usually held to have a responsibility for the overall coordination of Community policies – although they have frequently been unable to impose their will on some of their Ministerial peers – as well as external affairs in what is known either as the Foreign Affairs Council or the General Council.

Since 1974 the institutional character of the Community has been significantly affected by the creation of the European Council. This Council, unlike the Council of Ministers, had no legal status under the Treaty of Rome. Formerly it tended to meet three times each year, although twice a year is now more common. At a minimum, the European Council has provided a regular opportunity for the heads of the twelve governments (Prime Ministers and, in the case of France, the President – together with the French Prime Minister after the elections of 1986) to meet and discuss any issues relating to the Community and other subjects of common interest. The European Council has gradually assumed a far more important role in the decision-making process of the Community than was originally envisaged, although the Council of Ministers formally remains the body responsible for taking decisions that have legal effect.

There is therefore an element of ambivalence in the role of the European Council, which owes much to its origins. In part they result from the long-standing French desire to limit the supranational character of the Community and to subject the Council of Ministers to a more obviously inter-governmental body. At the same time, however, Giscard d'Estaing when President, also wished to allow for more informal discussions on the longer-term objectives of the Community. Summit meetings had achieved such a purpose in the past. One of the most notable was that held in Paris in October 1972, immediately before Britain, Denmark and Ireland joined the Community.

It was there that existing and new members agreed on a wide range of new policy areas for the Community, and set the vain goal of full European Union by 1980. But there has also been a further element involved in the growing importance of the meetings of Heads of Government. Even before 1974, summit meetings had been considered necessary on a number of occasions to settle outstanding issues of disagreement or sensitivity. The regularisation of summits, as the European Council, increased the temptation of the Council of Ministers to send issues 'upstairs' for Heads of Government to decide on.

The increased use of the European Council as a final arbiter or court of appeal was further encouraged by factors such as the greater publicity that the involvement of heads of government attracted. European Councils also increased public expectation that member governments would find it easier to agree with one another. The results have been patchy. The British budgetary problem was, for example, finally settled at the European Council meeting held at Fontainebleau in 1984. It had, however, been on the Council's agenda almost without fail for over four years. On the one hand, the greater glare of publicity can encourage heads of government to reach agreement, to act as the supreme court of appeal in the Community. On the other hand, it can also act as a reminder to each head of government of his or her national political responsibilities.

Yet in spite of the new role of the European Council, the Council of Ministers, remains the most significant decision-making institution, if only because of the frequency of its meetings and the formal requirement of the Treaties that the Council alone is competent to take decisions, except in those limited areas where authority has been delegated to the Commission or, over part of the Budget, to the European Parliament (see below). Meetings of the Councils of Agricultural and of Foreign Ministers take place at least once a month and sometimes last up to three days. Finance Ministers also usually meet monthly. The Council in its various forms is thus almost in permanent session. And yet national ministers can devote only a part of their time to Community business; they have equally pressing domestic responsibilities. These serve as a reminder that their function in the Council is primarily to make sure that their particular national interests are recognised and taken fully into account in any decision.

The Presidency of the Council of Ministers rotates every six months among the twelve governments in strict alphabetical order, according to the name of the country in its own language. National ministers from the country holding the Presidency chair their respective Councils, and their officials chair all the Council's subsidiary bodies and working groups. The Presidency has gradually assumed considerable significance in the Community decision-making process. Its primary task, is, with the help of the Council Secretariat and in cooperation with the Commission, to arrange meetings and their agendas, and generally to coordinate business. The six-month period in office thereby provides some opportunity, albeit limited and not always taken, to bring particularly favoured issues to the Council's attention, or even to delay less favoured issues – although revised Council rules of procedures limit a Presidency's ability to stall on an issue.

Particular interests or policies can also be promoted by the Presidency either through the initiation of a proposal which is then taken over by the Commission or by paying extra attention to the possibilities of mediating among the member states and their interests, a task previously carried out largely by the Commission. The Presidency also represents the Council at meetings of the European Parliament, answering parliamentary questions and reporting on meetings. It also often represents the Community in dealings with third countries together with the President of the Commission – the so-called bicephalous Presidency. The Presidency of the Council also represents the member states in European Political Cooperation, a task commonly carried out with representatives of the immediately past and immediately succeeding Presidencies, the 'troika' (see Chapter 17).

The method by which the Council of Ministers takes its decisions is formally laid down in the Treaties, and, in theory, differs according to the issue under discussion. The Treaties envisaged gradual movement towards majority voting although on certain particularly important and sensitive issues, such as the admission of new members, amendments or revisions to the Treaties and agreement on new areas of policy, unanimous decision-making was upheld. Before the signature of the 1986 Single European Act (the SEA), which provides for wider areas of majority voting, measures to establish the Internal Market under Article 100 were taken on a unanimous basis (see Chapter 5). The possibility of majority voting in areas not referred to in the original Treaties, such as environmental policies, was also opened up by the SEA. In these and in other instances, each state's vote is weighted in proportion to its size and importance. Under this formula, Britain, France, Italy and West Germany each have 10 votes, Spain has eight votes, Belgium, Greece, the Netherlands and Portugal each have five, Denmark and Ireland have three and Luxembourg two votes. Out of a total of 76 votes, 54 are now required for a qualified majority. This prevents the smaller states from being outvoted by the larger. The accession of Spain and Portugal has also meant that two of the larger states can no longer block a decision by themselves. However, it remains the case that while majority voting has been on the increase, and has been given further encouragement by the SEA, decisions of major importance are likely to continue to be taken on the basis of a consensus.

The pace and efficiency of Council proceedings depend heavily on thorough advance preparation, the primary task of the permanent national delegations to the Community, 'the permanent representatives'. These Brussels-based missions are composed of senior officials from national administrations, the heads of which are usually seconded from national foreign offices. The Ambassadors and their Deputies meet weekly in the Committee of Permanent Representatives (COREPER: COREPER I in the case of Deputies; COREPER II, the Ambassadors). While their major task is to prepare Council meetings in advance, in between they carry out the vital and necessary task of reconciling national positions through endless discussions and contacts at the official level. Indeed, the formal, much publicised Council meetings are only the tip of the iceberg, for below COREPER are the myriad of Council working groups. As the volume and complexity of Community decision-making increases, so the number of 'expert' committees, drawn from national officials (many of whom commute regularly from their national capitals) increases. As a result, COREPER has come to be seen as a kind of substitute decision-making body. Certainly, whenever possible, less contentious issues are resolved at the level of COREPER, being passed to the Council of Ministers as an 'A' point for formal agreement without discussion. Ministers are then left with the more controversial items and the real political battles.

The institutions of the European Community are in some respects very distinctive, if not unique. This is particularly the case in the relationship between the Council of Ministers and the Commission. The incomplete nature of both bodies – the Commission can only propose, while the Council retains the right to dispose or decide – requires their continuous collaboration. One of the most vital functions allotted to the Commission was to act as a mediator among governments in the Council, both in support of its own proposals and in an attempt to reconcile opposing national positions in the construction of a 'package' which is acceptable to the Council as a whole. The Commission has, therefore, a formal right to attend Council discussions and has, indeed, often become referred to as an additional Council member, although it has no vote. In its mediatory role the Commission is now often complemented – and sometimes outshone – by the Presidency of the Council. Both rely on persuasion, exhortation and, most importantly, on the ability to offer rewards and incentives for cooperation by incorporating some, if not all, of the particular demands of each state in the final proposals or package. But the notorious marathon sessions of the Council, and the often protracted negotiations between member governments and Commission officials, indicate the relative weakness of the Commission when faced with a determined stand by one or more governments.

Since 1966 and the 'Luxembourg Compromise' (see Chapter 1) the Council has assumed the dominant role in the partnership. While the Commission's mediating function is still a significant factor in the decision-making process of the Council, the Commission has been reluctant to force a further confrontation on the issue of voting in the Council. Clashes of national interest, which have usually been the cause of so little majority voting, have limited the Commission's ability to get measures through, and in some ways have encouraged the Presidency to take a more prominent role in mediation although not always with any greater success. This undermining of the Commission's political status was taken further by the practice of holding ministerial meetings outside the formal Community framework so that the normal rules on the Commission's participation did not apply. The meetings of Finance Ministers within the European Monetary System have been a case in point. So too were the efforts to coordinate the foreign policies of the member states through European political cooperation. It was only in the London Report of 1981 of Foreign Ministers that the participation of the Commission was actually assured.

THE EUROPEAN PARLIAMENT

As the Commission is an appointed, not elected, body, and the Council of Ministers has only an indirect link with the Community electorate, the European Parliament was established (originally with the title European Assembly; it was formally changed only by the Single European Act) as the directly elected institution of the European Community. The duration of the battle after 1960 to persuade the member states to agree to direct elections was indicative of the marginal role of the Parliament in Community decision-making and its uncertain political status *vis à vis* other Community institutions. The Treaty of Rome called for direct elections to the Parliament under article 138 but it was not until the Paris Summit of 1974 that the heads of government agreed to look further into the possibility of introducing direct elections and so replacing national parliamentary nominations. It was only in 1979 that direct elections took place for the first time. Even then, there was no common electoral system; elections took place according to national procedures – which meant that in the UK (with the exception of Northern Ireland) the 'first-past-the-post' system was used while elsewhere varying forms of proportional representation (PR) were employed. Differences in electoral system reinforced the impression that nine separate national elections were taking place. The situation was not very different in 1984 when the second direct elections took place. The British Government in particular remains hostile to a uniform electoral system, largely on the grounds that the introduction of PR in such elections would run contrary to British practice and traditions – and might increase pressures for the introduction of PR in general elections. (PR was used in Northern Ireland in both the 1979 and 1984 direct elections in order to ensure the representation of both Protestant and Catholic sectors).

The Parliament of the enlarged Community is made up of 518 members. Britain, France, Germany and Italy each have 81 MEPs, Spain 60, the Netherlands 25, Belgium, Greece and Portugal 24 each, Denmark 16, Ireland 15 and Luxembourg 6. The allocation of seats, derived from a typical Community compromise, strongly favours voters in the smaller member states, especially Luxembourg, and penalises those in the larger members, particularly West Germany.

The MEPs themselves sit not as national delegates but divide cross-nationally into broad party groupings. They did so even when the Parliament was made up of 198 members appointed from national parliaments. The largest groupings are the Socialists (who have had representatives from each of the member states), the Christian Democrats (known also as the European People's Party), Liberals and Communists. The European Democratic Group which was largely made up of British Conservatives together with a few Danes have been joined by members of the Spanish Allanza Popular, leaving the European Progressive

Democrats, who are largely French Gaullists with some Fianna Fail supporters (Fine Gael being a part of the European People's Party) and the European Right (again largely French, led by M. Le Pen) as more nationally-based parties. Since 1979 there have usually been a number of independents, some of whom have joined together in order to participate more effectively in many of the Parliament's procedures. After the 1984 elections, for example, 20 MEPs from various environmental or 'green' groups joined to form the Rainbow Group.

The Parliament is not permanently in session but meets for plenary sessions, lasting five days, once a month, except in August. It now meets in Strasbourg. Meetings were at one point divided between Strasbourg and Luxembourg but the original Parliament building in the Grand Duchy became too small, and Parliamentarians seem reluctant to be drawn back to Luxembourg despite the construction of a new larger building. The headquarters and the Parliamentary secretariat none the less remain in Luxembourg. In between plenary sessions, the specialist committees of the Parliament hold regular meetings, usually in Brussels. The Parliament has suffered particularly from its travelling existence, with all the accompanying costs and inconvenience. While the Parliamentary majority have sought to establish more permanent roots for the Parliament in Brussels, most member governments, led by those of France and Luxembourg, have been opposed to any formal change of venue – Luxembourg in 1981 actually prepared to take the European Parliament to the Court of Justice to prevent it from establishing a single site. The ineffectiveness of the Parliament in the decision-making process, however, tends to be reinforced by its absence from the centre of Community political activity in Brussels.

The powers and functions of the Parliament belie both its name and role by comparison with national parliaments, despite a number of important reforms and the introduction of direct elections. It does not possess the power to legislate except on certain budgetary items. It has only limited authority to call the Community's political leadership (i.e. the Council of Ministers) to account. The political thrust of the Parliament was originally directed towards the European Commission, the putative executive of the new Community. Under the Treaties, the Commission can be removed – albeit only *en bloc* – by a two-thirds majority of the Parliament in a vote of censure. While this has been threatened on a number of occasions, it has not yet succeeded – many Parliamentarians recognise that, because their authority is only of a negative kind since they do not possess the power to appoint a new Commission, power remains in the hands of the member states.

The Parliament's main functions are advisory and supervisory. The Treaties require the Parliament to be consulted (along with the Economic and Social Committee – see pp. 42–3) by the Council. The Commission usually consults the Parliament in preparing its proposals. The two institutions tend to regard themselves as natural allies against the Council, in the 'Community' interest. Neither the Commission nor the Council, however, are obliged to accept Parliament's advice. This largely consultative role reduces the Parliament to the position of an interested, but powerless, bystander in the Council–Commission discussions. In practice, both the Commission and the Council follow the procedures of consultation rigorously. However, the Council's failure to consult (in that it did not wait for Parliament's Opinion) in the Isoglucose Case of 1980, led to the reaffirmation of the Parliament's role by the Court of Justice. That role has been further extended under the Single European Act. In the Isoglucose case (isoglucose being a liquid sweetener made from maize), the Court held that a Council regulation was invalid because the Parliament had not been able to give its opinion. Under the SEA, decisions in a number of instances, including further enlargement, need to be taken by the Council *in cooperation* with Parliament, an important if still constrained move towards 'co-decision' between Parliament and the Council. While the Isoglucose judgement suggested that the European Parliament had a significant delaying power, an idea that was built on by the Parliament itself in its Draft Treaty of European Union of 1984, the SEA limited the period of delay to three months. None the less, if the Parliament has rejected a Council position, the Council can only overturn the Parliament's vote on a unanimous vote. It must also make its reasons for rejecting the Parliament's decision known, a development on the Treaty although in the conciliation process that has evolved between Council and Parliament, the Council's reasoning usually becomes apparent.

The European Parliament appears still to be better equipped in its supervisory functions. Its procedures and effectiveness have improved markedly over the last two decades; it can now, for example, call on both the Commission and the Council to account for their actions by means of questions to both institutions and by requiring them to defend their activities before plenary sessions. A semblance of real political debate emerges when individual Commissioners and the President of the Council of Ministers are questioned in detail by members, although it needs to be recalled that the position of the Presidency is constrained by the agreement – or lack of agreement – reached in the Council. But more detailed supervision is achieved in the specialist committees; in particular the Budgetary Committee, the Committee for Agricultural Affairs and the Budgetary Control Committee (which scrutinises expenditure after the event) have been assiduous in subjecting the work of the Commission to close examination.

The one area where the European Parliament has been able to strengthen its powers is that which is traditionally most associated with parliamentary control, the power of the purse. Until 1970 the Parliament was required only to give its advice to the Commission and the Council on the content and size of the Community budget, leaving the Council largely free to determine the Community's revenue and expenditure. With the agreement on the system of 'own resources' in 1970 (see Chapter 12) the Parliament was given limited powers to determine a part of the Community budget by having the final say (subject to a two-thirds majority) over that part of the budget not already committed by the requirements of the Treaties. In practice this covers only a very small proportion of the budget, even though it accounts for expenditure on nearly all Community policies except the Common Agricultural policy. In 1986 several member states led by the UK took the Parliament to the Court of Justice for attempting to raise that proportion of the Budget beyond acceptable limits imposed by the 'maximum rate' (see Chapter 12). More significantly, the 1975 Budget Amending Treaty confirmed the right of the Parliament to accept or reject the budget as a whole. Since direct elections in 1979, the Parliament has rejected the Budget several times so that, in the absence of agreement in the Council–Parliament concertation procedure, the Community has been obliged to exist on the expenditure level of the previous year – the system of provisional twelfths – until agreement is reached.

The Single European Act appears to mark a further step towards the idea of co-decision first mooted in the 1972 report on strengthening the Parliament's powers drawn up by the Group chaired by Professor Georges Vedel of the University of Paris. From Parliament's perspective, the SEA and the 'cooperation procedures' envisaged in the Act, mark a very limited step. The Parliament itself has attempted to develop its role on two fronts, sometimes against considerable hostility on the part of some member states. First, it has attempted to explore and exploit its treaty-given powers. In this, the Parliament's right to determine its own rules of procedure has been of considerable importance, not least through establishing the practice of holding debates and passing resolutions on its own initiative on issues that lie outside the framework of the Treaties as well as within it, on, for example, defence and security questions. Secondly, the Parliament has adopted a more confrontational approach especially since direct elections. The initiative of Altiero Spinelli, the veteran Italian federalist, and the Crockadile Group in instituting the debate which led to the Draft Treaty on European Union was of particular importance. The Single European Act bears only limited resemblance to the Draft Treaty on aspects such as co-decision. To many, therefore, the Parliament has been left as, essentially, a talking shop with some limited powers over the Budget. There also remains what has become known as a 'democratic deficit': national parliaments have faced growing problems in keeping their governments accountable on Community issues, while the European Parliament has not been able to assume responsibility.

THE COURT OF JUSTICE

The fourth major Community institution, the Court of Justice, is the most supranational of the four in the kind of authority it exercises over member states. In spite of this, it is also probably the least contested. The need for a Court of Justice stems from the character of the Treaties creating the three Communities and the fundamental objective of substituting a common set of rules for separate national procedures in the creation of a common market and an economic union.

The Court's main function is to ensure that the Treaties, as legal documents, are implemented and interpreted correctly and uniformly throughout the Community. This requires the Court not merely to interpret the Treaties themselves in cases of ambiguity, but to rule, if necessary, on the activities of the Community institutions, and indeed the member states, to make sure that these do not conflict with the obligations or intentions of the Treaties (see Chapter 4).

The Court of Justice is a permanent institution with its seat in Luxembourg. There are thirteen judges, one nominated by each member state, plus one other. The President of the Court is elected from among their number by the judges themselves. The Court's decisions are taken in secret by simple majority and no dissenting opinion is published. The consequence of this is to reinforce the independent authority of the Court and its role as the Community watchdog. In addition to the judges, there are six Advocates General, for whom there is no real equivalent in English law, whose job it is to sum up in public the case before the Court and give an expert legal opinion before the judges make their ruling.

While the other Community institutions have been considerably affected by the changing political climate of the 1960s and 1970s, and the consequences of enlargement, the Court has ridden these changes remarkably well, although its workload has grown considerably. Its authority and influence over the development of the Community has been persistent, while unobtrusive. When called upon to interpret the intentions of the Treaties, the Court has generally favoured an interpretation consistent with the promotion of further integration and the expansion of the authority of the institutions of the Community.

OTHER COMMUNITY BODIES

Quite apart from the four major Community institutions, there are a large number of other institutions and more informal groupings. The Economic and Social Committee is treated below. A major innovation in terms of organisation and financial control was the 1975 Amending Treaty which set up an independent Court of Auditors to scrutinise the financial operations of the Community. The nominations of the Council of Ministers to the Court have to be approved by the European Parliament. Other bodies have grown up in an equally *ad hoc* manner, sometimes within and sometimes outside the Community framework to form part of the complex and amorphous political arena of the Community. During the 1970s, the growth of regular meetings among officials and ministers outside the formal Community framework has been a distinctive feature of Community politics. The reasons for these 'extra-Community' fora were partly that some issues, such as foreign policy, lay outside the legal competence of the Community. Officials and ministers in areas such as economic and financial policies also met, and indeed, continue to meet, regularly in wider international organisations such as the International Monetary Fund, or, in the case of the Community central bankers, have their own informal 'network'. In some cases, this involves the same ministers wearing different hats during one meeting, for example, when ministers for foreign affairs meet to discuss Community matters and then, in a different part of the agenda, discuss foreign policy cooperation. In the case of European Political Cooperation, the Single European Act brought it within the Community as such, although to a considerable extent the workings of the European Monetary System remain outside it (see Chapters 17 and 13).

The much more informal foreign policy machinery has been considered a success and at least some governments have preferred to avoid the pressures and rules of the formal Community institutions. This has given rise to a great deal of discussion on the future institutional framework of the European Community. The creation of the European Council confirms the trend away from the precise balance, created by the Treaties, between the interests of member states (represented in the Council) and the wider Community interest (sponsored by the Commission). One of the biggest question-marks hanging over the further enlargement of the Community, to include Greece, Portugal and Spain, is the effect this will have on the Community institutions. It remains to be seen if the Commission and the Council can respond to the needs and demands of the three new members as well as those of the older member states, and, at the same time, reach decisions reasonably quickly and efficiently in the interests of the Community as a whole.

SUGGESTIONS FOR FURTHER READING

S. Bulmer and W. Wessels, *The European Council* (Macmillan, 1987)

D. Coombes, *Politics and Bureaucracy in the European Community* (Allen & Unwin/PEP, 1970)

J. Fitzmaurice, *The European Parliament* (Saxon House, 1978)

J. Fitzmaurice, *The Party Groups in the European Parliament* (Saxon House, 1975)

S. Henig (ed.), *European Political Parties* (George Allen & Unwin/ PSI, 1979)

V. Herman and J. Lodge, *The European Parliament and the European Community* (Macmillan, 1978)

R. Hrbek, J. Jamar and W. Wessels (eds), *The European Parliament on the Eve of the Second Direct Elections* (De Tempel 1984)

L. Lindberg and S. Scheingold, *Europe's Would-Be Polity* (Prentice-Hall, 1970)

J. Lodge (ed.), *Direct Elections to the European Parliament 1984* (Macmillan, 1986)

A. Morgan, *From Summits to Councils: Evolution in the EEC* (Chatham House/PEP, 1976)

C. O'Nuallain (ed.), *The Presidency of the European Council of Ministers* (Croom Helm/EIPA, 1985)

M. Palmer, *The European Parliament* (Pergamon, 1981)

G. Rosenthal, *The Men Behind the Decisions* (Lexington, 1975)

For the Treaty references to the institutions see: Treaty of Rome, Part I Article 4 and Part V Articles 137–198; and the Single European Act 1986.

3 The Policy-making Process in the European Community

The European Community is probably still better known – at least in the UK – for its failure to make decisions, for taking decisions too late or for taking the wrong decisions rather than for its speed, efficiency and success in reaching a consensus among the member states. The occasion is rare when ministers emerge from a Council session with a completed, agreed agenda behind them to announce to the press that all their demands had been satisfied. Council meetings are frequently adjourned with no major decisions having been reached (although ministers might have agreed to a number of so called 'A' points, those issues resolved at the level of COREPER). Contentious issues are referred back to officials for further scrutiny, and the various interested parties regroup for another round of bargaining and lobbying. Such a picture of deadlock and delay may be exaggerated, but it retains an element of truth in some areas of Community decision-making – the annual price review of the CAP, for example, or the continuous efforts at all levels, including that of the European Council, to reform the CAP and the Community's budget.

But such a picture underestimates the difficulties, and the achievements, of this new form of policy-making among governments whose interests cannot always coincide. Some issues are, in fact, agreed relatively quickly and smoothly by ministers. Moreover, the European Council is only the political peak of the decision-making process, which tends to obscure the much wider

36

framework within which Community politics operate. Most Councils will have been preceded by extensive discussions at the Council of Ministers level, which in turn are preceded by discussions among government officials both in Brussels and among different government departments in national capitals. These will have been followed up by meetings with Commission officials who will themselves have already gone through the Commission policy-making process, and will have consulted or been lobbied by various interest groups. The formal policy process has developed into something considerably more elaborate than that suggested by the Treaties. Informally, it is even more complex.

Formally, only the Commission initiates legislation. Although the impetus behind a proposal may come from elsewhere, such as a member state or from the European Council, it is within the Commission that the outline of a formal proposal is prepared. This outline will then be used by the Commission as the basis for consultations with interest groups, both informally and via the consultative committees, to test initial reactions; and with national officials, not to commit their governments at this stage, but to take advantage of their expertise. These preliminary discussions may be routine on all sides or be used by the Commission to drum up support in anticipation of government resistance at a later stage. Alternatively, for their part, interest groups or government officials are well placed to warn the Commission of likely opposition and problems. Depending on the political sensitivity of the issue, the Commission will then decide on its detailed proposal, either through a purely formal circulation of its contents among all Commissioners, or after a full internal discussion.

The Commission's proposal is then given to the Council, which invariably passes it directly to its Committee of Permanent Representatives (COREPER). Simultaneously, the Council asks the European Parliament and the Economic and Social Committee for their opinions. This interim stage of scrutiny and commentary by political, socio-economic and official groups is, in principle, supposed to separate the more 'technical' issues from the political problems, and to resolve the former, leaving the Council of Ministers to make their final decisions. While this remains the case, certain procedural changes will be required as a result of the implementation of the Single European Act, since, in a number of instances relating to the Internal Market in particular, the Council acts 'in cooperation' with the Parliament. However, the principle remains the same, that the technical difficulties of one government are the real political problems for another. In the inevitably slow process of reconciling national interests and traditions, governments issue instructions to their Permanent Representatives to defend particular positions from the beginning. Some less contentious proposals may be resolved at the COREPER level and go to one or other of the Councils to appear as 'A' points on their agenda. Unresolved issues may be placed on a Council agenda in the hope that ministers will find some grounds for compromise. But, if the gulf between national positions revealed at official level is so great that any Council discussion would be fruitless, issues may not reach the Council for some time.

If and when proposals finally do appear on the Council's agenda, the debate is then between national ministers and the Commission, in secret. Despite the Council's role as a legislature, their deliberations remain largely confidential. There are, of course, various briefings by the Presidency to the press at large and to their own national press in particular, together with briefings by other national ministers to their press corps, so that there is frequently an abundance of information on what went on behind closed doors – much of it appearing in *Agence Europe*, which is published daily. But the continued reluctance of government, to open up Council proceedings reflects the strength of the inter-governmental tradition still prevalent in most national administrations. Few wish to reveal their policy 'hand' too early; open meetings might reduce substantially their freedom of manoeuvre and their capacity to reach a compromise. The Council is in some ways, therefore, more like a national cabinet than a legislature, even though it is creating legislation. The result of open discussion, it is argued, would bring decision-making to a complete halt as each minister, conscious of his electorate, would be obliged to defend his national position to the last. But, in making their meetings inaccessible, the Council creates considerable difficulties for pressure groups and, indeed, national parliaments, as well as the public, to keep in touch with Community discussions. So far they have been left largely dependent on briefings, either from the Presidency or other individual governments intent upon bolstering their own positions or from (often frustrated) Commission officials. It remains to be seen in the post-SEA environment, how 'officially' informative Commission officials will be when reporting to the Parliament. The Council is inevitably attempting to take decisions against often very tight schedules. It used to be a marked feature of Council proceedings that Ministers would impose deadlines on themselves, to force some kind of compromise, or at least, to refer back an issue for further investigation by their officials. The 1992 deadline for the introduction of a genuine Internal Market reverts back to that practice (although in a Declaration attached to the SEA, the member states made clear that setting the 1992 deadline did not create any automatic legal effect). The use of deadlines, however, has its origins in the original Treaty deadlines which required the Council to take decisions by certain dates. Today, deadlines are more likely to be imposed by pressure of time on busy ministers with a full agenda awaiting them in national capitals. Since 1974 there has also been the additional opportunity to delay decisions, or to allow agreement to be sought at a different level when ministers have been defeated, by passing them to the European Council. As a result, the European Council has frequently found its meetings overburdened with issues exhaustively debated but still unresolved from 'lower down the ladder'. Finally, even if the European Council has given its go-ahead, the Council of Ministers has then to agree to the text implementing the decision, even while particular Ministers might be attempting to claw back as much as possible in the national interest.

The length of time involved in the preparatory discussions and ultimately decision-making states can vary enormously, from several years to only a matter of days if the emergency is recognised by all (as in the Falkland Islands conflict of 1982 when economic sanctions were drawn up and agreed within little more than a week). Throughout the process, whether long or short, issues are rarely treated in isolation, but overlap extensively with one another, either because individual governments have deliberately chosen to link proposals to increase their leverage, or because the Commission chooses to tie together proposals into a package which will gain the necessary support.

The process is generally so slow and unpredictable because of the diffusion of responsibility and interest in almost every policy area. Each of the twelve member states has to reconcile the proposal with its own political, economic and legal traditions. The competing interests and institutions at the national levels have then to be managed at the European level while at the same time the various institutions of the Community provide their own further checks and balances. This applies not only to the formal process, but also to the wider process of consulting interests and sounding out opinions in the initial staging of preparing proposals. The process is thus not only one of considerable complexity and one demanding no little dexterity on the part of practitioners, but one in which delays and protraction are endemic. The general picture of the Commission proposing and the Council disposing of issues is thus highly simplistic.

It also has to be remembered that, compared to any national government, the Community is incomplete in its decision-making scope. The three Treaties set limits to Community competence. Any extension of Community authority into new areas can only take place on a case-by-case basis, and with the unanimous consent of all member states. Yet, at the same time, the Treaties lay down detailed procedures in some areas which the Community institutions are expected to follow. In this sense the Community's 'constitution' is quite different from that of its member states. The major objective of the Treaty of Rome involved the creation of a customs union for which detailed targets and instruments were specified in order to remove tariffs and barriers to the free movement of capital, labour and goods. Agriculture, transport and economic policies, on the other hand, were scarcely defined at all and it was left to the Commission to propose new common policies and for governments to accept them. With the end of the transitional period for the first three new members (and still with only a common agricultural policy) the detailed guidance of the Treaties was either exhausted or overtaken by events. This situation was, to some extent, foreseen under the Treaty of Rome, in that Article 235 allows for totally new policies to be agreed by the Council of Ministers, on the basis of unanimity. But the decision-making process is now much less shaped and reinforced by Treaty obligations, although the SEA does bring a number of new areas within its purview. And yet it is still the case, even after exhaustive discussions on 'European Union' that there are opposing concepts of what union might entail and what should be undertaken at Community level.

The SEA also extends the degree of uncertainty into the decision-making process itself. The additional opportunities for majority voting (even with the safeguards that were sometimes re-emphasised in the provisions relating to the Internal Market) increase the need for individual member states to ensure that there are enough like-minded members to get a proposal passed or to block it. There is, in other words, an even greater need to build coalitions and alliances; there are fewer occasions on which a member state can simply rely on a veto. Given the propensity within the Community towards package deals, negotiating and bargaining skills will be at an even higher premium; alliances built on single issues, for example, may be too transient. If the European Parliament, say, under the new procedures laid down by the SEA, were to reject the Council's common position, and its amendments were accepted by the Commission and resubmitted to the Council, the amended proposal can be adopted by the Council on a qualified vote (it would require unanimity to change it). It presents the possibility of delicately-constructed deals coming unstuck as new pressures are brought to bear in circumstances that are constantly changing.

The implications of such changes can of course be exaggerated. The forces of inertia are strong. Perhaps equally strong, however, may be the determination of the Commission and the Parliament to explore the possibilities opened up by the SEA.

At the same time as internal Community negotiations threaten to become more complex, there remain the problems or pressures that are beyond the control of the member states. The fault may not always or even exclusively lie with the member governments. On some issues such as the international monetary or trade systems, the decision-making process inside the Community may be only a preliminary to international negotiations or may be dependent on decisions taken on a wider international scale.

COMMITTEES OF OFFICIALS

The complex network of committees made up of officials which has grown up around the formal Community institutions tends to reinforce the bureaucratic image for which the Community is regularly criticised. Yet, in many ways, this committee network only reproduces the procedures and channels of communication familiar at the national level. Governments rely on the expertise and advice provided by their civil services for making decisions. The many committees of government officials at the Community level, from COREPER to the highly technical working groups set up within the Council structure, are a predictable and unavoidable consequence of the attempt to coordinate national policies in which there is considerable government intervention, whether legal, administrative or economic.

Apart from the consultative committees, whose advice the Commission seeks when drawing up its proposals (see below), there are several other important committees of officials which play a vital role in the implementation of Community decisions. The functions of these vary from sector to sector. In an important sense they bridge the gap between the Commission and the member governments, with the latter advising or assisting the Commission in its management function – while at the same time being able to keep an eye on what is going on. The Commission chairs the management committees of the Common Agricultural Policy, for example, and the committees administering the Regional and Social Funds. There are also consultative committees midway between the Commission and the Council with both official and interest group representation. Some provide a sounding board for policy initiatives in major areas, where co-ordination of policy by the Community is just beginning. A foremost example of these is the Standing Committee on Employment, which has representatives from both the Commission and member governments as well as from both sides of industry throughout the Community (see Chapter 11).

INTEREST GROUP COMMITTEES

The channel specifically provided for under the Treaties for interest-group representation is the Economic and Social Committee. The Committee's composition and function is very similar to the committees created in France, Belgium and the Netherlands after the war to enable governments to discuss economic and social legislation in advance with those groups directly affected. The Economic and Social Committee now has 189 members appointed by the twelve governments to represent the interests of three main groups, the employers, trade unions and the so-called 'general interests', which include professional, consumer, agricultural and commercial interests. Each national delegation to the Committee broadly reflects this tripartite division of interest, although there have been complaints that this has been insufficiently adhered to. Members are appointed in their personal capacity and not as delegates of their particular organisation. To some extent, the members reflect the importance attached by governments to the particular interest group or organisation and the more general attitude towards the Economic and Social Committee itself.

In spite of the range and level of socio-economic interests represented in the Economic and Social Committee, its role in the decision-making process has remained purely consultative. Both the Commission and the Council of Ministers consult the Committee on almost every issue and since 1972 the Committee has been able to act on its own initiative in forwarding its views to the Council and speaking out in favour of changes in some areas of Community policy. Nevertheless its views and arguments, sometimes impressively documented, seem only rarely to be taken notice of, by the Council at least. The Committee's rather cumbersome procedures are frequently overtaken by the pace of the negotiations in the Council and the informal deals behind the scenes between governments. The Committee is, furthermore, very much an umbrella organisation. Lacking the teeth or leverage of governments or the Commission, it has great difficulty in exercising real influence at any stage of the policy-making process except perhaps on highly detailed issues where its expertise proves particularly valuable.

Two factors above all explain why the Economic and Social Committee tends to be by-passed. The first is the increased significance achieved by the directly-elected European Parliament. Not only has it sought to increase its powers and influence *vis à vis* the Council and the Commission, but it has succeeded in attracting the attention of many interest groups so that they now lobby the Parliament as well – and perhaps even more intensively. The second factor in the relative eclipse of the Economic and Social Committee has been the simple growth of other consultative committees. While farmers' groups, trade unions, employers organisations and consumer associations are represented in the Economic and Social Committee, they have also sought more direct means of exerting influence on Community policy. One of the most prominent features in the evolution of the European Community has been the growth of a kind of parallel 'non-governmental' Community of interest groups, some of which have set up elaborate Community-wide organisations and permanent headquarters in Brussels to monitor the work of the Community institutions.

Some 500 groups have been estimated to be active in one form or another at the Community level. Many have a dual function in that they are used both to transmit the views and demands of their members to governments and the Commission, and to scrutinise and respond to initiatives and proposals for Community legislation. In all the member states some sectional interests such as the farmers, trade unionists and employers have been well organised and have in the past benefited from close consultation with their governments. The need for these groups to coordinate their activities across national frontiers emerged very early in the development of the Communities for two main reasons. The first was the reaction of groups like the industrialists and farmers who shared a common interest, both in protecting themselves against the changes involved in the lowering of tariff barriers and the setting up of a common agricultural policy, and in trying to ensure that new policies would be to their advantage as far as possible. Trade unions have had a positive interest in common measures to improve the position of workers threatened with loss of jobs. Secondly, the Commission itself played a crucial role in stimulating the organisation of interest groups across national frontiers by refusing to deal directly with specifically national groups. Its strategy was based both on the need to avoid duplicating discussions on the same topic with separate national groups, and on the desire to encourage the emergence of a Community interest on the part of the interest groups themselves. This ensured the rapid creation of new Community organisations by the best organised and most affected interests, although the voicing of separate national and 'particular' needs has not diminished.

Among the largest and best-established of the Community-wide pressure groups is COPA, the *Comité des Organisations Professionelles Agricoles*, representing farmers (not farmworkers) and grouping under its umbrella influential national farmers' groups such as the National Farmers Union in the UK, the French *Fédération Nationale des Syndicates d'exploitants agricoles* (FNSEA) and the German *Bauern Verband*. For the employers' organisations, UNICE, the Union of Industries of the European Community, acts as spokesman for national bodies such as the CBI in Britain and the French *Patronat*. In addition, sectoral interests are also represented by influential organisations such as COMI-TEXTIL, representing national textile manufacturers and the European Council of the Chemical Industry Federation. On the

trade union side, the organisation of a single Community federation was severely hampered by the existence of several international trade union bodies which reflected political and religious
schisms in national trade union organisations throughout Western
Europe. However, the enlargement of the European Communities
brought new demands for a single trade union voice. In 1973 the
European Trade Union Confederation was formed on the initiative
of the TUC, embracing both Christian and non-Christian trade
unions and, eventually, representatives of the major Communist
unions in France and Italy. Strong Community-wide pressure
groups have generally built on the organisations of their members
in individual countries. The weakness and uneven organisation
of consumer interests in many Community countries explained
the absence for so long of any influential European consumer
organisation.

Both the effectiveness and representativeness of the Community
interest group organisations vary greatly. Although some like
COPA and UNICE have central headquarters and elaborate
procedures for drawing together the interests of their various
national groups, most are, in practice, loose-knit organisations,
frequently divided amongst themselves over immediate and
longer-term priorities. Thus COPA has often been split on national
lines over suggestions to reform the CAP, although on general
principles, such as the maintenance of farmers' incomes during
rapid inflation, it has tried to make use of its combined strength
and numbers to make its case in Brussels. Another factor inhibiting
the effectiveness of the umbrella organisation, arises from the
nature of the policy consultation and decision-making process
associated with the Community. The point at which decisions are
ultimately made – in the Council of Ministers – remains the most
inaccessible to Community groups, given the confidentiality of
Council meetings and its heavily-weighted national concerns.
Interest-group pressure is more likely to be effective at the other
end of the decision-making chain and lobbying Commission
officials on a regular basis is one of the main tasks of the Brussel-
based organisations.

Although the Commission still formally maintains its preference
for consulting only Community-wide interest groups, lobbying at
the Community level is, of course, not the only channel available
to interest groups. For many their ability to influence their own
government and parliament still remains the decisive factor. For

some vulnerable sectional interests – German small-scale farmers UK fishermen, or Belgian coalminers – their only chance may lie with pressing their case for special treatment with their own governments rather than see their particular need overtaken by the enthusiasm of the Commission and their competitors for a particular Community policy.

The internal machinery of governments has been quite significantly affected by the existence of the Community. Community issues cannot be conveniently classified into foreign or domestic categories or be clearly assigned to one government department or another. Most governments have had to introduce new internal methods of coordinating their positions on Commission proposals. The need for coordination is not purely, or even primarily, administrative. Participation in Community decision-making has involved national foreign ministries heavily, involved domestic departments such as agricultural ministries, and prime ministerial offices in domestic battles for the decisive influence over the preparation of national positions and the handling of Community negotiations. The French and British have developed centralised coordinating machinery. The Germans have settled for a more decentralised approach. A common reaction on the part of all governments, however, has been to try to confine divisions on Community proposals to 'home' discussions and to prevent them from surfacing in Brussels and so weakening a government's bargaining position. Most governments are also under great pressure from their domestic lobbies, either parliamentary or otherwise, to defend particular interests. This not only forces governments into choosing priorities but requires them always to appear to be in control of Community negotiations, or at least not to appear to be defeated.

Undoubtedly the losers in the quest for influence over Community decision-making are the national parliaments. This has been regarded as particularly unsatisfactory in view of the hitherto marginal role of the European Parliament. National parliamentary involvement has suffered partly because the Council of Ministers 'legislates' directly in areas such as agricultural policy, and partly because Community negotiations are confined to the executive or

to discussions between officials and interest groups. To some
extent complaints that parliaments are bypassed in Community
decision-making, made for example by many in the UK House of
Commons, lack consistency. Parliament's role in the detailed
administration of areas such as agricultural, commercial and
industrial policy was already weak before Britain joined the
Community.

National parliaments remain at an enormous disadvantage,
therefore, in attempting to participate in the Community process,
either by influencing negotiations in the Council of Ministers via
national governments, or by monitoring Community decisions.
In view of already overcrowded parliamentary timetables little
opportunity exists for Community issues to be debated. Debates,
even when they take place, are unlikely to be so timed or treated
by ministers as to tie their hands in Council discussions. Some
national legislatures have tended to rely, for information especially
on informal exchanges with their national MEPs. Others, however, have been more concerned to maintain or reclaim influence
over their executives. The Danish parliament, which because of
domestic political alignments and persistent reservations about
Community membership, has the most powerful parliamentary
body, the very active and vigorous Market Relations Committee.
The Committee cross-examines Danish ministers before Council
meetings and requires their adherence to a negotiating mandate
that can only be altered with the agreement of the Committee.

For the most part, the Danish committee is exceptional in that
national parliamentary scrutiny is either retrospective or limited
in impact or both. In Britain, the House of Commons and the
House of Lords both have scrutiny committees, that of the Lords
being generally the more successful in drawing public attention to
particular issues because it can report in detail on the substance of
proposed Community action. The House of Commons Committee
has a more limited remit and can only recommend that a proposal
be debated by the House before adoption; it cannot itself report on
the merit of proposals. The House of Lords' reports are frequently
well-researched and carefully argued. The House of Commons
committee, after initial problems over its role and hidebound by
party disagreement over British membership of the Community,
now has an effective scrutiny system although its impact is often
limited to causing ministers to delay their agreement to Community legislation. Other national parliaments, such as the

Bundestag, have appeared to be in a dilemma, reluctant to insist on having a powerful role lest it then adversely affects the position of the European Parliament, yet keenly aware of the European Parliament's lack of influence.

The decision-making process has altered considerably from the early days of the European Community in response to changing political attitudes, administrative demands and different policy needs. It is far from being the autonomous and self-sustaining process anticipated by the founders of the Community. It is also somewhat less than efficient and effective in producing decisions quickly and appropriately to meet what are frequently cited as urgent Community needs and interests. At the same time the visible deficiencies of Community decision-making mask the extent to which twelve governments have been prepared to alter their policies and practices to fit into a wider-than-national framework. Although most Community decisions take a long time to emerge, the great majority of them are ultimately accepted.

SUGGESTIONS FOR FURTHER READING

A. Butt-Philip, *Pressure Groups in the European Community* (UACES, 1983)

G. Ionescu (ed.), *The New Politics of European Integration* (Macmillan, 1973)

R. Pryce, *The Politics of the European Community* (Butterworth, 1973)

J. Richardson, *Policy Styles in Western Europe* (George Allen & Unwin, 1972)

C. Sasse *et al.*, *Decision-making in the European Communities* (Praeger, 1977)

H. Wallace, W. Wallace and C. Webb (eds), *Policy-making in the European Communities* (2nd edition, J. Wiley, 1983)

4 Community Law

The law of the European Community is, by and large, similar to any other legal system. What is peculiar about it is that it is not only a self-contained system of its own, running side by side with national legal systems (much as English and Scottish legal systems have operated in parallel), but it is also closely intertwined with the laws of the individual member states. In this way it follows the basic pattern in all Community affairs: the Community concerns itself with policy and rules, while their execution is the responsibility of the member states. This interrelationship is clearly revealed by the nature of Community law. The influence of national laws is strong. In the field of restrictive practices, or competition law, Community rules are heavily influenced by German (and even American) ideas and practices. But Community law does not make up a complete code covering the whole field of, say, company law, which wholly replaces national law. Community law, therefore, needs to be seen in the context of the national laws of all 12 member states.

This interdependence is even more marked in the process of creating new Community law. The formulation and taking of decisions involves a continuous interaction between Community and national organs. Similarly, judgements of the European Court of Justice evolve out of an amalgam of the differing national legal experiences of the 19 Justices (the 13 judges and six advocates-general), supplemented by a conscious turning to general legal principles common to all national systems, or to special principles from only one or two, where they seem most appropriate.

Community law is thus eclectic and *ad hoc*. The basic rules are in the Treaties. But neither these nor subsequent legislative or judicial decisions add up to a complete system of law – not even in the areas of agriculture, restrictive practices, or social security. The shape of these laws remains flexible and open to fairly far-reaching change as time goes by.

THE SHAPE OF COMMUNITY LAW

The range of institutions, committees and groups of the Community allow it a considerable flexibility in responding to social, economic and political forces. In law it is the same. The Community has a range of legal instruments at its disposal far wider than even the most advanced and complex societies. Since the political nature of the Community is itself extremely complex, there is fortunately an almost perfect balance between the political forces and the legal instruments available to reflect them.

There are three classical sources of law. These are, first, a written constitution; second, legislation; and third, case law, or the law as declared by the judges. There is a shadowy fourth source in the rules deriving from international law, particularly international treaties. The Community has all these, even the last. In this it follows the pattern of federal states, which also have a complicated power structure, which needs to be reflected in their legal forms. The Community, however, being even more complex than federal states, takes these structures a stage further.

1. *The Constitution*

The supreme law of the Community is its Constitution, the treaties setting up its three parts – the Coal and Steel Community (1952), Euratom and the Economic Community (both 1957). These three treaties have been supplemented by a number of others such as: the Merger Treaty (1965); the Budgetary Treaty (1970); the European Audit Court; and the Treaties of Accession – of 1972 when Britain, Ireland and Denmark joined the Community, of 1981 by which Greece joined, and of 1985 when Spain and Portugal acceded; and the Single European Act of 1986.

These form the written constitution of the Community, setting out: its form of government (the institutions and their powers); its legal structure; the guiding principles; the framework for the basic 'common policies' (agriculture, external trade, transport); the 'four freedoms' which are taken for granted in most Western states but are, at present, the most important elements of Community law (the freedom of movement of goods and of persons, of services and of capital); and certain special rules of ordinary law, such as those on restrictive practices.

It is from this Constitution that all other Community powers derive, and all laws are tested against it. As with most federal states, this testing is done by the judiciary. But the Constitution is not only the supreme law within the Community, as such. It is also the supreme law within the member states. Gradually, one by one, the supreme courts of each of the original Six member states have held this to be so. The process has been long drawn-out (the French Supreme Court did not get around to it until 1975–17 years after the founding of the Community). In part this is because time is needed for national judges to become accustomed to the idea that their national law is no longer untrammelled by any rules other than those decreed by their own national parliaments. The concept of the supremacy of Community law has caused particular problems for the British in view of the theory of parliamentary sovereignty, under which one Parliament cannot bind its successor. While a number of judges have pointed to the problem that could be created if Parliament passed legislation that was inconsistent with Community legislation and therefore inconsistent also with the 1972 European Communities Act by which Britain entered the Community and accepted the obligations of membership, British courts and tribunals have gradually accepted Community law as overriding contrary rules of English law.

There are exceptions to this rule of predominance. Germany and Italy have special 'Constitutional Courts' whose function is to protect their national constitutions against inconsistent legislation and conduct by the state. These have both held that the Community does indeed take precedence, even to the extent of upsetting the balance of power between the state and the federal *Länder* in Germany. But both countries have a Bill of Rights entrenched in their constitutions, which neither constitutional court has abandoned. Both, therefore, have reserved these fundamental human rights from the overriding power of Community law, until such time as the Community itself has its own Bill of Rights, which can then take over the burden of protecting the individual. The fact that all the member states have ratified the European Convention on Human Rights (drawn up under the auspices of the Council of Europe in 1950) adds a certain complication since there is some uncertainty as to the precise relationship between the laws of the Community and the rules of the Human Rights Convention. The Community itself has been moving slowly towards adopting its own code on human rights. This has been done partly by the European Court saying so as a general principle (although it has never applied such rights in order to strike down Community legislation), and acknowledging, especially in this field, that national constitutional rules are a source of the general principles of Community law. Intense interest in the protection of human rights was re-aroused during the second round of enlargement negotiations because of the relative fragility of democratic institutions in the applicant countries. The institutions of the Community, including the Court, responded in 1977 by solemnly declaring that they follow the principles of the European Convention in their conduct, although the statement as such has no overt legal force. The area remains therefore one in which there have been some strong pressures on the Community to develop its principles further. Human rights featured prominently, for example, in the European Union. The Single European Act, however, restricts to the Preamble its references to the European Convention on Human Rights and Fundamental Freedoms and to the European Social Charter.

2. *Legislation*

While the Constitution is mainly occupied in setting out the framework and general principles, and remains relatively unchanging, legislation spells out the detailed rules and is much more volatile. The Community has a very wide range of legislative instruments and two main legislative organs: the Council and the Commission.

The Council, in taking decisions, is the 'legislature' of the Community and thus is the equivalent in this respect of national parliaments (the European Parliament remaining largely consultative). The Commission exercises delegated legislative power and thus is the equivalent of the national government. Council regulations are similar to Acts of Parliament; Commission regulations are similar to statutory instruments, promulgated by a minister or, as orders-in-council, by the government as a whole. As in the UK, a Commission regulation must comply with the outline rules and powers set out in the enabling Council regulation, and can be attacked for going beyond its powers if it does not.

The 'regulation' is the standard type of legislation in the Community. It has direct binding effect on the individual in the same way as an Act of Parliament or statutory instrument and is their exact equivalent. It is, therefore, the most direct type of law there can be (to talk of a Council regulation as 'secondary legislation' – as is commonly done in Britain – is misleading). Regulations are used widely to lay down the detailed rules for the customs union and other important legal sectors contained in the Treaties, such as agriculture, transport, social security, competition. In the case of coal and steel it is called a 'general decision' but has the same effect. The great majority of regulations are issued by the Commission and concern either customs duties or the agricultural pricing system, most of which are of only limited duration (sometimes even a matter of days), and are, therefore of interest only to a very restricted group of people, mostly importers and exporters. Some, however, are of major significance (and picked out in bold type in the *Official Journal* of the European Communities to make them stand out from the majority). Regulations 1408/71 and 574/72, for example, provide a full Social Security Statute for workers who work in more than one member state. It is under these regulations that, e.g. an Englishman who has been working for a year in France or Germany can be entitled to social security benefit when he returns home as if he had never been away. Nevertheless, the main branches of law are not at present normally affected by 'regulations'.

But there is a second Community instrument, the 'directive', which is to be used to spell out other principles. The directive is described in Article 189 of the Treaty of Rome as 'binding' as to the results to be achieved, upon each member state to which it is addressed, but shall leave to the national authorities the choice of form and methods'. It is an indirect form of legislation which does not become binding on the citizen until his government or parliament has transformed it into national law. Thus, the First Company Law Directive became part of English law, not immediately on publication in the *Official Journal* (which would have been the case had it been a 'regulation'), but when it was passed as section 9 of the European Communities Act, 1972, an ordinary Act of Parliament. The original idea of the 'directive' was to enable the individual member states to translate that Community law into their own legal language, and to leave them discretion as to how they did it. It is a flexible instrument and reflects the active part played by member states in the Community legislative system.

The difference between directives and regulations has, however, become blurred. Because of certain provisions in the Treaties, directives have been used to a great extent to unify manufacturing standards (e.g. motor car components), where the directive has been so detailed that the member states have had no scope or discretion to do anything other than just say: 'So be it.' The European Court of Justice has also held in a number of cases that directives can be relied upon directly in the courts. Three grounds have been cited by the Court: the precision of the directive; its unconditionality in application; and whether the time limit allowed to the government to implement it had expired. In a test case brought by the Federation of Dutch Industries in 1977 which related to a precise if minor detail of the Second VAT Directive, the Court of Justice held that, although the Community rule was only a directive, the taxpayer could rely on it rather than the national law which brought it into effect but which had a slightly different meaning. In a judgement in 1986 on the dismissal of an Englishwoman who had reached the age of 60, the Court held that the directive on equal treatment was both precise in meaning and unconditional in its application and applied to both the public as well as the private sectors. There have also been a number of cases, such as the Ratti case of 1979, where, through the failure of a national government to implement a directive, the Court has held that it should be directly effective. In view of the substantial areas of law covered by Community directives, but which are not always identified as such, this has been a highly significant development by the Court.

This is important, for many substantial areas of law are being covered by directives. There are now Community directives on banking, insurance, doctors and nurses, lawyers, companies, rights of workers, adulteration of food, consumer protection, road transport, value added tax; there are proposals for directives on consumer credit, doorstep sales, product liability, company taxation, stock exchange transactions, agents. Many English implementing instruments do not identify their Community origin: but, whether they do or not, it is open to a citizen to query the meaning, or even the applicability of some of their provisions, if they do not seem to conform to the provisions in the Community directives.

The third type of legislation takes the form of 'legislative treaties'. In Community law there are, in fact, three types of treaty. A treaty is a legally binding agreement between states and is usually to be found at the level of international relations. That is why, when the Community was created by the six original member states, it took the form of treaties between them. Those treaties now make up the Community constitution, but still keep their inter-state international character. Amendments to them have to take the same form. The second type of Community treaty is the traditional international law one. It is a treaty entered into between the Community, on the one hand, and other non-member states, on the other, e.g. the trade treaty between the Community and India. The third type is the 'legislative treaty'. This is a treaty entered into by all the member states and by no others. Its purpose is to lay down legal rules which shall bind all the member states as part of Community law and, as such, is very similar to a directive. The choice of this form, instead of a directive or a regulation to legislate on a given subject, depends either on the seriousness of the subject matter or on specific requirements in the Treaty of Rome. Like a directive, it does not automatically form part of national law but, for the most part, has to be transformed into national law by the government or parliament. This, in the UK for example, can be done either by a statutory instrument defining it as a 'Community treaty' under section I of the European Communities Act, 1972, or by passing special UK legislation to make its provisions part of British law, as has to be done with any other ordinary treaty to which the UK is a party. Among the few legislative treaties so far agreed, the Community Patent Convention of 1976 was implemented by the 1977 Patents Act.

3. *Case Law*

The law is not only set out in written documents. Even if it were, it would still be necessary to interpret it and actually to apply it in practice. Much of the work of the courts is in deciding whether a particular set of circumstances is covered by one law or another law or no law at all. While doing this, the courts also find it necessary from time to time to state general principles (which are not contained in any of the written laws, but which are deduced from them and from the general legal climate) to help them to give a decision in the case before them.

In England such principles, and the individual sets of circumstances giving rise to them, are a source of law in themselves, which other lower courts are required to follow. A large body of English law has been developed by judges over the centuries and gives way only to Acts of Parliament. This approach is peculiar to English law and those legal systems derived from it (the 'common law') such as American or Australian.

The continental attitude is different, and indeed the French Civil Code specifically forbids a judge's ruling to be taken as a source of law. Nevertheless, the sheer practicalities of judging have caused some element of this to be followed in practice in most countries. In Germany a small district court can go its own way unless it is overruled by a higher court. In France, although in theory the small courts have the same independence, in practice the prestige of the Supreme Court (the *Cour de Cassation*) is so great that its decisions and rulings will normally be followed just as a county court follows the law laid down by the House of Lords in England.

The situation in the Community is interesting, because it was founded by six continental countries which followed a Franco-German approach. Nevertheless, because the Community is new and its law is still at an early stage of development, its legal system is little more than a set of bones. The only institution of the Community that can flesh out its skeleton is the Court of Justice, which does so by referring back to the words of the founding fathers and the 'guiding principles' to be found in the constitutional treaties. Whole branches of law have thus been developed by the European Court out of very sparse provisions in the Community Treaties such as the law on restrictive trade practices or the breaking down of the barriers to trade across the internal national frontiers of the Community. These have been accepted by courts everywhere in the Community as laying down the law for them. The French and German Supreme Courts have even said so expressly.

4. *International Obligations*

In English law this fourth category would not be a source of law at all. International treaties to which the UK is a party are kept firmly out of the internal legal system. If the treaty contains rules which are intended to affect individuals (whether private persons or businesses), then the government puts them into a Bill or an Order and they are made part of English law through legislation in the usual way. Elsewhere in the Community there is a much more welcoming approach to international obligations. As a general rule, if the state becomes bound by a treaty at the international level, then at the same time it becomes binding as part of the internal law of that state. The text of the treaty is published in the official gazette of the country and then forms part of its law.

The position of treaties in the Community system is not yet entirely sure. It seems, from a series of decisions by the European Court, that international treaties to which the Community as such is a party will be regarded as a direct part of internal Community law. Thus the free movements of goods between Greece and the Community under the Greek Association Treaty was secured even if there was no specific Community regulation on the particular point.

However, there is still a difference between treaties and other forms of written law. By its nature, legislation is usually of direct relevance to the individual and consequently has a direct effect upon him. This may not always be so. An Act of Parliament giving power to county councils to build roads will not entitle any private motorist to sue the council for not building a particular road. Such a law operates on a governmental or administrative level but not at a private level. In the case of treaties, most of their provisions will be at governmental level and only occasionally will their provisions be suitable for private individuals to involve themselves. There has developed (particularly in the United States) a whole series of rules to determine whether a given treaty provision gives rights to individuals or not. The European Court of Justice has followed the same line in deciding which articles of the constitutional treaties directly affect individuals, and now seems to be doing the same with international treaties. It held the Greek Association Treaty provision to be enforceable at the instance of a private importer; but in another case it held that an article of the General Agreement on Tariffs and Trade (GATT) was, because of its nature and context, not capable of giving rights to individuals but only to governments (including, of course, the Community government).

As a source of law, then, international treaties must be approached with caution. But they should not be ignored. And in some cases, for example the Free Trade Agreements between the Community and the EFTA countries (Sweden, Norway, Switzerland, etc.), they may provide some very important rights for traders.

THE APPLICATION OF COMMUNITY LAW

As Community law is part of the law which directly affects individuals, it is for the most part left to the usual procedures within the member states to handle its enforcement. The only exception is in the field of competition and particularly restrictive trade practices, where the Community rules are enforced by the Community itself. This is done by one of the Departments of the Commission: Directorate General (DG) IV, which has its own investigation division (with powers to obtain information and even to enter commercial premises and inspect documents). If the Commission considers that a firm has violated the Community rules on competition it is required to hold an oral hearing (somewhat similar to proceedings before an English administrative tribunal) at which the firm can argue its case, and then the Commission will issue a formal decision (which may go so far as to impose a fine). The firm can then appeal against the decision to the European Court of Justice.

The European Court of Justice is not a court of appeal from national courts; it is not 'above' for example the House of Lords. It stands alone, but it has very important links with national courts. Like most supreme constitutional courts, the European Court has a high constitutional function to enforce Community law against defaulting member states or the Community institutions (Commission and Council). This form of litigation is, however, reserved to governmental organs, and private individuals or firms have no access to it. The latter do have a right of access to the Court as a form of administrative control, in order to test the validity or correctness of decisions of the Commission taken against them. This is how one 'appeals' to the Court in restrictive practice cases. Since national courts apply, with little difficulty, Community law in the same way as they apply their other law, individuals are involved in Community law without necessarily realising the fact.

There is one difference, however. A national court faced with a relevant point of Community law may (or in some cases must) refer a question to the European Court to find out what the Community law means or whether a Community regulation or directive or decision is even valid (this is called 'Article 177 procedure'). There have been cases where the sole point at issue was one of Community law and the national court has immediately referred it to the European Court for an authoritative ruling, rather than waste time deciding it itself and perhaps seeing the parties go on to appeal. For such a decision of the European Court is final and binding on the particular point at issue. In this way, the meaning and content of Community law is kept uniform and it is not open to national judges to interpret it each in his own way.

It is in this way that individuals have their easiest path to the European Court. It is not an appeal procedure. The national courts remain masters of the particular case, and apply to the dispute before them the Community law as defined for them by the European Court. The relationship is a fraternal one, horizontal, not vertical. Nevertheless, it is a cheap procedure. In many 'Article 177' cases the parties do not appear, or even send in written arguments to the European Court, but simply let it decide. European Court judges often do their own research, and the Commission of the European Community always appears with both written and oral argument as a 'friend of the Court'. The problems raised by the national court receive careful analysis and treatment, whether the parties get involved or not. Reference to the Court of Justice has become increasingly common – in 1961 there was only one reference; by 1983 well over 900 cases had been referred. National court practices differ quite markedly with, for example, West German courts referring cases relatively frequently and British courts only sparingly.

Some of the important areas covered by Community law have already been mentioned. Their significance often goes unnoticed, in part because some Community instruments are translated into ordinary national law. But their effect can be felt at even the local level, whether in the field of social security, or local trading and consumer protection.

SOURCES OF COMMUNITY LAW

1. The Constitutional Treaties: these are published by HM

Stationery Office and by the Community. There are also several commercially published editions such as Sweet & Maxwell's *European Community Treaties*.

2. Legislation: all Community legislation has to be published in the *Official Journal of the European Communities* before it may come into force.

3. Case Law: the judgements of the European Court of Justice are published by the Court itself in *European Court Reports*, and in two commercial series, the English *Common Market Law Reports*, and the American *Common Market Reporter*.

4. International Treaties: all treaties entered into by the Community are published in the *Official Journal*. Some only are published elsewhere, by, for example, HM Stationery Office.

SUGGESTIONS FOR FURTHER READING

L. Neville Brown and Francis C. Jacobs, *The Court of Justice of the European Communities* (Sweet & Maxwell, 1977).

T. C. Hartley, *The Foundations of European Community Law* (OUP, 1981)

D. Lasok and J. W. Bridge, *An Introduction to the Law and Institutions of the European Communities* (3rd edition, Butterworth, 1982)

J.-V. Louis, *The Community Legal Order* (EC Commission, 1980)

P. S. R. F. Mathijsen, *A Guide to European Community Law* (4th edition, Sweet & Maxwell, 1985)

J. Usher, *European Community Law and National Law: the Irreversible Process* (George Allen & Unwin/UACES, 1981)

5 The Common Market

A free trade area and a customs union have in common the objective of abolishing the tariff and non-tariff barriers to trade between member countries. A customs union goes beyond a free trade area in adopting a common external tariff (CET). This provides a common barrier to imports from non-member countries which is designed to prevent any one country gaining a competitive advantage over the others by, for example, importing raw materials at lower prices.(This aspect of the common market is covered further in Chapter 14 on the Common Commercial Policy).

Although 'Common Market' is sometimes used as a synonym for customs union, a common market is more than a customs union. In addition to the removal of tariff barriers and a common external tariff, it includes both free movement of factors of production (movement of workers, flows of capital, establishment of enterprises and provision of services) and the gradual coordination of the economic policies of the member states. The basic theoretical economic assumption of a common market is that 'perfect competition' should prevail; no firm or group of firms should have a predominant influence on prices. With tariff barriers removed and factors of production moving freely, there will, according to the theory, be an optimal allocation of resources among member states, bringing increased efficiency and economic welfare. The larger tariff-free market is also designed to have dynamic effects by encouraging firms to exploit economies of larger scale, and to

61

increase their efficiency in order to prevent being undercut by new competitors. These objectives are set out in Article 3 of the Treaty of Rome as one of its principles. The free movement of persons, services and capital (Title III, Articles 48–73) and transport (Title IV, Articles 74–83) are among what are described as the Foundations of the Community (Part Two).

In going beyond the creation of a free trade area towards a common market, the aims of the founders were as much political as economic. The ultimate objective of the Community is, as stated in the Treaty, 'an ever closer union among the peoples of Europe'. And, although the basic principle of the Community was a single free-market economy, it was recognised that for political and social reasons adjustments would also be needed to soften the impact of the required changes. Agriculture was the prime example of a sector requiring intervention at Community level. In addition, the Treaty set up the Social Fund and a rudimentary regional policy and allowed for certain specific exemptions or derogations in order to alleviate problems which might be created by the common market. Such intervention and increasingly common or coordinated policies would, it was believed, create the conditions necessary for eventual political union.

FREE TRADE

The free movement of goods remains the most fundamental of the 'Foundations' of the common market. The Treaty of Rome provided a transitional period in which the original six member states were progressively to reduce and finally to abolish internal tariffs. The timetable was in fact accelerated and tariffs were completely abolished by July 1968, eighteen months ahead of the programme. There was a five-year transitional period for the elimination of tariffs between the UK, Denmark, Ireland and the rest of the Community ending on 1 January 1978; and Greece, a transitional period of five years for most products ending on 1 January 1986. For Portugal and Spain, industrial and some agricultural products were subject to a seven-year period starting in March 1986 and for other agricultural products (mainly fresh fruit and vegetables), seven to ten years (see the Annex to Chapter 6 for the arrangements for the principal products).

The elimination of customs duties has gone, so far, according to plan, and, for the original Six, somewhat faster. Trade among the Six rose dramatically during the 1960s, much faster than growth in GDP. But just as Britain joined the Community in 1973 the economic recession began. Unemployment started to rise. Trade between member states slowed down and governments resorted increasingly to protectionism, not so much by the reimposing of customs duties, but by erecting new non-tariff barriers, disguised, for example, as health or safety requirements. They also failed to press on with the dismantling of existing barriers to completely free trade as laid down in Title III of the Treaty and the articles quoted above.

This is not to say that there has not been progress towards a completely free market for products and factors of production. By 1980, freedom of movement for workers (employees) as laid down in Article 48 of the Treaty had been largely achieved, apart from some remaining problems over administrative procedures relating to residence permits and over the comparability of vocational training qualifications. A series of directives on harmonising or coordinating company law had been agreed so that national company laws did not stop the establishment of new companies or mergers between existing companies across national borders. In 1975 there was agreement on mutual recognition of medical qualifications which allowed doctors to practise in member states other than their own. Later directives gave the same possibility to dentists, nurses, vets and midwives.

TAX PROVISIONS

Following the undertaking to remove tariff barriers, member states undertook to eliminate fiscal barriers. Under the Treaty, member states are prohibited from imposing internal taxes on the products of other member states greater than those they impose on domestically produced goods, and from subsidising exports through tax rebates. The Treaty also called for harmonisation of indirect turnover taxes.

Community negotiations on indirect taxes were protracted. The system proposed by the Commission in 1962, after several studies, was that of a tax on the value added at each stage of production, i.e. Value Added Tax (VAT). Only the French, at that stage, had adopted a form of VAT, although several other member states were considering the introduction of similar schemes. But it was only when the West Germans overcame their initial doubts, and pressed for the adoption of the Commission's proposals, that progress was made. The Council of Ministers accepted a Community VAT, in principle, in 1965 and, two years later, adopted the necessary directives for VAT to be introduced by 1970. However, it was not until 1973 that Italy was able to implement these directives. The UK announced its VAT system in 1972 to take effect in 1973 following accession to the Community.

Although all member states now have a VAT system or are in the process of introducing it, there remain wide differences in the tax rates. This is partly because of differences in overall tax structures and partly because member states have been determined to relieve either different products, or different social groups, of the tax burden: many member states have three different rates, of VAT, a reduced, standard and a luxury band; food and children's clothing are exempt in the UK and some foods in Ireland. With the opening up of a genuine common, internal market, these differences will be all the more significant in terms of distorting trade (see below page 68). They also cause major problems in the effort to reach agreement on a common basis of assessment for the VAT element of the Community's budgetary revenues (see Chapter 12).

Some progress has also been made in harmonising excise duties, although it is the structures and not the rates of tax that have been tackled. One of the major problems is, of course, that taxes remain important tools of national economic management.

THE APPROXIMATION OF LAWS

Some advances have been made too in the difficult area of laws and regulations relating to health, safety and consumer protection. It is an aspect of the Community, that in the UK at least, has generated considerable hostility. The prospect of 'Euro bread' or 'Euro beer' are two of the more alarming proposals that have hit the headlines. There have been many accusations that the Commission has simply been proposing harmonisation for its own sake and seeking to impose the same tastes on consumers everywhere – Euroformity. Nevertheless, different national laws or customs procedures on quality and safety standards and so on affect the ability of producers to sell their goods in other member states and are, often, little more than disguised protection. The purpose of the Commission's proposals has been to ensure that products can be freely traded across frontiers, allowing consumers a wider choice and increasing competition. While some of its proposals for harmonisation have got nowhere, others have made progress, particularly in agriculture, where agreement on the CAP led to preliminary emphasis on adopting directives on foodstuffs, animals and plants. Among industrial goods, priority has been given to pharmaceuticals, motor vehicles and farm tractors. Progress has been slow not only because of protectionist opposition, but also because of the complexities of trying to harmonise national standards and practices.

From about 1980, pressure started to build up in the Community to make faster progress towards a genuinely common market. The British, for example, found the restrictions which existed in those areas where they believed they had an advantage, such as services, particularly onerous. In a series of speeches designed to overcome the belief that Britain was only interested in its budget refund, British Ministers argued strongly during 1982 that it was vital to create a genuinely free internal market in order to give industry the competitive edge it needed in the rest of the world. The European Council of December 1982, looking for a comprehensive strategy for dealing with unemployment, made one of the Community's priority goals 'Strengthening the common market and intensifying action to eliminate practices and measures which restrict trade and distort competition'.

There was considerable activity in the Community during 1983, including frequent meetings of the newly created Council for the Internal Market (largely composed of Trade Ministers). But in spite of the impetus, progress was patchy throughout 1983 and 1984, principally because the Community's attention was focused on the budget problem and the network of issues that came to surround it (see Chapter 12).

Nevertheless, far greater public attention began to be paid to the problem, due partly at least to the so-called Albert/Ball report presented to the European Parliament. ('Towards European Economic Recovery in the 1980s' by M. Michel Albert and Professor James Ball, European Parliament working document, dated 31 August 1983). This drew attention to some frightening (for Europeans) statistics about the decline of European economies and the greater size of unemployment relative to the United States and Japan. Among the causes it identified for Europe's backwardness were the absence of a genuine common capital market, of a genuine common market for purchasing by public authorities (public procurement) and for research and development. These defects and all other obstacles to free trade were equal, Albert and Ball argued, to a financial surcharge of one week's pay on average for every family in Europe. They pointed out that there were practically no firms for whom the European market was a homogeneous industrial base. 25 years after the Treaty of Rome had been signed, virtually no new transnational group had been set up, one reason being that there was no legal status for a European company (the exceptions include Airbus and the Ariane Launcher, both highly successful enterprises). The Report referred to the queues of lorries at frontiers between EC member countries, to the lack of common air space, to the lack of common standards and to a series of other obstacles to free trade in Europe which were expensive and which made Europe less capable of competing with the United States' large and homogeneous home market.

While the Albert/Ball Report lent some weight to the cause of reform, it was the Fontainebleau Agreement of June 1984 (see Chapter 12) which unlocked the next important phase of the internal market exercise by setting up the *ad hoc* Committee on Institutions (the Dooge Committee) and the *ad hoc* Committee on a People's Europe (the Andonnino Committee). Each covered a different aspect of the completion of the Common Market. The Andonnino Committee concentrated on the political task of making Europe more relevant to Community citizens, to 'visibly offer them tangible benefits in their everyday lives' as it was put in the Committee's first report to the European Council on 29 and 30 March 1985. The Committee concentrated on four main areas: freedom of movement for Community citizens; freedom of movement of goods, including transport services; administrative formalities for border-area traffic; and wider opportunities for employment and residence. The Dooge Committee, in its parallel report to the March 1985 European Council, argued again for the creation of a 'homogeneous internal economic area' so that Europeans could 'benefit from the dynamic effects of a single market with immense purchasing power'. Among its recommendations were that, pending the adoption of European standards, there should be 'immediate mutual recognition of national standards' on the principle that goods 'lawfully produced and marketed' in one member state should be allowed to circulate throughout the Community.

The two reports were endorsed by the European Council, which called for the creation of the Common Market by 1992 and directed the Commission to draw up a detailed programme of what had to be done. The Commission's 'White Paper' (entitled 'Completing the Internal Market' and published in June 1985 for the European Council which met 28–29 June in Milan) contained a series of proposals and a timetable for implementing them aimed at the removal of physical, technical and fiscal barriers to the free movement of people, goods and services.

On the physical barriers to free movement, the White Paper concentrated on frontier posts. The Commission proposed that, in a first stage up to 1988, the target should be to shift controls and formalities away from the frontiers (so that, for example, veterinary or plant health checks would be made before departure or on arrival at final destinations) by 1988; and in the second stage, to 'coordinate policies and approximate legislation so that internal frontier barriers and controls are eliminated in their entirety by 1992'. However, while referring to measures making for easier frontier-crossing for ordinary European citizens (such as the common Community passport, or the green 'E' disc on cars, which allowed them to be waved through at frontiers with the minimum of formalities), the Commission recognised that frontier controls could not be abolished altogether until adequate safeguards were introduced against terrorism and drugs.

On technical barriers, among a mass of detailed measures, the Commission's most important proposal was in relation to voting in the Council. Under Article 100 of the Treaty, the Council legislates by unanimity on the approximation of laws, regulations and the administrative actions of the member states which directly affect the functioning of the common market. The Commission proposed that the Council should be prepared to use majority voting. It also proposed, picking up the Dooge Committee's recommendation, that greater use should be made of mutual recognition of each other's standards, leaving harmonisation for only essential areas (for example, if a member state's standards were so obviously protectionist in intention that other states would not be willing to recognise them). Of particular importance to Britain, the Commission made progress for achieving a genuine free market in financial services, including insurance, and pointed out that this could not come about without a completely free market for capital.

The Commission's arguments on fiscal barriers are among the most difficult for member states to accept. Fiscal checks featured 'prominently among the functions carried out at the Community's internal frontiers'. As mentioned above (page 64) all the member states have adopted or are implementing a common turnover tax, VAT, but the Commission has claimed that the logic of a common market clearly calls for VAT and excise taxes to be levied on a common basis. If, the Commission argues, a principal objective of frontier controls is to allow member states to collect their individual and differing indirect taxes from travellers, then the abolition of frontier controls requires that the rates of indirect taxation are brought into line. The 'approximation' of indirect taxes has therefore been proposed, not harmonisation ('which has come to imply absolute identity in every respect'), and the construction of a 'clearing house system' to ensure that VAT collected by an exporting country and deducted in an importing state would be reimbursed by the latter.

Discussions on the completion of the common market continue; in one form or another they have gone on for so long that the pace of decision-taking was described as 'funereal'. In fact a number of useful steps have been achieved. In December 1984, for example, the Council agreed to the 'single administrative document', that is, a single customs document that from 1 January 1988 would replace the 70 or so documents previously required in intra-Community trade. In July 1985, the Council adopted a directive aimed at freedom of establishment for architects and freedom for them to provide services throughout the Community. It was regarded as something of a pilot project for the free movement of many other 'technical' professions and, according to the Commission, marks a real move towards applying the principle of mutual recognition of diplomas. Some bilateral steps also characterised a new mood within the Community with, for example, the French and Germans agreeing to press on together with the abolition of frontier controls and to join the Benelux countries in moving ahead on their own if Community-wide progress was too slow.

The European Council in Milan in June 1985 approved both the Dooge and the Andonnino Reports and the Commission's

White Paper. And, following the Inter-Governmental Conference on institutional and other reforms, the European Council of December 1985 agreed that the completion of the Internal Market should form part of the Single European Act. It meant that two principle objectives – the target date of 1992 and provisions for majority voting – should be buttressed by inclusion in the Treaty amendments designed to relaunch the European Community. To keep up momentum, three successive Presidencies of the Council of Ministers, the Dutch and British in 1986 and the Belgians in early 1987, agreed on a comprehensive programme for an 18-month period and each pushed hard to gain agreement. The pressure was further maintained by the Danes and West Germans with growing success, creating, perhaps, an irresistible impetus towards the establishment of single market.

TRANSPORT POLICY

Under the Treaty of Rome, a common transport policy was to apply to rail, road and inland waterway transport, with the possibility, if the Council of Ministers so decided, of extending it to sea and air transport. Whereas the Treaty made elaborate provision for a common agricultural policy (CAP), transport was treated much more generally. Unlike the CAP, therefore, the common transport policy is both limited and piecemeal.

A common transport policy was included in the Treaty on the grounds that, with the free movement of factors of production, competitive conditions would be distorted if significant disparities in national transport rates and systems were maintained. Transport can obviously make up a large proportion of total production costs. The attempt to iron out the most glaring anomalies in national practices in respect of the transportation of coal and steel had been a foremost preoccupation of the ECSC, though with only patchy results. Transport has always been a sector in which government involvement in management has been extensive. Railways, for example, are nationally controlled by all members of the Community (with the limited exception of some private lines in Italy), and have been regarded in particular as being as much a public service as a (possibly) profitable industry. But there have been differences as to how far governments should interfere in the competition between the different forms of transport, which have led to differences in licensing regulations for road transport and rules governing freight charges.

In order, therefore, to create equally competitive conditions, the Treaty provides that, within the framework of a common policy, common rules are to be adopted on transport in the Community. It lays down that all discrimination based on country of origin or of destination of products should be eliminated. Member states also undertook to eliminate forms of support which were to the benefit of a particular industry. Aids were permissible only if they were needed for the coordination of transport systems or were clearly intended to maintain transport as a public service. In order to advise the Commission in preparing its proposals to implement these somewhat general guidelines, a committee of national officials was set up.

It was not until 1965 that the Six agreed on the general principles to be adopted and the timetable for achieving a degree of harmonisation. Moreover, the timetable was soon ignored by the Council and only a piecemeal approach has been successful. In part this was because of the lack of precision in the Treaty on objectives and methods. Transport has also undergone important changes since 1957, particularly the increase in road transport and the decline of the railways. But progress has also been limited because of political differences among member governments, and a reluctance, expressed most strongly by the French, to allow transport to be taken from national control.

But since the beginning of the 1980s, transport has been increasingly treated as the important area it is in the drive towards the completion of the internal market, helping to revitalise European economies and to counter unemployment. Between 1983 and 1985, the Commission produced three papers on a common transport policy – on inland transport in 1983, on air transport in 1984 and on maritime transport in 1985. At the same time, after considering a complaint from the European Parliament made in 1983, the Court of Justice decided in 1985 that the Council of Ministers was in breach of the Treaty for failing to make progress on a common transport policy as laid down in the Treaty.

In its memorandum on inland transport (OJC 154, 13 June 1983), the Commission argued that the slow progress made towards a common policy stemmed not only from member states' differing historical and geographical circumstances, but also from more specific problems, in particular the conflict between them over the relationship between liberalisation of transport and harmonisation of the conditions of competition'; 'the pre-occupation of some Member States with their railway problems'; and 'the fear of strengthening community competence in transport'. They nevertheless pointed out the high cost to the community of divergent national policies. One of the principal difficulties is caused by various 'Member States whose budgets are weighed down by the financing of huge railway deficits and who are therefore not prepared to allow road transport to develop as it could in case it undercuts railways and causes even bigger deficits'. The Commission's main proposal for tackling this problem was to argue that governments should pay for railway infrastructure as they do for other transport infrastructure – especially, of course, roads. The railways could then develop their services to make them more attractive without having the additional burden of the full infrastructure costs (they would make some contribution). This would still be expensive for governments but at least it would clearly delineate their responsibility.

The principal blockage on road transport has been the system of quotas and licences for lorries crossing frontiers. Each member state acquires licences for a limited number of vehicles per year transporting goods across or into another member state. Four thousand Community licences were introduced in 1968 which means that some licence holders do not need a series of bilateral licences for crossing several countries. The number of these is to be doubled between 1985 and 1989 and restrictions have been abolished altogether on more than 40 per cent of road traffic. Transport Ministers agreed in November 1985 that all quantitative restrictions should be abolished by 1992 at the latest. Safety standards for motor cars have been harmonised. After long battles, still not entirely over, common standards on weights and measures of lorries were agreed in 1984 at 40 tonnes with a (temporary) derogation for British and Irish lorries at their existing maximum of 38 tonnes. The Community has set maximum driving periods and obligatory periods of rest policed by the tachograph which aroused such opposition in the UK (the 'spy in the cab'). In its 1983 memorandum, the Commission emphasised not only the importance of the removal of licences, but also of finding a system for compensating member states whose roads are used extensively for transit between other countries. Other proposals for speeding up road transport across frontiers have already been mentioned above. The Commission has made a number of proposals for inland navigation where the main problems have been sharing infrastructure costs and excess capacity. They have also proposed further Community financing of infrastructure projects of general Community interest. Among projects to which it has already contributed has been the M25 London Orbital Motorway.

In maritime transport, the main problem faced by the Community has been the decline of the Community's shipping fleet relative to world tonnage. The Commission's argument in favour of common action in the shipping industry has been based on the belief that Europe's dependence on world trade and the dependence of its shipping interests on international shipping markets requires the maintenance of a multilateral and commercially-orientated Community shipping policy. To that end, the Commission has looked to the use of the Community's weight in international negotiations to counter the protectionist policies of other countries and to ensure that there is equality of treatment of Community shipowners by member states. The Commission has also proposed that the competition provisions of the Treaty of Rome (see Chapter 8) should be applied to shipping in the Community. In December 1986, the Council adopted four maritime regulations which constitute the first stage in the development of a common shipping policy.

The emphasis on the application of competition policy is a major feature of the Commission's 1984 proposals for air transport. The ultimate objective of these proposals (which follow up those made in 1979) is the creation of a common air transport market. This was foreseen as likely to take a long time, and events have fully substantiated this somewhat cautious prophesy. However, they have attempted, with varying degrees of support from member states – the British having been among their strongest supporters –to introduce a greater element of competition between the airlines on routes within the enlarged Community only, in the hope that this might increase efficiency and lead to a reduction in fares. The difficulties in reaching even modest agreements on air transport reflects not only the strength of entrenched interests, but also the wider political consequences of accepting the liberalisation of trading policies and the opening up of national markets. They indicate the reasons why the competition of the internal market has been and continues to be a difficult and slow process.

SUGGESTIONS FOR FURTHER READING

M. Albert and J. Ball, *Toward European Economic Recovery in the 1980s* (Washington papers 109, Vol XII, Praeger/CSIS, Georgetown University 1984)

J. Pelkmans, *Market Integration in the European Community* (Martinus Nijhoff, 1984)

D. Puchala, *Fiscal Harmonisation in the European Community* (Frances Pinter, 1984)

P. Robson, *The Economics of International Integration* (2nd edition, George Allen & Unwin, 1984)

D. Swann, *The Economics of the Common Market* (5th edition, Penguin, 1984)

C. Cosgrove Twitchett, *Harmonisation in the EEC* (Macmillan, 1981)

For Treaty references see: Treaty of Rome, Part I, Article 3; Part II , Title I, Articles 9–37; Title III, Articles 48–73; Title IV, Articles 74–84; Part III, Title I, Chapter 3, Articles 100–101; Single European Act 1986.

6 The Common Agricultural Policy

The Common Agricultural Policy (CAP) has often been described as the cornerstone of the European Community. From the outset it was clear that agriculture would play a fundamental role, both because of its intrinsic importance to the economies of the Six, and as part of the basic Franco-German compromise on which the European Community was based. In 1958 agriculture accounted for 20 per cent of the jobs of the Community and some 10 per cent of its output. But, while the six member states agreed on the necessity of including agriculture in the common market, they were not prepared to accept the consequences of a completely free market which excluded governmental intervention, even if on a coordinated basis.

All the member governments of the Community had intervened in agriculture, in a variety of ways, and for a variety of reasons. European agriculture recovered rapidly from the devastation of the Second World War, especially with new techniques based on the application of scientific principles. The yield of crops such as barley and wheat rose dramatically; genetic selection and improved husbandry enabled a greater production of poultry meat, more milk per cow, more eggs per hen. Mechanised farming allowed for a reduction in the work-force. Improved drainage and irrigation, more fertiliser and more effective pesticides and herbicides, all contributed to increased production from the land. But in the countries of Western Europe, the gap between the minimum food necessary and the maximum food wanted is relatively small.

74

Extra food cannot, therefore, be sold at prevailing prices, and if substantial amounts of extra output are put on the market, prices may fall to levels so low that, without government intervention, farmers would be forced out of business until the quantities of food produced were reduced.

But, despite technology, agriculture still relies on processes which are affected by weather and disease. In a 'bad year' supplies might be scarce and high prices might result. In 'bumper years' low prices may force farmers to move out. If prices are volatile it is difficult to achieve a smooth, or orderly, transition to a more efficient industry as a consequence of technological improvements. Governments intervene, therefore, both to ease the hardships of farmers who cannot make an adequate income, and to protect consumers and producers from extreme price fluctuations.

Improved farm technology is only one aspect of the problem of European agriculture. The rising level of real income among the population also creates difficulties. Expenditure on food does not rise in proportion to increased income, yet the costs of farming, of labour, machinery and fertiliser, etc., rise at a rate which is closely related to the growth of the economy as a whole. The result is that, between rising costs and less rapidly rising revenues, a squeeze develops on farm incomes. Not all farmers are affected equally, but the actual or potential decline in real incomes places all farmers under great pressure to apply new methods. If they all increase output, prices will fall if not protected by government action.

The logical response of the agricultural industries to these long-term changes should be a shift of resources to other uses. But agricultural resources are less mobile than those in other sectors, particularly land. Farm capital, especially in land, represents an asset which farmers are reluctant to abandon, because it is both a security in times of food scarcity and a hedge against inflation. Farm capital may have a low 'salvage value'; the value of a second-hand milking parlour remains only as long as milk is produced, so that it may pay a farmer to continue to produce milk, since he can at least cover some costs, even if returns are small. The social implications of a decline in the farm labour force are highly significant: farming skills, for example, are not often transferable, so that retraining is necessary to avoid competing with other 'unskilled' workers. The relative immobility of men and capital, therefore, makes possible sustained differences in real incomes between agricultural and non-agricultural producers. This problem is especially acute where natural circumstances, such as hilly or mountainous countryside, handicap production. In all the member states agricultural policy was concerned, to a greater or lesser extent, with these consequences of economic change and, particularly, with the problems of low farm incomes.

Governments have also been motivated to intervene because of other factors which go beyond purely agricultural considerations. Agricultural policy cannot be divorced, for example, from questions relating to the rural environment, such as the appearance of the countryside, its accessibility to tourists, and its availability for leisure activities. In several countries extra agricultural output was wanted to reduce imports or increase exports. Security of supply has been a common goal for farm policy, which for many European countries has implied a high degree of self-sufficiency. Stable prices, together with high levels of employment and rapid rates of growth, have also been goals by which Western governments have sought to manage their economies. Food prices form a critical element in the cost of living, on which wage negotiations may be based. Still more important, since poorer households spend a higher proportion of their income on food, a rise in food prices is of greater social significance than a rise in prices in general.

The emphasis given to these reasons for agricultural policy varied among the Six. They were sufficiently important to all, however, for a common market to be unacceptable, if it meant completely free internal trade, and prices determined by supply and demand, rather than government intervention. Before 1958 the internal price levels of agricultural goods in the Six varied enormously and implied restrictions on imports. If free trade had been introduced, the effect of competition would have been to force the higher-cost producers to become more efficient, or to go out of business, while allowing the lower-cost producers to expand, with a tendency towards a lower price level than the previous average. Within the countries which were least competitive there would have been a transfer of resources towards other productive activities with a potential economic advantage to the Community as a whole. Such economic considerations had, however, to be balanced by the political significance of the agricultural sectors within the member countries. Since individual governments had intervened heavily to protect their agricultural producers, those separate national policies had to be replaced by a common policy which would regulate markets for the Community as a whole.

The Treaty of Rome did not define the mechanisms for such a common policy, but it did set out certain goals. The common agricultural policy (CAP) has five listed objectives:

  (i)   increase agricultural productivity through technological improvement, rational production, and the optimum use of the factors of production, particularly labour;
 (ii)   ensure a fair standard of living for the agricultural population;
(iii)   stabilise markets;
 (iv)   guarantee regular supplies;
  (v)   ensure reasonable prices and supplies to consumers.

The Treaty specified that, in working out the CAP, due account should be taken of the social structure of agriculture and the structural and natural disparities among the agricultural regions of the Community; adjustments should be made gradually; and that agriculture constituted a sector closely linked to the economy as a whole. These general objectives have been translated, after difficult negotiations, into common regimes for most of the major agricultural products of the Community.

THE CAP SYSTEM

In view of the common practice of the Six, the Community decided in favour of an agricultural policy that would guarantee farmers' incomes through the prices charged to consumers. Since agricultural goods would not flow freely between Community countries, even with the removal of trade barriers, if separate national pricing systems remained, the Community decided to set prices common throughout the Community for the main agricultural products. A range of instruments were agreed to control imports and to provide a safety net for Community producers should domestic supplies exceed those which could be sold at the price level determined by the Council of Ministers each year.

The Council, on proposals from the Commission, set what are called *target* or *guide* or *basic* prices, depending on the product concerned. These are the prices it is hoped farmers will achieve on the wholesale market for the next marketing year (which, of course, varies from product to product). The method used to maintain these prices is that of withdrawing the product from the market when market prices have fallen below a certain level. This price level, the *intervention price* (or *withdrawal* or *buying-in price*, again depending on the product), is set below the target price. It allows the Community, through national Intervention Authorities, to buy the product concerned. The farmer receives the intervention price, minus the costs of transport to the intervention centre and handling charges. The Community buys only those products which reach fairly rigorous specifications of quality. Goods not reaching these standards may have to be sold by the farmer for what they will fetch on the market. Those goods which cannot be stored because of their perishability are destroyed. Those that are stored are released when market prices have recovered sufficiently. They can also be disposed of in other ways, such as food aid, or they can be sold to non-Community countries. The intervention system is financed through the Community's budget, through the European Agricultural Guarantee and Guidance Fund (EAGGF or, more commonly, FEOGA from its French initials).

The internal Community market is protected from cheaper imports from third countries through *variable import levies*, or *countervailing duties* (depending on the product) – taxes levied on imports at Community frontiers. The levies are based on the average cost of the imports compared with the *threshold, sluice-gate*, or *reference price* (depending once again on the product concerned). These are fixed below the target price so that, after distribution costs have been added, the total cost is equal to the target price. The return from the levies is a part of the Community's revenues or 'own resources' (minus the costs of collection by national customs, which are retained by national exchequers) – see Chapter 12.

The application of these basic instruments varies from product to product: a list of products subject to common regimes is given in the Annex to this chapter. Some products are subject to a full ('heavy') regime, such as wheat; others have 'light' regimes, such as fruit and vegetables; and others none at all, such as potatoes and wool. Under some regimes certain quantities of imports are allowed into the Community free of levies, for example, sugar under the Lomé Convention (see Chapter 16). National variations are also sometimes allowed, such as the UK variable beef premium. They are all based, directly or indirectly, on the principles first established for cereals. The cereals regime was the first to be achieved, not only because of the importance of cereals *per se*, but also because of the dependence of other products, especially, of course, livestock, upon adequate supplies of cereals.

Certain other measures have also been agreed within the Community. The CAP, from the beginning, allowed for *export subsidies* or *restitutions*. These enable Community exporters to continue to sell in external markets, despite the higher price levels generally pertaining in the Community. The Community can, therefore, at least to some extent, avoid internal adjustments, intervention, or the disposal of intervention stocks at home, by sales to foreign markets. The subsidies can be varied according to the destination of the goods. They can also be substantial if world prices are low and Community production is considerably in excess of Community consumption. When world prices are high, as in 1974–5, *export levies* can be imposed on Community producers to restrain exports and, thereby, keep Community prices from rising to the higher world levels.

Further alternatives to intervention buying by the Community are measures which increase domestic consumption. Wheat surplus to direct human consumption, for example, can be sold for animal feedstuff at a lower price. Skim milk powder has sometimes been incorporated into animal feedstuffs (with a subsidy). It has, in addition, been exported to developing countries under the Community's food aid programme. Consumer subsidies have been given to increase butter consumption and specific sectors of the population have also been singled out for subsidies, such as pensioners (for beef), and schoolchildren (for milk). Finally, the Community has attempted to increase sales of one product by limiting competition from others. It has, unsuccessfully, attempted to define 'ice cream' as only those products which contain dairy fat. Although the scheme was later ruled as illegal by the Court of Justice, the Commission also obliged feedstuff manufacturers to buy a certain amount of indigenous feed before being allowed to purchase imported ingredients.

THE STRUCTURAL POLICY

Apart from attempting to regulate agricultural markets, the Community has tried to assist the modernisation of farming through a structural programme financed from the Guidance section of FEOGA. Initially, structural assistance was granted simply to supplement the efforts of national governments. In 1968, however, the Mansholt Plan (named after the then Commissioner for Agricultural Policy, Sicco Mansholt) was produced by the Commission, which envisaged more positive Community action in the field of structural reform. The Plan visualised that by 1980 there would be a substantial reduction both in the farming population and in the area farmed within the Community. The proposals were controversial, and it was not until 1972 that directives to implement some of its ideas, albeit in attenuated form, were actually introduced. Their objectives are two-fold: to assist in the modernisation of farming; and to reduce the numbers involved in farming. Aid is given by the Commission for the modernisation of farms by assisting the farmer to undertake developments which will enable the farm to earn an income per worker equivalent to that of employees in other industries in the same area. In order to qualify, farming must be the principal occupation of the applicant. The Community's contribution to these aids may be 25 or 50 per cent of the total grant. In order to reduce the numbers involved in agriculture, two schemes were introduced in 1972 which aimed to assist older farmers and farmworkers to retire, and to retrain younger farmers for whom no long-term prospect of satisfactory income exists. Since the enlargement of the Community, the structural programme has been strengthened in the case of 'less favoured regions', such as hilly and mountainous areas. In these regions additional aids, under the farm modernisation scheme, are given to allow funds to be used for craft or tourist activities ancillary to agriculture itself, and to allow direct payments per head of stock carried in these difficult areas.

THE DEVELOPMENT OF THE CAP

The CAP has, inevitably, had to respond to changes both within agriculture and the economy as a whole and as a result of the advent of new members. However, it has done so only slowly and with the utmost difficulty and reluctance. Throughout its existence the CAP has faced frequent crises. The very success of its mechanisms has resulted in surpluses which have in turn put intolerable strains on the Community budget. Yet high consumer prices have not necessarily meant adequate incomes for farmers in poorer regions, whose costs have risen steadily. These difficulties have been exacerbated by monetary (exchange rate) problems which have given rise to the arcane mysteries of 'green' currencies and monetary compensatory amounts. Advantages that the CAP has brought to farmers and consumers have been overshadowed by the difficulties, including acute monetary problems.

The introduction of supported prices at high levels, during a period of rapidly improving agricultural technology, tends inexorably towards the production of surpluses. This tendency has been reinforced since a level of prices above world prices has been the principal instrument in supporting the incomes of new or small, relatively high-cost, farmers. Larger, relatively low-cost, farmers are thereby stimulated to increase their output with the result that supplies exceed demand at the chosen price. If an excess is produced, a charge falls on the Community budget through intervention purchasing. Largely because of the costs of buying and storing surplus produce that could not be sold, and the actual costs (through export restitutions) of selling on the world market, the CAP has consistently taken some two-thirds of the total Community budget.

Agricultural expenditure has dominated the budget since the creation of the Community (see Chapter 12). The CAP is, of course, the only nearly complete Community policy. But it has continued to demand two-thirds or more of total Community expenditure despite strenuous efforts to reduce the proportions spent on it. The problem is inherent in the policy adopted. Both social and national interests inhibit price flexibility. Lower prices, if no other changes take place, reduce the income of all farmers, including those who are relatively poor and who remain politically significant in most member countries, including West Germany. Lower price levels also reduce the earnings of the agricultural exporting member states such as France and the Netherlands, even if they might benefit those who are net importers like the UK and Portugal. This is a major reason why the British campaign for lower agricultural prices, which would mean lower agricultural spending and therefore a lower British share of the budget has faced such powerful opposition from the other member states.

The difficulties are aggravated by what is, in any case, the unsatisfactory level of incomes for many farmers, especially in certain regions. This suggests that there are still too many farmers in the Community. Despite very substantial spending by both the Community and national governments, the gap between the income of farmers as a whole and the income of others has not, in general, narrowed. At the same time, within the agricultural sector, the differences between the prosperous and less prosperous farmers have widened.

Monetary problems have further added to the difficulties of the CAP. These first arose in the late sixties with the departure from fixed exchange rates. France devalued the franc but in order to hold back inflation, continued to translate agricultural prices in France from the Community unit of account into francs at the previous rate. This rate between the franc and the unit of account became known as the 'Green Rate'. As other member countries' national currencies were revalued or devalued, so their governments also manipulated the Green Rate, revaluing or devaluing or leaving it unchanged to suit their internal political priorities such as giving their farmers higher income or their consumers lower prices.

If left unregulated, floating exchange rates would have meant that there were no longer common prices. Cheaper produce from a weaker currency country would have undercut the more expensive produce in a strong-currency country. Produce from a strong-currency country could not have sold in a weak-currency country (unless, of course, producers in the former were to accept lower prices). The mechanism invented to correct this distortion was the 'Monetary Compensatory Amount' (MCA) which was, in effect, a tax levied on agricultural exports from a weaker-currency country and a subsidy paid to imports into a stronger-currency country. Countries with weak currencies have 'negative' MCAs, in effect a tax to bring the price of their exports up to the common price in units of account (now the ECU) and a subsidy to bring the price of imports down to local prices. 'Positive' MCAs for strong currency countries have the opposite effect, acting in effect as an export subsidy. At one point in 1978, Germany had a positive MCA of about 7 per cent and the UK a negative MCA of about 25 per cent which together corrected a price variation, arising from differences in currency values, of about 32 per cent.

At the outset of the system, governments were free to alter their Green Rates when they wanted and thus award their farmers' price increases (revaluations) or give consumer subsidies (devaluations) as they liked. Later it was agreed that changes could not be made without Community agreement. Most changes in Green Rates were meant to take place during the annual price fixing.

If MCAs corrected monetary distortions between member states, they reinforced distortions in production. Because farmers in strong-currency countries got higher prices than those in weaker-currency countries, production in the former increased, thus enabling countries like Germany to break into the traditional markets of others. As a result there was strong pressure to reduce the role of MCAs. France in particular pressed hard, and tried to make the abolition of German positive MCAs a condition of the entry into force of the European Monetary System in 1979 (see Chapter 13). France was not entirely successful and MCAs continued to cause problems.

Since the mid-1970s, there have also been other pressures for reform. Britain, for example, has consistently pressed for it, linking it with the campaign for refunds from the Community budget. Other member states have resisted equally strongly. The French, for example, have often argued that Britain was being *non communautaire* and have fought hard against what they regarded as attempts to 'destroy' the CAP. They argued that Britain wanted to enjoy the benefits of Community membership and the continued ability to import Commonwealth agricultural produce, in particular New Zealand butter, cheese and lamb without shouldering appropriate obligations. There was a particularly fierce confrontation between Britain and France over the introduction of the Community's 'sheep meat regime' (see the annex to this chapter). But the picture of constant battles over CAP reform between only France and Britain was increasingly overdrawn. On the one hand, France, too, began to urge reforms in the face of escalating costs. On the other hand, the agricultural sectors in other member states have been deeply engaged, not only in the Netherlands and in Ireland, but also in Germany where high CAP prices have been particularly important for small, often part-time farmers in the south if they were to stay in production at all. They have been consistently championed in Brussels by successive German Ministers of Agriculture, sometimes against the declared policy of the Federal Chancellor.

Where measures designed to curb agricultural production have been accepted, such as co-responsibility levies and quotas (see Annex under Dairy Products), they have so far been of only limited effectiveness. The one measure that could have effect (for which the British have consistently argued), support prices low enough to discourage production of the surplus commodities, has remained out of reach because, although prices have been reduced, yields have more than increased to compensate. Agricultural ministers, responsive to their farming lobbies, have for the most part taken decisions in a vacuum with little apparent regard for the budgetary consequences.

In the early 1980s, however, governments began to shift from their entrenched positions. The main causes of this movement go beyond the scope of this chapter and need to be seen in the context of continuing economic problems in Europe and changing attitudes to the Community budget. But the result was that a growing number of governments began to show concern over the high proportion of Community spending that went on agriculture and was not therefore available to support industry and combat unemployment. It also became only too clear that if the Community went on spending at the same rate, it would face bankruptcy. Finally, British pressure to reduce its budget contribution began to bear fruit. One of the effects of the decisions taken at the Foreign Affairs Council of 30 May 1980 was that France and Germany would pay more towards the Community budget. They thereby acquired a far stronger interest in keeping CAP costs down. Largely as a result, the average rise in prices in 1980 was below the average rate of inflation.

Negotiations to implement the 30 May mandate and find a long-term solution to the budget problem, and thereby the CAP, moved forward only slowly. Britain attempted to force the pace during the annual negotiations on agricultural prices in 1982/83, arguing that without a budget settlement, its contribution would be further increased by the proposed price rises which were therefore unacceptable. The Belgian President of the Council of Ministers then introduced majority voting for the first time in a price fixing. Britain, with the support of Greece and Denmark, invoked the Luxembourg Compromise (see Chapter 1) but was outvoted. However, a major crisis, in which Britain might have withheld its payments to the budget, was avoided, in part because of the need to maintain Community solidarity during the Falkland Islands crisis. In addition, the search for longer-term reform was given renewed impetus at the European Council at Stuttgart in June 1983. This led to the decision by the European Council in March 1984 that over a three-year period any future growth in agricultural spending should be less than the rate of growth of the own resources base; or put another way, that spending on agriculture should not grow faster than the rate of growth in the Community's revenue.

It was also in March 1983, in that year's price-fixing, that Agricultural Ministers agreed to farm prices that represented a reduction in real terms of between two and three per cent, the first time that there had been a cut of this size across the board. They also agreed on the introduction of a quota/supplementary levy scheme for milk, the most difficult of the surplus products, to be applied for five years with a review after three years. The scheme set a production limit for the whole Community divided into national quotas, based on their shares of production in 1981, with special provision for certain countries (Italy, Luxembourg and Ireland and also for Britain in respect of Northern Ireland). Governments then set quotas for individual producers who pay a levy on quantities in excess of their quotas which they sell to dairies. For a number of other products, 'guarantee thresholds' were set, whereby the Community guarantee prices only up to a certain level of production. Beyond that price, producers have to sell for whatever price they can get on the market.

Finally, the March 1983 Agricultural Council agreed that existing positive MCAs should be gradually eliminated and no new ones created. Since this meant that producers in strong currency countries (Germany and the Netherlands at the time) would suffer cuts in real terms in their incomes, they were allowed to pay certain national aids to their farmers. This element of 're-nationalisation' or 'regionalisation' of the CAP, with increased costs undertaken by national treasuries, was a major departure from basic principles. Governments have often been tempted to assist their own farmers on a national basis (and have sometimes succumbed to the temptation despite the watchful eye of the Commission) but the 1983 agreement may have set an important precedent for the future.

The decisions on the CAP taken by Agricultural Ministers and by the European Council in March 1983 formed an essential part of the wider agreement reached at Fontainebleau in June 1984 on relaunching and reforming the Community. But despite agreement on 'budgetary imbalances', enlargement and new 'own resources' (see Chapter 12) the agricultural problem was far from resolved. On dairy produce, for example, it became clear that the introduction of quotas had caused only a short-term fall in production, in part because the initial quotas had been generous, but also because regional milk boards or cooperatives had juggled individual production quotas. It therefore appears likely that the problem can be settled only when prices are set at a sufficiently restrictive level. This, however, was something the Germans refused to accept in the 1985 price fixing and they invoked the Luxembourg Compromise to block price reductions for cereals and rape seed agreed by all other countries; the first time the Germans had used the veto. Nevertheless, the trend towards lower support prices has continued, necessarily perhaps in view of the prospect once again of Community bankruptcy.

The conflict of interest between member states over the reform of the CAP has not therefore been resolved even though some measure of agreement has been reached over the last few years. The conflict is not likely to be settled quickly. Any particular set of arrangements for the development or reform of the CAP implies a gain to some members and a loss to others. The original six members of the Community, in fixing prices considerably above the prevailing world prices, established a system that was clearly to the advantage of agricultural exporters, and France and the Netherlands have benefited substantially. Since enlargement, the Danes and the Irish have similarly benefited. However, the growth of agricultural production, with the ensuing problems of surpluses, has led other governments to question a policy which appears lopsided in its benefits. Moreover, there are pressures not only from governments within the Community. The United States, supported by Australia and others, have been determined to put agricultural subsidies high on the agenda of the Uruguay Round of the GATT. External factors will also therefore have to be dealt with. The problem is political rather than technical. Technically feasible proposals for the more rational use of Community resources as a whole have often been put forward. The problem lies in making such proposals politically acceptable to the member countries. There is a tendency for negotiations between member states, within the Council of Ministers, to focus on trade-offs, rather than on new policies which might use Community resources more rationally. And, since any new policy involves the unanimous agreement of all the member governments, the position of those opposed to change is strong. The major bargaining weapon for those in favour of change is their resistance to price increases which might refuel inflationary pressures. Such a policy is damaging to the unity of the Community, both psychologically and in more material terms. Resistance to price increases over a substantial length of time could lead governments to assist their farmers in ways that are less equitable than under the present system.

The problems confronting the CAP are, therefore, extremely complicated. They became even more so with the accession of Spain and Portugal (see Annex II to this chapter). Nevertheless, there were signs during 1987 that there was greater unanimity in the Community about the need to reform the CAP than there ever was before. It was not, however, until February 1988 at a specially-called European Council that the means of reform were finally agreed. The agreement included a ceiling on agricultural spending and controls ('stabilisers' and a 'set-aside' scheme) on cereals and other crops as part of a more comprehensive budgetary agreement (see also Chapter 12).

SUGGESTIONS FOR FURTHER READING

A. E. Buckwell et al., *The Costs of the Common Agricultural Policy* (Croom Helm, 1982).

F. Duchene et al., *New Limits on European Agriculture: Politics and the Common Agricultural Policy* (Croom Helm/Rowman & Allen-held, 1985)

R. Fennell, *The Common Agricultural Policy of the European Community* (Granada, 1982)

T. Heidlines, T. Josling et al., *Common Prices and Europe's Farm Policy* (Trade Policy Research Centre, 1978)

B. E. Hill, *The Common Agricultural Policy: Past, Present and Future* (Methuen, 1984)

J. Marsh and P. Swanney, *Agriculture and the European Community* (UACES/George Allen & Unwin, 1980)

E. Neville Rolfe, *The Politics of Agriculture in the European Community* (PSI, 1984)

J. Pearce, *The Common Agricultural Policy: Prospects for Change* (RKP/RIIA, 1981)

M. Tracey, *Agriculture in Western Europe: Challenge and Response 1880–1980* (Granada, 1982)

For Treaty references to the CAP see: Treaty of Rome, Part II Title II Articles 38–47.

Annex I: the CAP System for Selected Commodities

Cereals

Each year the Council of Ministers sets a *target price* for each type of cereal relating to Duisburg in the Ruhr Valley, the area of greatest deficit in the Community, to apply for the following marketing year (starting 1 July). From the target price is derived the *intervention price* which is the price, set for each cereal at 12–20 per cent below the target price, at which intervention agencies are obliged to buy cereals and withdraw them from the market in order to support prices. When prices are high (for example, when products are out of season) the intervention boards release stocks on to the market.

In the effort to curb surpluses, two mechanisms in particular have been introduced. One has been *guarantee thresholds* introduced in 1982–3 whereby, if average production over the previous three years exceeded a threshold of 119.5m tonnes, the intervention price would be cut by 1 per cent for each 1 m tonnes excess (up to 5 per cent). It was also decided that if imports of cereal substitutes during the previous year exceeded 15m tonnes, the guarantee threshold would be increased proportionately. A *co-responsibility* levy was introduced in 1986–7 (after a record crop in 1985) for a period of five marketing years. The rate is set at a certain percentage of the intervention price (1986–7, 3 per cent of £3.37 per tonne).

To stop imports from outside the Community disrupting the market, there is a *variable import levy* or *agricultural levy* which is a charge, calculated daily, levied on imports so that the *threshold price* on arrival at Rotterdam plus transport costs to Duisburg and trading margin just exceeds the target price, thereby preventing imports from undercutting Community prices. The threshold price is therefore an import floor price calculated as a function of the target price.

Export restitutions are subsidies paid to Community exporters to make up the difference between the Community price and a lower world price for the product in question.

Milk and Milk Products

The regulations governing the milk market are basically similar to the above. The market is supported by intervention purchases of butter and skimmed milk products.

There have been a variety of mechanisms designed to curb the chronic surplus of milk:

(a) Subsidised sales to consumers in the Community (such as 'Christmas butter') or abroad (for example to the USSR).

(b) Co-responsibility levies; charges levied on all producers at a fixed percentage of the target price in respect of the quantities of milk delivered, the proceeds to be used for financing expansion of the milk products market and disposal of surpluses.

(c) Production Quotas: a production (maximum threshold) is set (in 1986 it was just under 100m tonnes). This is broken down into individual or collective quotas. Individuals producing above their quotas will only be paid 25 per cent of the target prices for their excesses; collectives will receive no payments at all for theirs.

Beef and Veal

The central instrument for controlling the beef and veal market is known as the *guide price*. This acts in the same way as the target price to trigger the application of variable import levies and intervention (or instead of normal intervention, aids for private storage). This system has been supplemented in the UK by a variable premium scheme (or 'deficiency payment' system) which allows for direct payments to beef producers when market prices fall below an agreed ('target') level.

Sheep Meat

Member states have the choice between an intervention buying system (with public and private storage) or a variable slaughter premium system, combined in either case with an annual ewe premium. France has opted for intervention, the UK for the variable slaughter premium. The rest merely apply the ewe premium system.

Agricultural ministers set each year the *basic price* on which are calculated the intervention prices and the *guide price* used to determine the variable slaughter premium. There used to be a separate reference price used for calculating the ewe premium which varied between different regions of the Community. The prices have now, however, been brought together.

The intervention price is set at 85 per cent of the basic price. Intervention has never so far taken place but can take the form of either public intervention or private storage. The variable slaughter premium is paid to producers when the market price falls below the guide price (85 per cent of the basic price). The premium is equal to the difference between the two prices. Payments in Great Britain (Northern Ireland is not included in the scheme) under the slaughter premium are deducted from the amount of the ewe premium. The premium has to be paid back if the meat is exported to elsewhere in the Community (known as 'clawback'). The ewe premium is based on the difference between the reference price (equals basic price) and market price.

There is no import levy but there is a customs duty. New Zealand is the principal exporter to the Community, also exclusively to the UK. The Community was unable, because of bindings in the GATT, to reduce New Zealand or other countries' sendings unilaterally, but negotiated voluntary restraint agreements with New Zealand and the other main traditional non-Community supplier countries in return for a reduced rate of duty (10 instead of 20 per cent).

Pig Meat

Intervention takes place at a reference price between 85 and 92 per cent of a *basic price*. Because of the relative volatility of the pig market, the basic price is usually below the lowest market price in order not to encourage pig production, but merely to put a floor in the market.

A *sluice-gate price* for imports is set each quarter, similar to a threshold price. If imports enter the Community below this, they are subject to a supplementary levy to bring them up to it. All imports are subject to a *variable levy*, based on the difference between world market and Community costs for cereals for pig feeding, plus 7 per cent of the sluice-gate price, in order to allow for an element of preference for Community producers. To guard against very cheap imports, a supplementary charge can be added to the levies. Export restitutions can be made.

Eggs and Poultry Meat

The Community makes no attempt to intervene internally in the market for eggs or poultry meat. Imports are, however, regulated through a system similar to that used for pigmeat (see above).

Fruit and Vegetables

There is a considerable element of flexibility in the market for fruit and vegetables, largely because of their perishability. The first line of market management is that producer organisations may set a price at which they can, with some Community support, withdraw goods from the market. The Council of Ministers sets basic prices for cauliflowers, tomatoes, cucumbers, apples, peaches, pears and table grapes. Member states may fix *buying-in* prices 40 to 70 per cent below the basic price, and if prices fall for three successive days below this, a crisis may be declared and the member states can intervene. Producer organisations may withdraw products from the market when prices fall below a withdrawal price they set themselves. Only goods reaching quality standards may qualify. The goods purchased are either destroyed or pulped and used for cattle feed.

Imports are regulated through customs duties and through countervailing duties when prices fall below the reference price over two successive days. There is a limited system of export restitutions.

These measures were amended, particularly by strengthening support for producer groups and adding to the products qualifying for Community in order to safeguard the interests of French, Italian and Greek growers of Mediterranean products when Spain and Portugal joined the Community.

Oils and Oilseed

The Community is not self-sufficient in oil seeds and protein seeds and imports a large proportion of its requirements. Although an intervention system exists, the principal method used to give producers a 'fair income' is that of deficiency payments (i.e. direct payments to producers reflecting the difference between a guide price and actual market prices). Towards the end of 1986 the Commission was giving increasing thought to the possibility of introducing a variable levy on imported oils and fats which would not only combine incentives for Community production and disincentives for imports, but which would also in the short term increase the Community's budgetary revenues (although complicating relations with the United States, a chief supplier of oils).

For olive oil, where there is no problem of self-sufficiency, there is a combined system of deficiency payments and price support. Olive oil imports are subject to variable levies.

Wine

There are two withdrawal systems for supporting the market; a limited form of intervention based on a guide price set by the Council, linked with aids for private storage; and *preventative* and *compulsory distillation* which are the principal methods to deal with surpluses of cheap table wine. A producer can decide on preventative distillation if he sees difficulty in selling all his crop and is paid at 65 per cent of the guide price. The Commission decides on compulsory distillation for individual regions when there is a serious imbalance in the market and producers are paid digressively from 50 per cent of the guide price for the first 10m hectolitres to be distilled.

Sugar

The CAP imposes a quantitative restriction on the production of sugar which qualifies for support within the Community. This is because of the tendency in the Community to produce more sugar than is necessary to meet consumer needs, and because of the undertakings given to developing countries which are signatories to the Lomé Convention and which are dependent on their sugar exports.

Within the Community a target price is fixed annually for sugar produced in the main surplus areas.The market is supported by intervention purchases at prices which are lowest in the surplus areas and which increase towards the deficit areas. Producers enjoy full intervention prices on only a limited amount of sugar, divided among the member states according to quotas. Member states divide these into quotas for individual sugar manufacturers. The full price guarantee is given to a limited amount for each producer known as the A Quota (the sum of A quotas is roughly equivalent to Community consumption). A reduced guarantee is given for a further limited quantity – the B Quota – which is roughly equivalent to the opportunities for selling outside the Community. Quantities produced beyond the A and B Quotas get no support, nor may they be disposed of on the internal market.

The Lomé sugar producers are guaranteed the purchase of 1.3m tonnes of cane sugar by the Community at prices linked to the Community's internal support price. Imports beyond these are subject to threshold prices with variable levies. Export subsidies may be paid when world prices are low, and levies on sugar exports may be charged when world prices are high. Export restitutions may be paid.

Annex II: Agricultural Aspects of the Accession of Spain and Portugal

With the accession of Spain, the Community gained a major new agricultural power. Its total land and cultivation is second only to that of France; 20.5 per cent of the Community's total compared with France's 23.7 per cent. Spain and Portugal bring to the Community 3 million farms and agricultural labour force of 3 million people and some 30m hectares of agricultural land. 18 per cent of Spain's total working poulation and 23.8 per cent of Portugal's is engaged in agriculture (compared with 2.6 per cent for the UK). Spain is the largest exporter in the world of oranges, mandarins and almonds, Spanish vineyards are the largest in the world and its production of olive oil enormous. Portugal agricultural assets are limited to wines, tomato products, olive oil and animal feedstuffs (for which it imports inputs from third countries at world prices). It is clear why the existing Mediterranean producers, Greece, France and Italy, feared Spanish competition, already strong but potentially even stronger within the Community. Equally, the existing northern members feared they would have to find the money to support ever-increasing wine and olive oil lakes and fruit mountains even if accession does bring some 48 million new consumers into the Community. Restructuring Portuguese agriculture will also be expensive.

Equally, there are serious problems for Spanish and Portuguese agriculture. Both countries have mountainous terrain (Spain is the second most mountainous country in Europe after Switzerland), poor soil in several regions and inadequate or uneven rainfall. Both countries have inefficient and old-fashioned farming structures and production techniques, although the picture is varied in Spain, with some very efficient agriculture. Irrigation is inadequate in Spain and particularly primitive in Portugal. Both countries have a preponderance of small farms and elderly farmers. In Portugal, the weaknesses are general and are compounded by widespread illiteracy among farmers. In both countries, the state plays a preponderant role in market management.

It is not surprising, therefore, that agriculture was the most difficult problem in the accession negotiations which were anyway further complicated with the cross-linkage with the budget and other issues. Briefly, however, the settlement reached on agriculture comprised the following main points:

(a) A 'conventional' transitional period of seven years for Spain in respect of all products except fruit and vegetables and for Portugal in respect of certain products only. During this period, Portuguese and Spanish prices will be gradually aligned to Community prices; tariff and non-tariff barriers will be eliminated; Spain and Portugal will adopt the common commercial tariff and Community preference (i.e. observance of reference prices and application of levies).

(b) For other products, there is a transitional period of 10 years divided into two stages. The first stage will be four years (possibly three for Portugal). In broad terms, in the first stage the two countries will make their domestic market organisations compatible with the EC system. During the second stage, lasting up to 31 December 1995, the Spanish and Portuguese markets in these products will be gradually integrated into the Community.

(c) The 'supplementary trade mechanism' whereby if imports of sensitive products into the old Community from Spain or Portugal or vice versa reach or exceed 'indicative import ceilings' established at the beginning of each year, various measures can be taken including curtailing or suspending imports. (The principal products concerned are from Spain, wine products, new potatoes, fresh fruit and vegetables; into Spain from the Community, wine products, certain meat and milk products, several types of fruit and vegetables and bread-making wheat; and in both directions, olive oil in particular).

(d) Spanish production will be subject to the same restraints (e.g. guarantee thresholds, quotas, etc.) as other Community producers. Portugal is allowed some leeway for increased production.

(e) The Community policy for agricultural structures has been applied to Spain and Portugal from accession.

7 The Common Fisheries Policy

Fisheries received only the briefest mention in the Treaty of Rome, by being lumped in with agriculture as one of the products for which there needed to be a common policy. However, in 1970, at the very beginning of negotiations on accession with the UK, Norway, Denmark and Ireland, and seemingly with a clear eye to securing their interests in British and Norwegian waters, the Six adopted the Common Fisheries Policy. The policy is in many ways similar to that for fruit and vegetables (see p. 91), covers only the main species, and includes regulations on the grading of fish. Producer organisations can withdraw fish from the market when prices drop below levels set by the Community, in which case the Community pays a proportion of the costs. Imports from third countries are monitored against a reference price and may be stopped by the Commission if prices fall below it. Community fish prices are set each year in the autumn to take effect from 1 January the following year. There are also provisions for structural assistance to the industry. More central to the problems which arose in revising the Fisheries Policy was the basic principle of equal access to each member state's waters by every other member state.

The applicants were, however, able to negotiate considerable modifications to the common policy for a limited period – until 1982. Under the Treaty of Accession, all member states were allowed a general zone of almost exclusive fishing rights of six miles from the coastline, extended to 12 miles for areas which were recognised as particularly dependent on fishing. Only historic rights in the 6–12-mile part of this belt were excepted. The 12-mile zones for the UK were to the north and east of Scotland, from Cape Wrath to Berwick, and the Shetlands and Orkneys, north-east England, south-west England and County Down. These modifications were to be reviewed before 1982, the implication being that they might continue after then. Under the Treaty special conservation measures were to be adopted by the end of 1978. While accepted by the UK and Ireland, the Common Fisheries Policy, despite these modifications, proved a major factor in Norway's rejection of Community membership in its referendum of 1972.

These arrangements, and the Common Fisheries Policy itself, appeared immediately caught up in the dramatic changes brought about by the UN Law of the Sea Conference. Major changes in the pattern of fishing had been under way for some time. They arose principally from the enormous expansion in the scale of fishing since the Second World War. High capital investment in modern equipment, especially for industrial fishing for fish meal and fish oil, as well as the appearance of new fleets such as those of Eastern Europe, led to high catches and overfishing. Efforts had been made to control fishing through voluntary quotas but they were not particularly successful. As a result, there was a sustained campaign by a number of countries, of which Iceland was the one to affect the Community most, for 200-mile fishing limits. Iceland, indeed, took a series of unilateral actions to extend its control of fishing beyond territorial waters, culminating with the formal extension of its limits to 200 miles before this became acceptable under international law during the Law of the Sea Conference. This in turn led to the last of the 'cod wars' between Britain and Iceland. This was formally ended in June 1976 by a six-month agreement that allowed Britain only considerably reduced fishing rights in the Icelandic 200-mile zone. Hopes of a Community agreement with Iceland to replace the six-month bilateral agreement proved unrealisable.

Other countries, notably the US and Canada, also expressed the intention of extending their limits to 200 miles. As the trend grew there was a shift in customary international law. The result was that those countries which extended their fishing limits were then able not only to limit foreign fishing but, where necessary, to use access to their fishing limits as a bargaining counter to obtain access to other fishing grounds for their own fleets. At the same time, fleets denied access to their usual fishing grounds hurried to take fish from other waters, including their own home waters. It was therefore becoming imperative for the major Community fishing countries that they should also declare 200-mile fishing limits. This would have allowed fishing by non-Community countries to be controlled. But it gave no extra protection to member states because, as a result of the equal access provisions of the CFP, they would still be allowed to fish in all Community waters up to six or twelve miles of each other's coasts. The extra area gained would still be subject to Community rules. In anticipation of an extension of limits, therefore, both Ireland and the UK, not without difficulty, got the Community to agree that the CFP should be revised to take account of the new situation. It was also agreed that the Community should bring forward proposals on conservation as envisaged under the Treaty of Accession.

It was clear from the outset that there was no likelihood of a quick agreement on changing the common policy on the terms the UK and Ireland wanted. But the need to negotiate with non-Community countries for mutual access to waters was pressing. At the Hague in October 1976, the Council agreed, therefore, on a concerted extension of fishing limits to 200 miles from 1 January 1977 in the North Sea and the Atlantic, thus creating what is loosely known as the Community 'fish pond' but which is in fact the sum total of areas under member states' jurisdiction. The Commission was instructed by the Council to begin negotiations with third countries broadly on the principle of obtaining a balance of fisheries advantage. The result was a series of agreements with both developed and developing countries, of which the most important were with Norway, Sweden, the Faeroes and Spain, all concluded in 1980. The agreements established annual consultations at which the yearly catch that each side may take from the other's waters are fixed; licences are granted, and permitted fishing zones and cooperation on preserving fish stocks established. By its agreement with the USA (1977), the Community was given access for Italian and German boats to some US East Coast fishing. With Canada (1981) the Community agreed on reduced tariffs for certain Canadian fish exports in return for access to Canadian waters. The Community had issued fishing licences to Poland, the GDR and the USSR but when negotiations on agreements broke down in 1977, no further East European

fishing was allowed in Community waters. Following its withdrawal from the EC, the Community concluded an agreement
with Greenland (and Denmark) which took effect on 1 January
1985. This gives Community fishermen some access to Greenland's waters, while Greenland is entitled to sell fish and fish
products to the Community free of customs duties and quantitative
restrictions.

Agreeing common positions for the negotiations with third
countries was difficult. There was considerable debate on whether
negotiations could open before the Community had decided on
how much fish would be left to third countries after it had agreed
on an internal policy. Force of circumstances, however, soon
made the issue one of how much fish would be left to Community
fleets after agreements had been signed with third countries, but it
was in facing up to the need to agree on an internal policy that the
real differences of interest between the member states emerged.

With the extension of fishing limits by others, British, German
and Belgian fleets lost the major part of their distant-water
fishing. Distant-water fishing made up 36 per cent of the British
total catch, twice the volume of the French catch and three times
the volume of the West German catch. But the West German
proportion of distant-water fishing was some 69 per cent of its
total catch. The prospect for deep-sea fishing fleets was, therefore,
either to be laid up, with the men seeking employment in other
industries, or to attempt to find compensation in medium-distance
fishing grounds in Community waters of the North Sea and the
North East Atlantic. These were largely in the UK and Irish
zones – waters already overfished by existing fleets. Loss of catch,
and the claim that the UK contributed some 60 per cent of fish
stock in the North Sea and North Atlantic area subject to the
Common Fisheries Policy, were the main arguments in Britain's
demand for special treatment. The British Government first
proposed a belt of variable width but with a maximum of 50 miles
around the coastal state to be reserved for that state's fishing only.
When this was not agreed, Britain asked for a 'dominant preference', i.e. a 12- to 50-mile belt, with historic rights under 12 miles
phased out over a long period. This, too, was not agreed by the
others and the question of access, particularly acute between
France and Britain, was the single most important issue in the
negotiations on the new CFP and caused them to drag on until the
last moment and beyond. Besides this, and agreements with third

countries, other key issues were conservation, 'total allowable catches' (TACs) and quotas. A subsidiary but still important problem was that of aids for restructuring member states' fisheries.

The agreement on a new CFP finally came into effect on 23 January 1983. In fact, of the ten member states, nine had agreed on a package in the autumn of the previous year but the Danes had held out for better catch quotas. There was the usual Community cliffhanger with the possibility that, if no policy was in place on 1 January 1983, some member states like Britain and Ireland would resist attempts by others to fish 'up to the beaches' in a hideous free-for-all. There were suggestions that to avoid this, majority voting might be used to get the nine's package through, but Britain resisted as a matter of principle, and so overall agreement had to wait on the decision of the Danes. The main elements of the new package were as follows.

On access, it was agreed that while in principle all waters within the Community's two-hundred-mile zone were open to fishing by all member states, in practice there would be certain derogations. These allowed each member state to have exclusive fishing rights in the waters up to 12 miles from its coasts, subject to the traditional, 'historic', rights of fishermen from other Community countries. These historic rights were listed and detailed provisions made as to the species that could be caught by whom, when and where. Those rights that had not been exercised were abolished. As part of the conservation measures, a wider area, (known as a 'box') was established around the Shetlands and Orkneys at the entry of larger fishing vessels into it was restricted. These provisions were to last twenty years with a review after ten years, in 1992.

Conservation was the next most difficult problem after access. All member states in theory recognised the importance of conservation but some are stricter than others, in theory and in practice. The British have tended to pursue stricter measures. Under the Treaty of Accession, it is for the Community to determine conservation measures, although some national measures are not ruled out. With the extension of fishing limits some member states argued for Community measures only. This was considered premature by others, including the British, and as part of the Hague settlement of October 1976 member states retained the right, in the absence of agreed Community measures, to introduce their own, on an interim and non-discriminatory basis. But many of the British unilateral measures were disputed and led to cases in the European Court. They also led to conflicts, sometimes violent, with other member states in the fishing grounds, between, for example, France and Britain over Dublin Bay prawns (or langoustines).

The conservation package is based on TACs and quotas. The Commission proposes and the Council decides on yearly TACs for all threatened species. The TACs are divided into quotas for each member state, taking account of criteria such as the traditional activities of Community boats; the special needs of certain fishermen, especially in regions where there is little or no alternative employment; and the losses suffered in third countries from the extension to 200 miles. (In order to provide a basis of comparison between different species, the six main categories of edible fish are divided into cod equivalent; for instance, 1 haddock = 1 cod, 1 mackerel = 0.3 cod). These arrangements had been in effect before 1983; the agreement confirmed them and added the principle of 'staying power' for shares, so that each member state is allocated the same percentage share of TACs each year. The UK share of TACs varies according to species and sea area.

A number of technical conservation measures were agreed on, for example, mesh sizes. A system of surveillance had already been agreed which relied principally on national activities. The Commission has its own team of inspectors but they have to act with national inspectorates.

The Community also agreed on general measures to help the fishing industries of the member states. These include aids for modernisation (of boats, for example, or of fish storage facilities); fish farming; 'mothballing'; scrapping old vessels; exploratory voyages and joint ventures.

There had been earlier agreement on a new marketing policy made necessary by the shift to consumption of processed and frozen fish rather than fresh fish and the change in the types of fish caught by Community fishermen as a result of the loss of traditional fishing ground. The new policy introduced new marketing standards (on the size and quality of fish); and was based, like the previous policy, on producer groups who apply common rules on production and marketing. At the beginning of each fishing season, the Council of Ministers sets guide prices for the principal species, much in the same way as prices are set for agricultural produce. They also set 'withdrawal' prices, usually between

70 per cent and 90 per cent of the guide price. Producer organisations can withdraw produce from the market in order to firm up market prices on the basis of the Community withdrawal price; or, in order to take account of seasonal fluctuations, they may set their own withdrawal prices within a range related to the Community price. There is a Community system of compensation for organisations who withdraw produce. This is designed so as not to encourage overfishing and so far the cost of the market support policy has been relatively small.

The pressure to reach agreement on 1 January 1983 was not just because of the fear of an uncontrolled scramble for fish if the deadline set in 1972 was not met. It was also to ensure that the Community had a policy in place before Spain and Portugal became members (shades, perhaps, of the first enlargement of the Community). When negotiations on fisheries started in 1983, both countries were told they would have to accept the *aquis Communautaire*. Greece had already done so but its accession had not raised any great fisheries problems. The accession of Spain and Portugal was a different matter. Spain had the third largest fishing fleet in the world and therefore a capacity far larger than the resources it could find in its own waters. It already had an agreement (1980 – see above) with the Community, which gave it some fishing rights in Community waters. All the fishing members of the Community but especially France, Britain and Ireland feared they would be swamped by Spain's fleet. For example, the French fleet fishing in the Bay of Biscay was estimated in 1984 to be about 60 000 tonnes compared with the Spanish fleet of 600 000 tonnes. Portuguese fishing activities were much smaller, with the main fishing effort by small boats in coastal waters and with limited capacity in third country waters (off Canada, Norway and Africa). Thus the fisheries negotiations turned out, as expected, to be among the most difficult and in large part were responsible for the delay in reaching overall agreement.

The final settlement was not overgenerous to the applicants. The number of Spanish boats allowed to fish in other member states' waters and the types of fish they can catch are severely limited. A zone off the coasts of the UK and Ireland, for example, is closed to Spanish and Portuguese boats until 1996. The two countries adopted the common marketing policy from the date of accession, although the narrowing of price differences and the dismantling of customs duties is to be spread over seven years (ten years for sardines).

The next major landmark will be the review of the CFP in 1992 by when the Commission has to submit a report on the fisheries situation to the Council. This could lead to changes, although Britain in particular will be concerned that the access provisions and quota shares should not be altered to its disadvantage. The Commission may also in the next few years make proposals for the development of the CFP for the Mediterranean where the marketing policy applies but not TACs or quotas and where, of course, there are no 200-mile limits. In the meantime, there have been signs, like the blockade of the French fishing port of Hendaye by Spanish fishing vessels in June 1986, that there will be strong pressures to modify the CFP before 1992.

SUGGESTIONS FOR FURTHER READING

J. Farnell and J. Elles, *In Search of a Common Fisheries Policy* (Gower, 1984)

M. Leigh, *European Integration and the Common Fisheries Policy* (Croom Helm, 1983)

M. Shackleton, *The Politics of Fishing in Britain and France* (Gower, 1986)

M. Wise, *The Common Fisheries Policy of the European Community* (Methuen, 1984)

For Treaty references see: Treaty of Rome, Part II, Title II, Articles 38–47, with particular reference to Article 38.3.

8 Policies Relating to Industry and the Environment

Community involvement in policies relating to the industrial structure of the member states stems both from the Treaty of Paris, establishing the European Coal and Steel Community, and from the Treaty of Rome. Under the Treaties the emphasis was placed particularly on the removal of practices which adversely affect trade within the common market. In 1972, the Heads of Government attempted to give added momentum to the process of achieving the goals set out in the Treaties. They sought also to extend Community involvement in more 'positive' policies towards industry and the environment. Neither appeared to carry the Community far before the economic recession significantly altered the preoccupations of member governments. Reactions to the recession were mixed: on the one hand, member governments were determined to safeguard their own industrial interests, and to contain inflation and unemployment. On the other hand, it was clear that most of the member states were facing common problems, the resolution of which was to at least some extent (and the extent differed from one government to another) beyond the reach of each government by itself. Moreover, the Community itself had some legal competence or responsibility in a number of sectors, including, for example, the steel industry, so that, encouraged by the Commission, the member states were obliged to seek more common solutions.

COMPETITION POLICY

The politics of competition policy have been much less dramatic than those of policies such as agriculture. A significant body of competition law now exists affecting both local and Community-wide trading. (See also Chapter 4.) Yet in some ways the Community's competition policy has been removed from both the attention of national governments and their intervention. Its rules and their interpretation are executed by the Commission and the Court of Justice. At the same time, since the policy is directed against both private companies and national governments, the Commission has had to show some sensitivity to national needs and demands, particularly with the onset of the recession. In addition, the Commission was presented with a dilemma. In some sectors there had been a longstanding concern that, by international standards, many European enterprises were too small to maximise efficiency and to challenge successfully their international competitors, especially Japan and the United States. Yet in other sectors, there was anxiety that smaller and medium-sized companies in Europe were not able to exploit new technologies as they have often done in the United States because of the position of the larger established companies. The Community has, therefore been somewhat ambivalent in its attitudes towards concentrations of industry.

The basic rules governing competition among private enterprises are included in Articles 85 and 86 of the Treaty of Rome. They are designed to control any agreements between companies that are liable to affect trade between member states, and which 'have as their object or effect the prevention, restriction or distortion of competition within the common market', and to prevent any enterprise with a 'dominant' position in the market from abusing that position. The Commission is given the responsibility under the Treaty to ensure the application of these rules and to end any infringements. In 1962 the Council granted the Commission both initiative and decision-making powers in relation to both articles. Since 1962, therefore, the Commission has been able to build up its policy without the need for continual references to the Council of Ministers. In doing so it has often been supported by the Court of Justice through its interpretation of the Treaty on appeals from those contesting the Commission's decisions.

The Community's rules on competition owe much to the

influence of United States anti-trust laws. This is particularly so within the ECSC Treaty, where the powers of the High Authority were both wider and more detailed than those of the EEC's Commission. The reasons for this were largely political: to prevent any revival of concentration in German heavy industry. The Treaty of Rome, on the other hand, is concerned more with general principles. This, too, reflects the political climate of 1957, including the lessened enthusiasm for granting supranational powers to the Commission. But it also reflects the belief that the large unified market would allow for the reconciliation of the aim of greater competitiveness with the establishment of industrial structures capable of taking advantage of economies of scale.

The Commission, like member states, has for the most part developed its policy on restrictive practices in a highly practical manner. It has combined test case decisions with a regard for Treaty provisions allowing for exemptions where agreements between companies can be held to be in the Community interest. Those agreements which can be so exempted are those which contribute to 'improving the production or distribution of goods, or to promoting technical or economic progress, while allowing consumers a fair share of the resulting benefit'. Through this combination of intervening and standing back the Commission has evolved a policy which, among other things, bans price-fixing, market sharing, production quotas and vertical distribution agreements. A major innovation in the law of restrictive practices has been in the field of distribution; the Commission has ruled illegal the traditionally accepted practice of exclusive dealing arrangements in foreign countries as liable to create artificial barriers within the market.

As in other fields, the Commission has not been working in isolation. All member states have some form of legislation on restrictive practices even though they may vary in strictness. Such parallel legislation in the member states has created few major political problems. Contact between Commission and national experts is frequent and takes place within a framework where the Commission's authority is clearly defined. Indeed, if the Commission begins to investigate a case already being investigated by national authorities, the principle has now been accepted that the Commission proceeds and the national authorities accept its decision. This can, however, cause some irritation, not least in view of the sometimes inordinately long time Community cases can take. Theoretically, it is possible for a firm to be fined both by the Commission and by national authorities, especially under Article 85 of the Treaty where Community and national interests are often the same. Such an identity of interest has not, however, been so marked in other areas of competition policy, including the control of mergers.

The Commission's proposal to control concentrations and mergers between companies, introduced in 1973, has aroused considerable controversy. The proposal itself came only after several years of legal argument over the basis for such a regulation. Systematic control over concentrations was provided for under the ECSC Treaty in relation to the coal and steel industries, but was left very much more vague under the Treaty of Rome. Under Article 86 the Commission can challenge an enterprise for abusing its dominant position, but a dominant position as such is not regarded as unacceptable. The Commission proposed to go beyond this to control mergers which might lead to an abuse, on the proposition that extending a dominant position as such is not regarded as unacceptable. In 1984, for example, the Commission after an investigation begun in 1974 reached a settlement with International Business Machines (IBM) which left the company in a clearly pre-eminent position *vis à vis* European computer manufacturers. However, the settlement did wrest some concessions from IBM, such as accepting a timetable for the disclosure of technical details, and it also allows for the Commission to review IBM's business practices. None the less, the Commission has been intent on establishing controls over mergers which might lead to an abuse. In this the Commission has been supported by the Court of Justice and the European Parliament. In the Continental Can case, although the Court found in favour of the company, it supported the Commission's view that effective competition required the control of concentrations and, therefore, mergers. It was in order to be able to deal effectively with the question that the Commission introduced its proposal.

Although the Commission modified the proposal in 1981, it remained unacceptable to the Council of Ministers. Member governments were reluctant to allow the Commission to expand its authority in such a sensitive area and at a time when there was (and still is) a general desire to create stronger industrial units to combat increased international competition. Such a policy would provide the Commission with significant responsibilities, backed up by legal sanctions, to inhibit mergers. Since the policy would influence the structure of industry, it has been considered by some to be premature when there is no complementary, coherent Community industrial policy. Moreover, the policing aspects of the proposal, to safeguard the interests of competition within the Community, can be undertaken, if desired by member governments themselves.

It is thus in the area of restrictive practices, where there are no great political difficulties for member governments, that the Commission has moved ahead. There appear to be no sufficiently compelling reasons for member governments to allow it to go further in other, if related, directions. But, as with much of Community law, the direct effects of possible gains for the consumer or the economy are not easily discernible. Aware of this, and as part of the battle against inflation, the Commission has extended its methods of detecting restrictive practices by publishing comparative prices of selective products within the Community. This has not only increased the opportunities to exercise its investigatory powers, but may reduce the very wide gap between the Commission and its actions and the general public.

INDUSTRIAL POLICY

The Community's involvement in a positive industrial policy derives in part from the Treaty of Paris establishing the Coal and Steel Community. The emphasis was placed not only on removing trade barriers and eliminating the highly complex series of national pricing systems, but also on improving the structure of the industries. Under the Treaty of Rome, Community intervention was limited. The basis of the Treaty was economic liberalism, despite the traditions of government intervention, especially in France and Italy. However, it became increasingly clear during the 1960s that market forces by themselves would not bring about the intended result of a single industrial base within the Community. The application of the Treaty coincided with the growing intervention of nearly all governments even, though to a limited extent, on the part of the West German government. Although, therefore, the ideological differences between West Germany and France especially were somewhat narrowed, it remained sufficient to prevent the adoption of any coherent industrial planning at Community level.

Other factors have, however, come increasingly to the fore. Particular industries have come under increasing external competition: steel and related industries, such as shipbuilding, from Japan and several other of the Newly Industrialising Countries (South Korean shipyards, for example, produced a similar tonnage to those of all the European member states together in 1984); and textiles and clothing from many older developing countries in Asia, the Mediterranean, and from Eastern European countries. The general world recession, beginning in the early 1970s, intensified many of the problems. While the measures taken mark a significant step in the Community's development, agreement has been only on a piecemeal approach, based on the common commercial policy, rather than any comprehensive industrial policy.

Industrial policy is, of course, difficult to isolate from other economic and social policies. In the absence of an agreed overall framework, a limited approach is perhaps unavoidable. Difficulties are created by the fact that the member states are industrial competitors. In addition, Community debates have often been polarised between the advocates of the free market and of government intervention. This division at government level has been reinforced at interest-group level. Employer groups, for example, represented at the Community level in the Confederation of Industries of the European Communities (UNICE), are constitutionally committed to free enterprise. In contrast, trade unions have differed on the extent of intervention necessary, while, in general, heavily preoccupied with the more immediate consequencies of industrial policies for their members.

None the less, since the mid-1960s, there have been several attempts, particularly by the Commission, to introduce coherence in a Community industrial policy. In 1970 the Commission produced the Colonna Report, which defined five main areas which needed to be tackled: the elimination of technical barriers to trade; the harmonisation of the legal, fiscal and financial frameworks; the encouragement of transnational mergers; the adaptation of industry to changed economic circumstances and demands; and greater solidarity towards technical collaboration and in controlling multinational corporations. The latter was often particularly stressed, especially a Community policy towards advanced technology industries, such as electronics, aeronautics, and computers. Many considered it of the highest priority to reduce the gap between the US and Western Europe in these areas in the interests both of Community industry, and of further integration in Europe. It raised the issue, however, of whether the Community is the most relevant unit for industrial cooperation in view, for example, of the significance of the roles of the US and Japan. Where there has been collaboration within the Community it has tended to be between individual countries or industries, such as French, German, Spanish and British industries (with varying degrees of governmental support) in the Airbus. The importance of the US market remains particularly clear, and many member states have, perhaps inescapably, been attracted towards cooperation with US aircraft manufacturers on large new projects.

Although little progress was made in discussion on the Colonna Report, within a purely Community framework, the Paris Summit of 1972 appeared to give a strong political commitment to greater progress. On the basis of that commitment the Commission presented its Action Programme on Industrial and Technological Policy in 1973. This continued many earlier preoccupations, including the tendency for mergers to take place, not between companies across national borders, but within member states. Greater information on merger possibilities was, therefore, held to be necessary – especially for smaller and medium-sized firms. A legal framework for a European Company was also considered a priority. The need to meet the challenge of especially American-dominated multinationals strongly reinforced the Commission's desire for more mergers. However, at the same time, the Commission also proposed a greater control over mergers (see above). This implied ambiguity in the Commission's approach towards mergers reflected, in part at least, the divisions within the Commission between the interests of the Industrial Affairs Directorate General and those of the Competition DG.

The Action Programme also emphasised the need to take a more sectoral approach to industrial policy to tackle the problems of particular industries. A distinction has been frequently made between 'sunset' and 'sunrise' industries, those suffering from structural decline and those in the advanced technology sectors. Attention often shifts from one to the other, especially when the former face further crises. The world economic recession made many of the problems facing the traditional industries particularly acute. The problem of unemployment resulting from technological advances and increased productivity and the increasing penetration of European markets by industrial imports from developing countries had already become apparent. Member states have tended to react against problems individually. Each has inevitably pursued policies which met its particular needs, concentrating on improving the viability of its own national industries, influenced by traditional structures and attitudes. In reinforcing these individual approaches, the recession made progress towards common policies even more difficult.

None the less there has been movement at the Community level. Under powers derived from the Treaty of Paris, the Community became involved in efforts to tackle the grave problems affecting the steel industry. It became ever more apparent that the industry was not suffering from merely cyclical problems and that severe restructuring was inevitable as a result. Productivity, for example, compared poorly with its competitors, notably Japan. Investment to re-equip and adapt the industry had also been lower in Community countries than in other members of the OECD. The industry has been working consistently well below capacity, dropping to only 58 per cent in 1980 and to 57 per cent in 1983. Various plans were put forward to establish some sort of market discipline by means of voluntary guidelines but with little success. In 1980, therefore, after a further collapse in prices, a 'manifest crisis' was declared under the Treaty. This allowed the Community to set product and delivery quotas (which eventually covered some 80 per cent of production within the Community) and to control prices set by producers and wholesalers (controls on imported products had in fact been introduced in 1978).

The problems involved in restructuring have been severe. The 1985 targets involved cutting some 18 per cent of the total capacity for 1980. Even that figure has over-estimated demand so that further cuts are likely, particularly for the industry in France and Italy, and although it was the intention to begin the process of liberalisation in 1986, that has become increasingly impractical. The repercussions of closures, whether political, economic or social, fall, inevitably, on the member states with varying degrees of severity and with only limited assistance from Community funds. Considerable efforts, however, have been made to control state aids to the industry. At the same time, the international repercussions of the Community's policies have been significant, especially as, with only a minimal growth in world demand, competition has become intense. Relations with the United States over trade in many steel products became particularly strained, with restrictions and countervailing duties being imposed by each side, until agreement on Community export curbs was reached in 1985.

There are both external and internal elements to the Community's policy towards industries such as steel, shipbuilding, and synthetic fibres. The common commercial policy has been employed to block cheaper imports in order to allow at least a breathing space for the industries most hard pressed. Various negotiations have been undertaken to introduce quotas and voluntary restraints which might allow for the burden of competition to be spread more equitably among the member states. In the case of textiles, the thicket of quotas on imports from developing countries has been replaced by the evolution, within the General Agreement on Tariffs and Trade (GATT), of the Multi-Fibre Arrangements. Under these arrangements, which have been several times renewed, the last renegotiation having taken place in 1986, importing countries have concluded a number of multi-fibre agreements with supplying countries which allow for only a slow and controlled increase in the level of imports. The European Community has signed such agreements on behalf of the member states (see Chapter 14).

It has often been difficult to reach a consensus among member states on using the opportunities created by the MFA. This is perhaps not surprising given the scale of restructuring involved. Between 1973 and 1985, for example, some 33 per cent of jobs were lost in the textile industries of the Community. The restructuring of the industry has been a protracted process, with inevitably, national governments reacting individually. The major concern of the Commission has therefore been to try to prevent 'beggar-my-neighbour' competition in state subsidies and to allow only those aids which clearly aim to adapt industry to changed economic conditions. Similarly, the Commission sought to curtail pressures towards the establishment of cartels in the synthetic fibres sector of the industry, although largely at the behest of the Industrial Affairs DG it allowed the 10 leading manufacturers briefly to coordinate their reductions in capacity.

The Community has necessarily therefore been concerned with the most vulnerable sectors of industry. In place of long-term and ambitious goals, the Community has often been obliged to lower its sights to immediate problems even if on a limited and pragmatic basis.

SCIENCE AND TECHNOLOGY

Community involvement in science and technology, which originates from the European Coal and Steel Community Treaty of 1951, was reinforced by the establishment of the Joint Research Centre (JRC) under the Euratom Treaty of 1957. The JRC now has four sites, the largest of which is at Ispra in Italy.

Pressures for joint action beyond that of the JRC increased steadily during the 1960s. A committee of experts was established in 1967 to investigate the possibilities. However, it was not until 1972, against a background of increasing international collaboration, that Heads of Government gave political impetus to the issue of a purely Community research and development programme (although R & D was not more generally included within the competence of the Community until the Single European Act of 1986). In 1972, member states were called upon to coordinate national policies, and a Science and Technology Research Committee (CREST) was set up. CREST advises both the Commission and the Council of Ministers, and is chaired by a representative of the Commission. It has been supported by a number of sectoral sub-committees covering such subjects as energy, raw materials and medical research. All programmes are watched over by Advisory Committees on Programme Management, composed of specialists, which also advise the Commission on the preparation of proposals for new action in their fields.

The period 1974–76 was very much an experimental phase, providing useful experience on which the Commission, supported by the Advisory Committees on Programme Management, could draw when framing its subsequent proposals. However, CREST was of the opinion that caution was required before the introduction of a specifically Community R & D policy. While a number of proposals were put forward by the Commission the great majority that were agreed lay in the field of energy, and it was not until 1983 that a broader-based multi-annual framework programme was agreed.

But, limited though the Community's involvement in R & D was before 1983, it had not been wholly excluded from earlier developments. It had become involved via three main ways: through direct, concerted and indirect actions. Direct actions included those carried out through the JRC and have covered a wide range of subjects, inevitably still influenced by the JRC's origins and its continuing expertise and facilities in the field of nuclear energy. Under concerted action, member states have agreed to exchange information about relevant work within national programmes. The research itself remains under national control and funding, but through coordination at Community level, the several components can reinforce one another. Examples include studies of the physical properties of foodstuffs and several aspects of public health. The Community budget meets only the relatively modest costs of coordination. Indirect actions are carried out through cost-sharing contracts between the Commission and laboratories in the member states. Projects cover aspects of environmental research, energy, raw materials, scientific and technical information, agriculture, standards, and reference materials.

Special arrangements have been made for the management of the Joint European Torus (JET) fusion project located at Culham in Oxfordshire. The project was finally agreed in May 1978 and was formally opened in 1984. In view of its significance as a major part of the Community's thermonuclear research programme, and its costs and time-scale (the first experimental stage is to last 15 years), the responsibility for running the project lies with a special JET council. This is composed of two representatives from each of the participating states and the Commission. The JET project in many ways represents the most advanced element of a common Community policy.

After considerable pressure from the European Commission, usually strongly supported by the European Parliament, and in circumstances that clearly showed that Europe was lagging seriously behind in a number of critically important areas, the programme on forecasting and assessment in science and technology (FAST) was introduced in 1979. An information network, Euronet Diane, was set up in 1980 with national PTTs. And in 1982 a five-year programme in bio-technology was introduced. Also undertaken in 1982 was an experimental phase of the European Strategic Programme for Research and Development in Information Technology (ESPRIT), although it was not until two years later that the Council of Ministers somewhat reluctantly agreed to a larger programme, and then as part of the multi-annual framework programme agreed the previous year. ESPRIT was designed for pre-competitive collaboration between companies with the Community providing 50 per cent of the funding.

The results of the research are then made more widely available. Although the programme was widely acknowledged to have been a success in bringing about closer collaboration among a number of enterprises, efforts to increase the funding of ESPRIT substantially for 1987–91 were not met with unanimous enthusiasm.

The multi-annual programme agreed in 1983 set out seven priority areas including the promotion of agricultural and industrial competitiveness, and the improvement of energy and raw-material management. The framework programme was for a three-year period beginning in 1984, contributions from the Community budget being some Ecu 4.5 billion. Within the general aim of promoting industrial competitiveness, the development of new technologies has received particular attention. In addition to ESPRIT, other programmes begun were Basic Research in Industrial Technologies for Europe (BRITE) which was also designed to encourage joint projects between companies in different member states. Again the Community has funded 50 per cent of the costs incurred in companies introducing new technologies.

Research and Technology was another area brought within the Treaty framework by the Single European Act. It was a clear indication of the importance attached by all the member states to the need for greater collaboration in R & D in one form or another to meet American and Japanese competition. However, a number of difficulties have arisen, in part because of the procedures laid down under the SEA whereby once the framework programme is agreed on the basis of unanimity, agreement on individual programmes, such as ESPRIT, can be reached by a qualified majority. The problems that have arisen reflect deeper suspicions both of the Community's involvement as such in R & D and the costs of that involvement. Each member state, particularly, of course, the more highly developed, have for many years encouraged national leaders or champions. While international collaboration has been seen as increasingly necessary and desirable, there has been considerable ambivalence about the precise form of that collaboration, whether it should be on a government-to-government basis, an industry-to-industry basis, within Europe, with American companies, etc. No consistent line has been pursued; governments sometimes lead and at other times are led by, their industries. For those member states with a solid R & D capability, there is therefore considerable interest in retaining flexibility. For other member states, there is inevitably a far greater interest in the dissemination of information and the diffusion of technology and they have often looked to the Community as a means of such transfer.

There is, in other words, an incipient north–south dimension to the issue which has been exacerbated by budgetary considerations. On the one hand, West Germany and the UK have been strongly in favour of strict budgetary limits; on the other hand, Italy and Greece have pressed strongly for increasing budgetary allocations to R & D. The issue inevitably became entangled with other issues, not least the reform of the CAP and the budget. Effective agreement on the framework programme could not therefore be reached until June 1987.

The Community's policy remains modest in financial terms. But it needs to be remembered that a great deal of collaboration already takes place within a wider European framework and, moreover, the Community itself is increasingly playing a part in such collaborative efforts.

In 1971, before the Community had settled the general lines of a policy towards science and technology, it coordinated the establishment of a Committee of senior national officials, known as COST (*Cooperation Scientifique et Technique*). COST now has a membership of 19 European countries. Its technical sub-committees cover a wide range of subjects, including telecommunications, transport, oceanography, and meteorology. In terms of cost, its major project has been the creation of a European Centre for Medium Range Weather Forecasting at Bracknell in Berkshire.

Outside the Community framework the member states have been involved in a wide variety of bilateral and multilateral collaborative projects. In aerospace, for example, the European Space Agency was established in 1975 out of two earlier organisations, the European Space Research Organisations (ESRO), and the European Launcher Development Organisation (ELDO) with a membership wider than that of the Community. The European Nuclear Research Centre (CERN) was founded in 1954, again with a wider membership, to carry out research on pure science aspects of nuclear physics. The European Molecular Biology Laboratory (EMBL) brings together ten countries to collaborate in a major field of basic research. Fundamental research as a whole is the concern of the European Science Foundation (ESF) set up by non-governmental bodies from 16 countries in 1974. It is composed of 44 national research councils and academies, and is concerned with stimulating and coordinating research and encouraging collaboration rather than undertaking research directly. The Commission is represented on the ESF council.

Finally, the Community as such has no role in EUREKA, the initiative launched by President Mitterand largely in response to the Strategic Defense Initiative (SDI) of the United States. The major concern was that the SDI programme would have profound implications for the civil as well as the military sectors' position in high technology industries through cross-national collaboration. National governments determine their own funding levels and no Community funds are involved. The Commission none the less sits alongside the other 19 countries that belong to the organisation.

ENVIRONMENTAL POLICY

A Community environmental policy began only in 1973, when the Commission's proposals for an Environmental Action Programme were largely accepted by the Council of Ministers. Significantly, Ministers acted not only as the Council but, formally, as representatives of their governments. Competence or responsibility in environmental matters was – and in important respects, remains – 'mixed', part Community, part national. Environmental policies were brought within the framework of the Treaties only with the Single European Act and even then their 'mixed' character continued to be recognised.

By 1973, many member states had already taken a variety of unilateral measures, but directed towards differing aspects of the environment, according to different standards, and using different methods. Much work had also been accomplished within international organisations such as the Organisation for Economic Cooperation and Development (OECD), especially on pollution, the Council of Europe, especially on the protection of the environment, and within the UN's Environmental Programme (UNEP). In 1972, however, the Heads of Government meeting at the Paris summit declared themselves in favour of a Community policy, on the grounds that 'economic expansion is not enough. . . . It must emerge in an improved quality as well as improved standard of life. In the European spirit, special attention will be paid to non-material values and wealth and to the protection of the environment so that progress shall serve mankind[1]. Very clearly pollution did not recognise political frontiers so that Community involvement was a logical step. At the same time, the aim of safeguarding and improving the environment was complemented by the need to ensure a free market among member states because of the increasing number of different regulations.

Three principles have come to underlie the Community's environmental programmes: the necessity for preventive action, which carried with it the implication that environmental protection should be a factor taken into account in assessing new industrial projects and technological advances; the responsibility of the polluter to pay for the pollution caused, a principle first agreed in the OECD and formally incorporated in the SEA; and the need for action as early as possible, preferably at source. From an initial programme of studies, the Community's policies have gradually encompassed an ever-wider range of issues, from water pollution, to air pollution, noise levels, the control of chemical products, nuclear safety (a concern intensified by the Chernobyl disaster of 1986), and conservation. The Community's Third Action Programme began in 1983. The year 1987 has been designated the European Year of the Environment in order to promote greater awareness of environmental needs and the Community's policies.

While an increasing number of decisions have been taken, agreement on common and/or minimum standards throughout the Community has been often extremely difficult. In part this has been because of conflicting expert opinion on environmental risks and on the actual causes of pollution. The latter is well illustrated by the position taken for so long by the British government against those who accused British power stations, etc., of causing the acid rain that fell in Scandinavia and elsewhere. As a result there has been deadlock in the Council of Ministers on power-station emissions, with the Commission supported by Denmark, West Germany and the Netherlands calling for a 60 per cent cut in sulphur dioxide emissions by 1993, while the British were prepared (at least in 1986) to agree to a cut of only 30 per cent by 1995, rising to 45 per cent by 2015 and only after that to 60 per cent. In this case, as in others, differences over expert advice have coincided with problems of cost – it is expensive, for instance, to 'clean' power station chimneys. The costs involved in preventing pollution or improving environmental standards have been a particular concern for the industrially less-advanced member states. Greece, for example, has called for specific Community funding for environmental improvements, and aid has in fact been given by the European Regional Development Fund for such purposes (examples include contributions towards cleaning the Mersey and the Bay of Naples). But the position of Greece and other Mediterranean countries underlines the very different attitudes towards pollution: in the case of the still industrially-developing countries, development is considered simply more important in the short and intermediate term than the environment. In some instances such an approach is backed up by differing social standards; the netting of wild birds in Italy might cause affront in England; concern over lawnmower noise might simply cause bewilderment in Greece. Some member states have been very much more active than others, in large measure in response to new political movements such as the Greens. As a result West Germany, for example, has been a pacesetter in several areas, such as controlling the lead content of petrol. Since many anti-pollution measures are expensive, it is natural that those member states which have adopted them wish to see others follow suit, so restoring their competitive position. Equally clearly entrenched interests which have not adopted such measures can often exercise strong influence against governments' accepting them. But there are strong grounds for adopting generally acceptable rules, which allow for the free flow of goods from one member state to another, so overcoming any 'non-tariff barriers' caused by different national regulations.

Although the Commission was originally in favour of harmonised measures applicable to all, in the interests of measurability, a more flexible approach has in fact been adopted. Indeed, such flexibility has been formalised in the SEA, largely to meet the concerns of Denmark, for Article 130T provides that protective measures agreed for all should not prevent a member state from introducing more stringent protective measures. There is however a qualification that such measures should be compatible with the Treaty, including the establishment of a genuine Internal Market by 1992.

The Community's policies under the first Action Programme tended to be largely exploratory and to some extent reactive, as, for example, in the case of measures to counter pollution by oil tankers, which were expedited somewhat after the *Amoco Cadiz* accident caused Heads of Government to discuss the issue in April 1978. Water was, indeed, the main area of concern under the first Action Programme, fresh as well as salt water, and the setting of 'quality standards'. From 1975 onwards a considerable range of proposals relating to water for drinking, swimming, farming, fisheries, recreation and so on were gradually accepted, together with restrictions on the discharge of pollutants into water. It was over the latter that there was particular difficulty, the British, for example, remaining unconvinced that measures necessary for the already heavily polluted Mediterranean were appropriate to faster-moving rivers that flowed into the Atlantic and the North Sea with their strong tidal movements. Agreement was only reached in the case of titanium dioxide (a 'whitener' used in the manufacture of paints, which when discharged is often known as 'red sludge') on the basis that disposal at sea – condemned by the Italians and supported by the British – was possible, but only if continuous monitoring failed to reveal any significant pollution. Such an agreement raises serious questions, in turn, about the effectiveness of the implementation by member governments of decisions once reached.

A second area tackled at the Community level was, and continues to be, that of air pollution. While general guidelines, resolutions and studies on sulphur dioxide emissions, on transboundary pollution and pollution by lead have been agreed, the Commission's attempts, supported by Denmark and West Germany especially, to introduce tighter controls have been deadlocked in the Council of Ministers.

Pollution of the air and sea can obviously not be contained within the Community. Norway has, for example, been greatly concerned over air pollution derived from foreign sources, including British plants. Other international organisations have also been active, particularly within the various Specialised Agencies of the UN. In some ways such international activity creates problems for the Community. Some member states have been reluctant to establish purely Community rules if there are already international rules in existence – such as those agreed under the aegis of the International Civil Aviation Organisation (ICAO) on, for example, noise levels. There is also a reluctance on the part of some member states to allow the Community, as such, rather than the individual member states, to negotiate in such fora, particularly on those issues where there are no internal

Community rules. The Commission has often, therefore, had only observer status as, for example, at the Law of the Sea Conference. With the acceptance of Community rules and the increasing number of international conventions, the Commission has, however, begun to play a larger role. The Community participated, for example, in negotiations for the Barcelona Convention on the pollution of the Mediterranean and became a signatory to the Paris Convention on sea pollution from rivers.

It was only in the third Action Programme, agreed by the Council of Ministers in December 1982, that the Community began to move towards preventative actions. The key measure from the Commission's perspective was that agreed in 1985 under which approval for major industrial or infrastructure developments is subject to a prior assessment of its environmental impact. Further preventative measures are likely under the fourth Programme although their adoption is likely to continue to be slow. It is significant, for example, that the SEA specifies certain elements that need to be taken into account in any Community action, including the (different) 'environmental conditions in the various regions of the Community', 'the potential benefits and costs' of actions, and the 'economic and social development of the Community as a whole and the balanced development of its regions'. In addition, it is left to the Council to decide on the basis of unanimity what action is to be taken and whether or not they should continue to be decided on that basis. Member governments are therefore effectively left with a veto in environmental matters.

SUGGESTIONS FOR FURTHER READING

G. Hall (ed.), *European Industrial Policy* (Croom Helm, 1986)

The Fast Report: Eurofutures – the Challenge of Innovation (Butterworth for the European Commission and *Futures*, 1984)

N. Haig, *EEC Environmental Policy and Britain* (IIEP/IIED, 198)

A. Jacquemin (ed.), *European Industry: Public Policy and Corporate Strategy* (Clarendon Press, Oxford 1984)

S. P. Johnson, *The Pollution Control Policy of the European Communities* (2nd edition, Graham & Trotman, 1983)

V. Korah, *Competition Law of Britain and the Common Market*

(3rd edition, Martinus Nijhoff, 1982)

D. H. McKay, *Planning and Politics in Western Europe* (Macmillan, 1982)

M. Sharp (ed.), *Europe and the New Technologies* (Frances Pinter, 1983)

G. Shepherd et al., *Public and Private Strategies for Change* (Frances Pinter, 1983)

D. Swann, *Competition and Industrial Policy in the European Community* (Methuen, 1983)

R. Williams, *European Technology: the Politics of Collaboration* (Croom Helm, 1973)

D. Willson, *A European Experiment: the Launching of the JET Project* (Adam Hilger, 1981)

For Treaty references see: Treaty of Paris; Treaty of Rome, Part III Chapter I Articles 85–90 and 92–94; Euratom Treaty.

9 Community Energy Policy

Progress towards developing a Community energy policy has been both limited and slow. This has been despite the profound importance of the establishment of the European Coal and Steel Community (ECSC) and the European Atomic Community (Euratom). The reluctance of the member states to take decisions in common energy matters was most clearly revealed during the aftermath of the Arab–Israeli War of 1973 when member governments (but not the major oil companies) failed to agree on a common response to the discriminatory cutback of oil supplies by Arab countries. While strenuous efforts have since been made to build up a common energy policy, especially by the Commission, agreement remains limited. In view of the obvious importance of energy, member states have been reluctant to pool their national authority further, particularly when the distribution of resources within the Community is so disparate. Vested interests have also encouraged strong national positions in the Council of Ministers, while the worldwide context of energy has led governments to find solutions outside the purely Community framework.

Western Europe emerged from the Second World War with its energy supplies in ruins. Mines had been bombed, sabotaged or poorly maintained; the transport system was in disarray, so disrupting the distribution of coal. The priority, therefore, was reconstruction. By the end of the 1940s it had become increasingly difficult politically for the Allies to continue to control West German coal and steel. The result, which overcame French fears of an uncontrollable, resurgent Germany, was the Coal and Steel Community (see pp. 3–4).

The timing of the establishment of the Coal and Steel Community was propitious. Its success was of vital importance to the future of European integration. Although coal was scarce, output rose fast. The ECSC's High Authority thus presided over the distribution of an expanding resource in strong demand. It was, therefore, able to reach agreement on dismantling protective regimes and to break up cartels of buyers and producers.

Its success stimulated further movement towards integration, stimulated by a report in 1955 published by the Organisation for European Economic Cooperation (OECC). (The report, written by Louis Armand, was entitled *Quelques Aspects du Problème Européen de l'Energie.*) The underlying thesis of the report was that Europe was moving from a period characterised by a shortage of a single fuel to an era of competition between fuels, and asserted that the development of nuclear power was of vital importance to Europe's future. This was enthusiastically taken up by the European Federalists, led by the Action Committee for a United States of Europe under Jean Monnet (see p. 5). They considered that it was of the highest political significance that European authorities should be seen to be presiding over fundamental changes and leading Europe into new fields. As Monnet declared: 'The United States of Europe means a federal power linked to the peaceful exploitation of Atomic Energy.'

This emphasis by Federalists on nuclear energy was echoed by French opinion, even though their aims differed markedly. While the Federalists saw Euratom as leading the exclusively peaceful development of nuclear technology in Europe, French nationalists tended to view it as supporting the French military effort to establish a nuclear presence. The objectives of French policy towards Euratom were, therefore: to obtain technical information (especially if the UK could be persuaded to join); to obtain access to the rich uranium deposits in the then Belgian Congo; and to obtain access to West Germany's financial and industrial strength. Euratom came into being in 1958, at the same time as, but separate from, the Economic Community. In some French circles Euratom was considered to be by far the more important.

The establishment of Euratom alongside the ECSC created high expectations of the evolution of a common energy policy. But progress was hampered by the fact that coal and nuclear energy, in the years before 1967, were dealt with by different Communities with different powers and separate bureaucracies. Oil was, seemingly, the responsibility of no one and had been ignored in the negotiations leading up to the Treaty of Rome. There is no mention of oil in the Treaty, let alone of a common energy policy. Yet oil became what so many had expected of nuclear energy, that is, a cheap fuel which enabled rapid economic expansion. This had, in fact, been pointed to in a comprehensive and prescient study of oil, prepared in 1955 by the United Nations Economic Commission for Europe, to which all European countries belonged. The report (*The Price of Oil in Western Europe*) suggested the likelihood that oil prices in Europe would eventually fall because of a large potential over-supply at low cost. This study was followed by a report of the OEEC in 1956 which analysed the potential of oil and elaborated on the possibilities of mutual interdependence between Europe and the Middle East. Although these papers discussed many of those issues which were later to preoccupy the Community, they appear to have been ignored when the EEC and Euratom were founded.

The growth of imports of cheaper oil had a profound effect on both the Coal and Steel Community and Euratom. It coincided with the fall in energy consumption in 1958–9. The volume of coal and oil imports, however, continued to increase because long-term contracts had already been concluded. In view, therefore, of the difficulties which faced domestic coal industries, the ECSC's High Authority sought protective measures. It failed. It did so in part because it was working in relative isolation. While there was some support for protection against oil imports within Euratom, the Economic Community gave a higher priority to general expansion, based on cheap fuel, and was more preoccupied with establishing the common market. The High Authority was refused powers to take crisis measures because the member states themselves, depending on the importance of indigenous coal to their economies, were taking their own, uncoordinated, measures. A common approach to coal was not actually agreed until well after the crisis when, in 1964, the Council of Ministers agreed on a Protocol of Agreement on Energy Policy. The principal significance of the Protocol was the acceptance of the need to subsidise indigenous production, thereby attempting to maintain the coal industry in being, while not interfering with low overall prices set by imports. The element of common policy introduced was that the Community was provided with the responsibility for supervising the subsidies and ensuring that they satisfied certain requirements.

The greater emphasis on national policies also contributed to the decline in importance of Euratom. The three most important objectives of Euratom had been: a nuclear common market; a common programme for research and development; and the establishment of an agency to control the supply of nuclear fuel. Euratom was successful in creating a common market and certain common standards for nuclear technology, but these relatively minor successes were undermined by its failures elsewhere. Lack of agreement was perhaps not surprising given the differences among the member states. The French tended to concentrate on their national programme for military objectives, and, subsequently, like the West Germans, had to compensate for their lack of research by building US designs under licence. Divergences further increased with the growth of the commercial significance of nuclear power, a factor that some governments later had to balance against growing public concern, and the rise of 'Green' movements hostile to nuclear energy. As a result, the member states have been unable to agree on common procedures for licensing, or on standards of safety or quality controls, although in the aftermath of Chernobyl, the Commission proposed a number of new safeguards. While Euratom research establishments have been set up (sometimes after considerable argument over their location), their research has tended to be on peripheral issues, and has been bedevilled by constant wrangling over finance. (See also pp. 113–14.) Because of the plentiful supply of uranium ore, the supply agency has been redundant, despite the efforts of the Commission to revive it.

National policies have frequently been pursued outside the Community framework. This has in part been due to the role of the oil companies which have provided secure and improving supplies, often with little regard to national boundaries or even national governments. There has been little purely Community stimulus in respect of electricity. The various consortia operating in the gas and nuclear fields link up a variety of Community and non-Community combines. Spain, Sweden and Iran, for example, have been involved in Eurodif (European Gaseous Diffusion Consortium) for enrichment. As regards oil, the International Energy Agency was established under the auspices of the OECD, after the

Yom Kippur War of 1973 had revealed the vulnerability of Western economies. Although a member of OECD, France refused to join the IEA in order to preserve its independence of action and, it argued, to avoid confrontation with the producers. The Community as such, therefore, is not represented and the Commission attends IEA meetings only as an observer. There have been other differences between France and its partners as, for example, on IEA efforts to set a minimum selling price for oil to protect investments and over emergency oil-sharing.

But before 1973, the success of the oil companies in providing secure supplies at stable prices was an important element in making any progress towards a more comprehensive energy policy unnecessary. The 1973 Arab – Israeli war and the subsequent quadrupling of oil prices, changed the position markedly. The Commission's analysis was that the only way to reduce the Community's dependence on imported oil was a dramatic expansion in nuclear energy. Its strategy was to reduce consumption of energy and to increase the nuclear power capacity for generating electricity fourteen-fold. Indigenous natural gas and oil production should be increased as rapidly as possible, imports of gas should be increased, supplies of oil diversified, and indigenous coal production maintained. These ambitious goals were accepted with some modifications by the Council of Ministers in 1974.

In addition to pressing for a comprehensive energy policy, the Commission has also proposed initiatives in the various energy sectors, particularly to deal with the recession in oil refining, the financing of investment and the social and political implications of nuclear energy.

But the fact is that the differences between member states' energy resources and needs and their administrative and legislative approaches to the energy sector have been so varied as to make a genuinely common energy policy impossible. The lack of any comprehensive Treaty framework has not helped. The Commission has argued that the differences that exist, and in particular differing taxes and duties on hydrocarbons, distort competition in the Community. On the one hand, the member states have generally proved reluctant to give up controls over energy. On the other hand, the Commission has consistently regarded the adoption of a common energy policy as an important political step towards European unity. It was perhaps significant – although it also reflected the considerable easing of the energy situation in the mid-1980s – that energy was not referred to in the Single European Act. The most the Commission has been able to persuade member states to accept is the coordination of national policies, the setting of Community targets and some Community finance (apart, that is, from loans from the EIB) in fairly limited fields for helping energy projects of general Community interest in member states.

The overall policy objective that the Community has set for itself (or that member states have agreed for themselves) has been security of energy supplies at minimum cost. To achieve this, it adopted a number of targets for the period from 1974 and then again from 1980–90. In September 1986 the Council adopted targets for the period up to 1995. The targets have in essence consisted of: reduction in oil consumption, represented by a reduction in the proportion of oil used, compared with other fuels; development of alternatives to oil, especially nuclear power and solid fuels; and price transparency to try to ensure the economic use of energy.

Community funds are spent primarily on research and the development of new technologies, especially those aimed at energy saving and alternative energy sources. The Community also finances 'demonstration projects', or pilot schemes used as a testing ground for the industrial and commercial viability of new methods and technologies arising from research, for example, in new energy systems, like solar energy or geothermal energy or in energy savings in buildings or industry or transport. Some member states, especially the British, have looked for substantial support for coal from the Community, but because imported coal is cheap, because some member states do not produce it at all and because production is expensive in some of the member states, agreement in principle has never been translated into agreement in practice. Nevertheless, Britain received a large proportion of its budget refunds in the period before the Fontainebleau agreement through Community expenditure on energy projects in the UK.

The main source of Community oil remains the Middle East, with which the Community has close geographical and historical ties. Europe's need for oil and gas and the Middle East's need for manufactured goods provided the economic dimension to the unsuccessful Euro–Arab Dialogue (the political element of course being the Arab attempt to get the Community more closely involved in the Middle East peace process and to recognise the PLO). This economic interdependence provides further justification for the Arab part of the Community's Mediterranean Policy and for various efforts to conclude commercial (but not preferential) agreements with other parts of the Middle East, for instance with the Gulf Cooperation Council (GCC) and, at one time, with Iran. The Community has tried to achieve common energy policies towards third countries as it has in other areas, but one of the difficulties confronting it arises from the independent policies of member states, particularly in relation to procurement. This is of course reflected in the formal French absence from the IEA which makes a common Community policy there difficult to achieve, although in fact there is close collaboration, especially via the Community's and the IEA's emergency oil-sharing schemes.

The second 'oil shock' of 1979 took oil prices upwards again but there was no overall shortage of oil to test the IEA's or the Community's oil-sharing schemes. The Community's targets for 1990 look like being achieved, but this is as much due to the economic recession as to the Community's own efforts, so the Community's role remains limited. The debate about what energy policy is appropriate for the Community will continue. In part, it has to reflect the changing world situation; the fall in the price of oil in 1985–6 and the doubts cast on the generation of electricity by nuclear energy following the Chernobyl disaster. More fundamentally, it still reflects differing attitudes of the member states. In addition, the conception of the Economic and Atomic Communities proved a severe handicap. Euratom was founded on expectations which proved misguided and so was deserted. No specific powers were provided to the Economic Community to deal with oil. Moreover, the nature of the decision-making procedure has also caused problems and remains unchanged by the Single European Act. The technical details of Community energy policy are referred by the Committee of Permanent Representatives (COREPER) to the high-level Working Group on Energy. These senior national officials are impeded from going much further than COREPER on technicalities, which are often based on political differences, because of the lack of political guidance from the Council of (Energy) Ministers. The Council itself is often unable to deal with either the political or technical problems and so refers the issues back to COREPER for further discussions. Thus the circle begins again. The Commission in drawing up its initial proposals has increasingly taken care to consult the various national interests involved. These remain strongly entrenched, ranging from oil companies, gas and electricity public or quasi-public enterprises, atomic energy authorities, equipment manufacturers and unions – the mining unions in Britain and Germany being particularly strong. In such a highly technical, yet politically and economically vital area as energy, negotiations are necessarily arduous. It is both a sign of continuing disagreement among the member states, and an indication of the limitations of a Community perspective, that so many important discussions in the energy field are taken outside the Community.

SUGGESTIONS FOR FURTHER READING

N. J. D. Lucas, *Energy and the European Communities* (Europa, 1977)
N. J. D. Lucas, *Western European Energy Policies* (Oxford, Clarendon Press, 1985)
H. Maull, *Europe and World Energy* (Butterworth, 1980)
T. Weyman-Jones, *Energy in Europe: Issues and Polices* (Methuen, 1986)

For Treaty references see: The Treaty of Paris; Euratom Treaty.

10 Regional Policy

Until 1975 regional policy was left almost entirely to the member states. The Treaty of Rome, while recognising the need for the development of less favoured regions, concentrated on the means of expanding trade. It was more concerned with ensuring that member states' policies did not adversely affect that expansion. The only real exception to this seemingly *laissez-faire* approach was the special attention paid to the Mezzogiorno, the south of Italy, and this was as much for political reasons as economic ones. However, at their meeting in Paris in 1972, the Heads of Government agreed to a more generally positive approach to regional policy within the Community. It none the less took two years of hard bargaining, especially on the part of Ireland and Italy, before a modest Community approach was agreed. It comprised an extremely small European Regional Development Fund (ERDF) and a Committee on Regional Policy consisting of national officials, staffed by the Commission. But the decision did equip the Community, for the first time, with a means of financing regional development. It also provided an institutional framework, within which the regional policies of the member states and the Community's own policies could be progressively coordinated and developed, in order to reduce regional disparities within the Community.

But even before the 1972 agreement, regional development beyond that of the Mezzogiorno had not been wholly ignored. The ECSC Treaty, for example, had included provisions for financial

131

aids to assist regions suffering from declining employment in the coal and steel industries. The European Investment Bank (EIB), created under the Treaty of Rome, had responsibilities to finance projects in the less developed regions. But the major concern of the Rome Treaty was to promote expansion through free trade. Regional subsidies were permitted under Article 92 where they were considered necessary to allow all regions to participate in, and benefit from, the expansion of trade; that is, when used to promote the economic development of 'areas where the standard of living is abnormally low or where there is under-employment', or to facilitate the development of 'certain economic activities or of certain economic areas'. But the member states were not, and are not, free to grant whatever financial assistance they wish, to promote regional development. Under Article 93 of the Treaty of Rome, the Commission was granted the power to review, and, if necessary, call for the withdrawal of any state aid granted to particlar firms in order to prevent any distortion of trade and competition incompatible with the Treaty.

Agreement was reached among the Six in 1971 on rules to govern regional aids granted by member states. These reflected a consensus among the member states on the economic principles governing acceptable regional aids, and on how to measure, compare and assess them on a uniform basis throughout the Community. Initially control was exercised over the aids granted in the most highly industrialised areas of the Community with the highest levels of income per head. These aids were considered the most likely both to lead distortions of trade, and to harm the economy of poorer regions. After enlargement in 1973 the system of controls was further developed. In 1975 four categories of region were defined with differing limits on aids. Maximum aids were allowed for Greenland, Ireland, the Mezzogiorno and Northern Ireland, although the Commission could examine any individual cases where investment projects involved expenditure costs of more than £10 million, and where aids exceeded the equivalent of 35 per cent of the total cost of an investment. A second category, with an aid ceiling of 30 per cent of investment costs, applied to the Assisted Areas of the UK, French regions eligible for industrial grants, and certain assisted areas in Italy. West Berlin and the frontier regions of West Germany were allotted an aid ceiling of 20 per cent as were all other regions.

The rules governing state aids also required that the aids

should be measurable and 'transparent', so that their compatibility with the Treaties could be determined. 'Opaque' aids, or those which cannot be measured, were deemed inadmissible. This requirement caused a number of problems because many of the aids extended to the less developed, peripheral regions of the Community tended to involve a large proportion of indirect aid which was not easily measurable. A compromise formula was agreed which recognised the complexities of the issues involved and accepted some 'opacity' but the Commission was a reluctant partner to the agreement on the grounds that the aids often concealed subsidies to current operating costs and therefore slowed down the adaptation and restructuring of declining industries. The Commission's fundamental conception of regional aids remained that they should be directed towards new projects in industries and in locations where the firms concerned could survive competition, not only from other regions but also from other Community countries.

This rigorous stance, while maintained in principle, was somewhat relaxed in practice during the later 1970s and especially during the recession of 1978–9 when pressures on the member states to strengthen their regional policies increased. A delicate balance had to be drawn by the Commission between accepting on the one hand that regional aids were often popularly regarded as necessary, especially when they sought to avoid severe social and economic dislocation, and that they could play an important role in attracting new capital and new industries, and, on the other hand, maintaining its position that such aids should not distort trade and have adverse repercussions on other perhaps equally badly-hit regions of the Community. The Commission had already put forward new proposals to the Council in 1977 and these were largely accepted in February 1979. The proposals went beyond the consensus on the criteria on which regional aids should be based, i.e. that aids to new investment should not exceed certain ceilings, expressed either as a percentage of the value of the investment or expressed in terms of the investment cost per new job created. They upheld the need for the coordination of national regional aids, so often closely linked to national industrial policies since they sought to help declining industries rather than to tackle regional underdevelopment as such. They also introduced the idea of periodic reports from the Commission so that the Community's policies could be based on a more comprehensive system of analysis, and also the notion of regional impact assessment, so that the impact on each region of all Community policies could be assessed. The latter, in implying the need for the closer coordination of Community instruments, has been a recurring theme.

Under the Treaty, the Community is also empowered to examine the compatibility of public undertakings with the rules of competition (see Chapter 8). The growth of state intervention in private industry during the 1970s, much of it with a regional objective, inevitably concerned the Commission. It was, however, cautious in its approach although such bodies as the National Enterprise Board in the UK were closely scrutinised. In 1980 the Commission adopted a directive, based on Article 90 of the Treaty, requiring member states to supply it with information on the financial relationship between them and public undertakings. This search for greater 'transparency' caused considerable opposition from especially France, Italy and the UK who took the Commission to the Court of Justice. However the Court supported the Commission, whereupon the Commission sought information on motor vehicles, man-made fibres, textiles machinery and shipbuilding among other sensitive industries.

A positive Community regional policy, distinct from the coordination of state aids, had not been considered necessary before the end of the 1960s. Apart from the South of Italy, which was treated in a special protocol, and to which the EIB was to devote particular attention, the problem of regional disparities was considered a national responsibility to be resolved by national policies. At the Community level the regional problem was treated largely as a territorial dimension of agriculture and the coal and steel industries. Provision to offset any adverse effects of the common market on peripheral areas was made in a number of measures: the Guidance Section of FEOGA; in the finance of training and retraining provided by the Social Fund; in the regional development objective of the Statute of the EIB; and in the interest rebates allowed on loans available under the Treaty of Paris to create jobs and retrain workers rendered unemployed by closures in the coal and steel industries.

The justification for a general and positive Community regional policy derives largely from the adoption at the Hague Summit in 1969 of the objective of Economic and Monetary Union (EMU) – see Chapter 13. There was considerable concern (expressed even more strongly at the 1972 Summit) that continued divergence between the richer and the poorer regions of the Community would make it impossible for some governments to surrender control over their economic policies. A regional policy was, therefore, considered a vital complement to monetary union. It was recognised, however, that in the context of EMU the really significant problems would be the 'national regions', for the UK, Italy and Ireland had lower levels and rates of growth in productivity, and a higher propensity to inflation than other Community members. Clearly, economic convergence depended – and continues to depend – on coordinating monetary and fiscal policies, incomes and price policies and other instruments executed by member governments. But while a regional policy was seen as unable to correct fundamental imbalances among national economies, it was regarded as capable of making some contribution. It was a contribution that, with the second enlargement to the Mediterranean, was of enormous symbolic importance, even if its economic impact might be limited.

Regional policy first became a high priority, however, largely because of the accession of the UK. Although the Commission and Italy had pressed hard beforehand, a Community regional policy, from which the UK would benefit financially, was seen as necessary compensation to offset the disproportionate British contribution to the Community budget, and especially to the financing of the CAP. But the British also brought with them into the Community a relatively new regional problem of industrial decline and urban decay. This was adopted as an appropriate economic argument to underpin the political claim to a larger share of Community budgetary expenditure.

In March 1975 the Community established the European Regional Development Fund (ERDF), its first instrument of positive regional policy. The Fund provides investment grants, under prescribed conditions, to industrial and service activities, and either grants or interest rebates on EIB loans for infrastructure. The grants match national aids and are in addition to them. At the same time as establishing a small Fund Management Committee, the Council of Ministers set up a Regional Policy Committee composed of senior civil servants from national administrations with a secretariat provided by the Commission. The Committee provides a planning framework for the operations of the Fund and coordinates the

Community's own policies and expenditures with national regional policies.

The ERDF, and the rules governing it, were agreed only after considerable haggling. Indeed, it took the threat of a boycott of the European Council by the Italians and Irish to win final agreement on the actual establishment of the Fund (the British, by then under a Labour Government, were more preoccupied with renegotiating the terms of British entry). National quotas were the inevitable result of the insistence of member states on 'fair' shares. The British, for example, once the Fund became established, were determined to be a net beneficiary, particularly during the transitional period when its contributions to the Community budget and therefore to the CAP, were rising by stages. But no member state was content to be wholly excluded from the Fund. The linking of ERDF aid to national regional aid programmes was agreed only after the failure of prolonged attempts to define 'objectively' those regions of the Community which should be eligible for Community aid. The negotiating bids on the size of the Fund ranged from the ambitious sum of £1500 million put in by the UK to only £300 million suggested by West Germany.

The Fund was – and remains – small. It was endowed with some £540 million for the first three years. To put it in perspective, in those three years the UK received £152 million, compared with an annual UK expenditure on direct regional aid of £600 million. When the Fund was renewed in 1978, it was with an endowment of £1200 million for a further three years. Thereafter, it became subject to annual increases as part of the Community budget, haggled over by the European Parliament (on the side of large scale increases) and the Council of Ministers (on the side of limiting any significant increases). Until the reforms of 1984, the Fund disbursed its resources on the basis of national quotas. These were modified in 1979 when, after strong pressure from the Commission, a small (5 per cent) non-quota element was added which allowed the Commission a certain additional discretion, and again in 1981 with the accession of Greece. Although the size of the Fund was not significantly increased in real terms in 1984 (its annual increase was only 6.5 per cent as against 14.2 per cent in 1983) a number of important reforms were introduced, perhaps the most notable of which was the formal abandonment of quotas in favour of 'indicative ranges', i.e. ranges of maximum and

minimum amounts. Insofar as the latter are guaranteed, they are
quotas in effect, but they allow for a possible 'quota-free' element
of up to 12 per cent for the Commission to determine – although
subject to the advice of the Regional Fund Committee made up of
national officials. It provided a typical compromise between
Commission efforts to respond to criticisms of the lack of impact
made by the Fund, to increase its own involvement and discretion
in the Fund and to create a greater Community dimension to
regional aid, against a general reluctance on the part of member
governments to give up the idea of quotas.

Table 10.1   The European Regional Development 1975–86

	National quotas (in percentage terms)			Indicative ranges	
	1975–78	*1978–80*	*1981–84*	*1984–85*	*1986–*
Belgium	1.5	1.39	1.11	0.90–1.20	0.61–0.82
Denmark	1.3	1.20	1.06	0.51–0.67	0.34–0.46
FRG	6.4	6.00	4.65	3.76–4.81	2.55–3.40
France	15.0	16.86	13.64	11.05–14.74	7.48–9.96
Ireland	6.0	6.46	5.94	5.64–6.83	3.82–4.61
Italy	40.0	39.39	35.49	31.94–42.59	21.62–28.79
Luxembourg	0.1	0.09	0.07	0.06–0.08	0.04–0.06
Netherlands	1.7	1.58	1.24	1.00–1.34	0.68–0.91
UK	28.0	27.03	23.80	21.42–28.56	14.50–19.31
Greece			13.00	12.35–15.74	8.36–10.64
Portugal					10.66–14.20
Spain					17.97–23.93

The impact of the ERDF has been difficult to assess. Inequalities
of income and economic activity between regions have tended to
widen rather than the reverse. To some extent, national quotas
undermined the ability of the Fund to have any great impact. Aid
has been diffused over a multitude of projects – by 1984 over
25 000 of them. Member states have been reluctant to regard the
aid as additional to, rather than indirectly replacing national aids.
There was a strong tendency to look on the quotas as little more
than drawing rights. The ERDF has traditionally provided aid in
Assisted or similarly designated areas largely on a project by
project basis, contributing to up to 50 per cent of the total aid

expenditure, subject to the percentage ceilings on the level of subsidies to industrial projects which applied to combined national and Community aid. Under the 1979 reforms an element of flexibility was allowed in the amount of aid allocated to infrastructure projects and, in the non-quota section, assistance was extended not to projects but to multi-annual programmes designed to tackle specific regional problems.

Several of these elements were taken up and extended under the 1984 reforms, agreed not only with Greece, already a member and pressing strongly for a more integrated programme for the Mediterranean, but also with the prospect of Spanish and Portuguese membership in the near future. While, as suggested above, many member states were reluctant to give up the idea of quotas, there was a broad acceptance of the need to concentrate aid where it was most needed. The Commission's priority areas continued to be the same as those in 1973 (plus parts of Scotland and Wales, the overseas departments of France, which had been allotted additional funds in 1979, and Greece apart from Athens and Thessalonika), itself an indication of the limited impact made by the Fund as well as the inherent difficulties of developing peripheral regions. The non-quota element under the Commission's responsibility provides it with considerably greater flexibility to introduce Community programmes rather than individual projects. This creates a further incentive perhaps for national governments to coordinate their programmes more closely with the Commission.

At the same time, after considerable criticism of duplication of effort in some cases and of contradictory efforts in others, the Stuttgart European Council in 1983 called upon the Commission to undertake a study on improving the effectiveness of the Community's structural funds – the ERDF, the Social Fund, the Guidance Section of FEOGA, etc. – within the framework of both enlargement and of the future of the Community's budget. This was again taken up in the negotiations on the Single European Act where Article 130D called for a decision to be taken on the coordination of financial instruments within a year of the SEA coming into operation. While that decision is to be taken on the basis of unanimity, subsequent decisions on the ERDF are to be taken on the basis of a qualified majority in cooperation with the European Parliament.

The inclusion of the commitment in the SEA to reduce regional disparities and of references to the ERDF were of particular importance to the newer Mediterranean members, all of whom had looked to considerable returns from the structural funds on their accession to the Community. Greece had already used its membership and the threat of a veto on any further enlargement in order to win further assistance by means of what became known as the Integrated Mediterranean Programme (see Chapter 15). The clear determination of the northern member states to work for a genuinely free internal market in which they, rather than the southern member states, were likely to benefit in the immediate and intermediate future led to an insistence by the south on the inclusion of the commitment to greater 'co-hesion' within the Community, by which they meant a commit-ment to the redistribution of funds towards the Mediterranean. While the commitment may have been regarded as a *quid pro quo* for the commitment to the Internal Market, the latter is considerably less costly. There is once more an important dis-tinction between 'negative' integration (the removal of barriers), and 'positive' integration (the establishment of new policies). While the Community faces repeated financial crises largely because of the expenditure on the CAP, few member govern-ments of the northern states will willingly acquiesce in additional spending on regional issues.

Financial rectitude in this instance has been compounded by a more ideological antagonism to public spending. Just as several member governments, most notably that of West Germany under Chancellor Schmidt believed that British regional policy tended to be a thinly disguised welfare operation, so other governments in the 1980s, including that of Mrs Thatcher in the UK, have expressed doubts about the long-term benefits of public as against private investment. To some extent the Commission in its 1984 guidelines sought to assuage potential criticisms by emphasising the need for internally-generated development in the regions, for using local resources and for tying in Community aid with small businesses, etc., rather than concentrating so heavily on infrastructure projects. There remains, however, considerable difficulty in reconciling the views and interests of the northern member states and those of the south, which, given the institutional changes brought about by the SEA, may create even greater complexity and confusion in the relationship between member states, the Commission and the European Parliament.

SUGGESTIONS FOR FURTHER READING

M. Keating and B. Jones, *Regions in the European Community* (Oxford, Clarendon Press, 1985)

D. Keeble et al., *Centrality, Periphery and the EEC Regional Development* (Cambridge University Press, 1982)

W. Molle et al., *Regional Disparity and Economic Development in the EEC* (Saxon House, 1980)

D. Pinder, *Regional Economic Development and Policy: Theory and Practice in the European Community* (George Allen & Unwin/ UACES, 1983)

D. Seers et al., *Integration and Unequal Development* (Macmillan, 1982)

For Treaty references see: Treaty of Paris; Treaty of Rome, Protocol concerning Italy.

11 Social Policy

All members of the Community have long-established and extensive social policies of their own. Many of the social problems they
have faced were, and remain, common to all of them, even if in
different degrees. On signing the Treaty of Rome in 1957, they all
had to face the social effects of establishing a common market.
The Treaty made no mention of creating a common social policy.
It was generally believed that the functioning of the market itself
would improve working conditions and standards of living. It was
expected, therefore, that this would also lead member states
gradually to coordinate or harmonise their social policies. In this
they were also to be encouraged by the Commission.

Such optimism was not to be borne out. Even by the end of the
1960s it became clear that the problems of global competition
demanded the adjustment of many of Europe's industries and a
greater emphasis upon training and skills within the Community's
workforce. With enlargement in 1973 to include the UK, the
problems arising from the decline of traditional industries were
exacerbated. And the general recession of the 1970s increased the
social problems facing the Community still further, particularly
in the field of unemployment, unemployment among women and
those under 25 being recognised as having special priority. It
became increasingly clear also that traditional redistributive
policies were failing to deal with the problem and that the social
impact of all sectoral policies both at national and Community
levels needed to be assessed and taken into account.

Initially, however, it was to the extent that national social policies affected, or were affected by, the common market that the Community was involved. This meant a considerable number of references to social matters throughout most of the Treaty: for example, the Council was called upon to adopt measures in the field of social security in order to ensure freedom of movement for, and end discrimination against, migrant workers; in the section on state aids, possible exceptions to the rules were noted for those aids designed to promote the economic development of areas where the standard of living is abnormally low or where there is serious unemployment. Within the specific Social Policy section of the Treaty (Articles 117–28), the Commission was given the job of encouraging closer cooperation between member states on subjects including employment; labour law; vocational training; social security; safety and health; and collective bargaining between employers and workers. The aim, by means of closer consultation and studies, was gradual harmonisation, but without any timetable imposed. More specifically, member states agreed to give equal pay for equal work under Article 119, inserted at the insistence of France, which was the most anxious of the member states about possible differences in costs of production arising from different social security systems.

The Treaty also established the Social Fund. The Fund's purpose was to assist with the improvement of employment opportunities by making it easier for workers to change jobs or to move from one part of the Community to another. Lying behind this was the thought that, as the common market began to work, uneconomic businesses would fold; others would be restructured, and new ones would be established. The detailed rules for the implementation of the Fund were left to the Council to determine.

Neither the Social Fund nor the other provisions of the Treaty relating to social policy were able to make much impact on the social problems of the 1960s and the problems grew steadily worse with the economic recession of the 1970s. A major reorganisation of the Social Fund occurred in 1971 and a second in 1983. In both instances the Council of Ministers accepted that the Social Fund had been unable to meet the tasks set for it and that reorganisation was necessary in the effort to respond to new conditions.

Under the 1971 reorganisation the basic purpose of the Social Fund remained that of providing financial support for training, retraining and settlement schemes to help the unemployed and the under-employed. The scope of the Fund was, however, widened. Two types of assistance were distinguished: under article 4 of the 1971 Decision, the Council could decide on assistance to particular sectors or groups of people affected by Community policies; under article 5, assistance could be given where employment conditions in particular regions or among groups of undertakings threatened to inhibit further Community development. Applications to the Social Fund were channelled through member governments. If accepted, and applications began to outgrow the monies allotted to the Social Fund in the Community's budget, the Fund financed 50 per cent of the costs of the project with the public authority involved. Following a review of the Fund's activities in 1977, it was enabled to contribute up to 55 per cent of the costs of schemes in particularly disadvantaged areas and was also allowed to help towards employment subsidies and job-creation schemes.

The continued increase in the rate of unemployment, especially among people under 25, led to a more radical review of the Fund in 1983. The Commission proposed a Fund with considerably more flexibility within guidelines agreed by the Council and to a certain degree this was accepted. The commitment to vocational training was reaffirmed and the Fund was recognised as playing a part in assisting and/or complementing national employment or labour market policies. A number of areas were picked out for particular attention. These included a greater concentration on the alleviation of unemployment among the under-25 year-olds, for whom some 75 per cent of the Social Fund was to be designated. Other sectors of concentration were the long-term unemployed, women, the handicapped and migrants. The needs of employees in small and medium-sized businesses were also to be taken more into account. In addition, the Council of Ministers allowed the Commission to allot a part of the budget to innovative and demonstration projects. However, they restricted it to only 5 per cent of the Fund.

More controversial was the proposal to concentrate a greater part of the Fund on particular geographical areas of needs. Although quotas as such had been eschewed in the case of the Social Fund, unlike the Regional Development Fund, particularly disadvantaged areas had been increasingly accorded greater funding and this had been recognised in the 1977 review of the Fund. In 1983, some member states proposed a more formal quota system but the Council finally decided to continue to concentrate resources, with 40 per cent of the fund reserved for supporting measures in the most deprived areas, these being determined as: Ireland, Northern Ireland, the Mezzogiorno, Greece and French overseas *départements*. Portugal and parts of Spain were added in 1986.

The Social Fund is financed from the Community Budget, being considered a part of the non-compulsory part of the Community's expenditure (see Chapter 12). Like everything else, its size is small in relation to spending on the Common Agricultural Policy, even though it has been rising in real terms. The Social Fund is administered by the Commission under general guidelines from the Council of Ministers. Like the Regional Development Fund, the Commission is also advised by a committee, the Social Fund Committee, which is made up of national officials. In the case of the Social Fund Committee, representatives from employer and trade union groups also participate. There have generally been more applications than funds available so that the Commission, on the Social Fund Committee's advice, has had the task of choosing the projects to be supported. The bias of the guidelines before 1983 were very much towards public sector projects so that those member states with more developed public sectors, such as the UK, tended to get the larger number of projects accepted. While the 1983 guidelines took a greater account of other enterprises, a bias remains insofar as public authorities are more likely to command the resources necessary to wait upon the Fund's sometimes slow procedures.

The successive reorganisations of the Social Fund have been only one aspect of the Community's efforts to become more responsive to social needs. Many in Western Europe became increasingly concerned that while some national budgets continued to grow and others were being curtailed, in both cases certain groups, such as the elderly, migrants (whether from inside or outside the Community) and the handicapped, continued at severe social disadvantage. At the same time there was a growing incidence of social disorders such as drug and alcohol abuse. At the 1972 Summit, Heads of State and Government recognised the need for a visible sign of the development of the social conscience of the Community for both political and social reasons. It was a move fostered by the enlargement of the Community in 1973 when many groups within the new member states were anxious to see the Community confound the criticism that its goal was solely material.

As in other policies, the 1972 Summit meeting appeared to give considerable impetus to these and other improvements with the general aim of giving the Community more of a 'human face'. In 1974 the Council adopted the 'Social Action Programme' prepared by the Commission, which had three main themes: the improvement of living and working conditions; greater participation by workers and employers in Community decision-making; and the provision of full and better employment. This overall programme had then to be implemented against a background of increasing structural problems and with a number of governments adopting the fight against inflation as the highest priority. None the less a number of highly significant measures have been adopted such as those on the equal treatment of men and women in access to employment in employment and training. In 1974, for example, the Council approved a first directive on the approximation of laws relating to equality of earnings. However, by the beginning of the 1980s it was recognised that the economic crisis had made inequalities in the employment of women even worse, with female unemployment rising to some 40 per cent, a figure similar to that of people under 25. A new action programme to promote equality of opportunity was adopted in 1982, introducing, albeit in a qualified way, the idea of positive action in favour of women.

Other areas tackled included improvements in working conditions such as measures to improve health and safety at the workplace and improving the situation for those seeking employment elsewhere in the Community. Measures have also been taken to help workers who migrate into the Community from Third World countries. In addition, the Commission has been active in introducing measures to safeguard the rights of workers, for example in relation to mass dismissals and where businesses change hands or collapse. Areas of particular controversy, which arose from the Commission's concern over the establishment of a single European base and the existing role of multinational corporations in the Community, have included those falling under the general heading of worker participation, of access to information, consultation and formal participation on company structures. Despite lengthy discussions in all the institutions of the Community, the member states have failed to achieve a consensus on the Commission's proposals for work-sharing; early retirement and so on have also been put on the Community agenda, measures which have sometimes been characterised conceptually as adding up to *l'espace social Européen*. The Community has also established three institutes with the aim of studying and encouraging Community activity: the European Centre for the Development of Vocational Training in Berlin; the European Foundation for the Improvement of Working and Living Conditions in Dublin; and the European Trade Union Institute in Brussels.

The aim has been to try to set minimum standards in such matters applicable throughout the Community. The objective has not been to set unrealistic uniform standards on, for example, women's salaries, or to change employment structures so that opportunities might be exactly the same for men and women throughout the Community, but to ensure that all women receive the rate for the job and possess an effective right of redress where necessary.

The involvement of workers and employers in Community decision-making is not, of course, restricted to social affairs. But consultations with both the European Parliament and the Economic and Social Committee are specifically provided for in the Social Policy section of the Treaty of Rome.

While at least one general debate is held annually, on the Commission's *Report on the Social Situation*, the Parliament's Committee on Social Affairs, Employment and Education continuously scrutinises Community proposals in detail. It has often been highly critical of the lack of progress made by the Council of Ministers and has pressed hard for the allocation of more Community resources to the Social Fund. The Economic and Social Committee, representing employers, trade unions and other interests, has, as its name would suggest, been closely involved with social issues. Its great value, apart from representing the interested parties, is the expert attention to detail it can give to proposals. The Committee's right to be consulted is stated in the Treaty of Rome, although it tends to be involved only at a relatively late stage in the development of Community legislation. In line with the 1972 Summit agreement on the importance of involving the 'social partners' the Economic and Social Committee has been given the right to initiate its own discussions rather than wait upon being consulted.

Other committees and groups have also been established. (For a general discussion of this phenomenon see Chapter 3.) Of particular importance is the Standing Committee on Employment, established in 1970 'to ensure . . . a continuous dialogue, joint action and consultation between Governments, the Commission and the Social Partners to facilitate coordination by the member states of their employment policies in harmony with the objectives of the Community'. Ministers of Employment attend the meetings of the Committee, which are held usually once every six months. There has, however, been a certain decline in the importance attached by some member states to the involvement of both sides of industry. Largely in response to trade-union demands that they should be able to meet Ministers of Finance too, Tripartitie Conferences were created but only four have been held.

The Social Action Programme was drawn up at a time when there were few signs of the approaching recession. Decisions on its implementation were taken against an increasingly gloomy back-drop. Under the Programme for example, allowance had been made for only pilot studies to be undertaken on action to counter poverty within the Community. One pilot study, the European Social Policy Observation, Information and Research (ESPOIR), reached the conclusion that poverty worsened considerably during the recession of the 1970s, that poverty was not confined to marginal groups of the population and that high unemployment coupled with rapid technological change was likely to increase the number of those in need. However, the Community's social policy and the Social Fund have been able to deal only with some aspects of these problems. It has been able, for example, only to attempt to remedy the effects of large scale unemployment rather than the causes which have to be tackled by the full range of national, Community, and international instruments. The Community's social policy, therefore, can have only a limited role to play. But it offers, none the less, an important, though undramatic, contri-bution to the task of improving living and working conditions in the Community.

SUGGESTIONS FOR FURTHER READING

D. Collins, *The European Communities: The Social Policy of the First Phase* (Martin Robertson, 1975)
D. Collins, *The Operation of the European Social Fund* (Croom Helm, 1983)

J. Dennet et al., *Europe Against Poverty* (Bedford Square Press, 1982)

J. Holloway, *Social Policy Harmonisation in the European Community* (Gower, 1981)

C. Saunders and D. Marsden, *Pay Inequalities in the European Communities* (Butterworth, 1981)

M. Shanks, *European Social Policy: Today and Tomorrow* (Pergamon, 1977)

J. Vandamme (ed.) *New Dimensions in European Social Policy* (Croom Helm, 1985)

For Treaty references see: Treaty of Rome, Part III, Chapters 1 and 2, Articles 117–28.

12 The Community Budget

It was reasonable to hope in early 1978, when this chapter was written for the first edition of the book, that the budget problem faced by the whole Community and the particular case faced by Britain were on the way to solution. In the case of the latter, agreement had been reached at the European Council in Dublin in December 1975 on the 'Financial Mechanism' which was designed to set a limit to any excessive discrepancy between a member state's contribution to the Community budget and its ability to pay. By the end of 1978, however, and the end of Britain's transitional period, it had become clear that the mechanism was not having the effect the British had desired. In 1979, the Commission calculated that during 1980, Britain would be the largest net contributor to the Community, paying over £1000 million. In the Queen's speech in May 1979, the new Conservative government said it would 'press for a fairer pattern of budgetary and resource transfers in the European Economic Community.' The so-called 'British problem' proved a particularly difficult one to resolve. But it has to be set against a wider context and other controversial issues, not least, the continuing (and rising) costs of the CAP and the financial problems of enlargement, which have threatened the Community with bankruptcy, and the struggle for influence between Community institutions especially on the part of the European Parliament.

EXPENDITURE

The total size of the budget for 1985 was 28 433.2 million ECU. It represented less than 1 per cent of the total GDP of the 10 Community member states and was equivalent to about 2.8 per cent of the 10 national budgets. It is not, therefore, as in the member states, a primary instrument for managing the economy. None the less, the budget embodies the results of all Community decisions to embark on joint financing of common policies; it is therefore a key measure of integration within the Community. Agriculture – the European Agricultural Guidance and Guarantee Fund (FEOGA) of the CAP has dominated spending and in 1985 accounted for 70 per cent of the total, despite attempts at greater budgetary discipline. This predominance of FEOGA expenditure reflects the fact that agriculture is the only important area of expenditure policy for which the member states have accepted any substantial pooling of authority. In other words, the cost of FEOGA to the Community Budget can, broadly, be regarded as replacing a similar total of national expenditures. This over-whelming proportion of expenditure is itself dominated by payments from the Guarantee Section of the Fund which supports prices and farmers' incomes (see Chapter 6). Many proposals have been made to increase the amounts paid from the Guidance Section, which supports structural adaptation, in the hope that such spending could, in part at least, reduce the production of costly surpluses. The Guidance Section has remained, however, less than 10 per cent of total FEOGA spending; in 1985 it was less than 3 per cent.

The agricultural part of the budget is difficult to control because it is based on 'open-ended' policies. Once intervention prices have been determined by the Council of (Agricultural) Ministers in their annual price review, the budgetary consequences follow automatically. Budget estimates for the Guarantee Section can only be preliminary guesses. The budget has, therefore, to be amended frequently to take account of the success or failure of harvests, for it is only then that the sums needed to fulfil the earlier decisions of the Council are finally known.

The other areas of expenditure from the Community budget itself are each relatively small compared with agricultural spending. This reflects the reluctance of the member states to transfer responsibility for other 'domestic' policies to the Community in the same way as they did for agriculture. 'Structural' funds – that is, the European Regional Development Fund and the Social Fund (together with the Guidance Section of FEOGA) – accounted for merely 12.84 per cent of expenditure in 1985. Research, energy and industrial policies took up only 2.49 per cent of expenditure. Most Community expenditure is in the form of grants to the member states. Other activities are financed by means of loans rather than grants, principally through the European Investment Bank (see Annex I to this chapter). Community access to capital markets has gradually been accepted. In 1977, the Community, through the Commission, was authorised to borrow money on the markets to onlend to member states for nuclear power stations. The Community was then given further powers to raise money for member states to finance investment projects in the energy, industry and infrastructure sectors, particularly to help regions in difficulty and to combat unemployment. This was called the New Community Instrument (NCI) or, more commonly, the Ortoli Facility after the then Vice President of the Commission, responsible for Economic and Financial Affairs, who had been particularly active in pressing for the introduction of the scheme. The European Development Fund is financed outside the Community Budget on the basis of a different contribution key.

REVENUES

The Community's revenues were originally derived from national contributions. This, it was agreed, would be only a temporary arrangement. The Treaty of Rome indicated that the Community should eventually have its own resources to implement its common policies, and specified in particular the revenues of the Common External Tariff (CET) – see Chapter 14. With the introduction of the Common Agricultural Policy it was decided that the Community should also receive the income from the variable import levies (see Chapter 6). The present structure was finally laid down in the Council Decision of 1970. Under this agreement the Community's own resources are made up from: the proceeds of the customs duties; the agricultural levies (less 10 per cent repaid to member governments to cover the costs of collection); and a rate of value added tax (VAT) set originally at a maximum of 1 per cent of a theoretical figure of the total VAT raised in each member state and applied as if VAT rates were harmonised throughout the Community. This piece of fiction was devised as a compromise to allow individual member states to maintain different rates on different products. A Community-wide value added tax had been recommended as early as 1962, but it was not until 1967 that the Six finally agreed that all member states should adopt VAT, and while the original deadline had been 1970, Italy only introduced it in 1973. A consensus on the harmonised basis of assessment necessary for the collection of VAT for Community revenues had been agreed to in principle in 1970 but it was not until 1977 that the compromise was reached and embodied in the Sixth VAT Directive. In 1984, as part of the Fontainebleau settlement (see below), the VAT ceiling was raised to 1.4 per cent (providing an increase of some 24 per cent in the overall budget). It was also agreed that the ceiling might be raised to 1.6 per cent on 1 January 1988 if there was unanimity in the Council.

There have been many criticisms of the own resources system from the point of view of equity, reliability and adequacy. Revenues from customs duties and agricultural levies are proportionately higher for member countries that import most. Passing these revenues to the Community was considered unfair in the case of the Netherlands and Belgium because many imports enter the major European ports of Rotterdam and Antwerp in transit to other member countries. It clearly weighs more heavily on countries which import, say, a high proportion of their food (and indeed was meant to, in order to encourage Community preference). This means that not only has the amount raised through agricultural levies varied because it depends on the gap between world and Community price levels but also, through the operation of Community preference, it is bound to continue to fall. From the point of view of revenue, customs duties are also unsatisfactory; as the CET is reduced as a result of international trade negotiations, so Community revenue diminishes.

VAT revenues are generally considered more equitable than duties and levies because they are more closely related to gross national products, a good indicator of each member country's 'ability to pay'. But the VAT is not particularly progressive, in that it is levied at a flat rate. It is even slightly regressive, since it penalises countries, such as the UK, where private consumption is a high proportion of total consumption, where there is a relatively low rate of investment, and where there is, usually, a balance of payments deficit. Moreover, VAT revenues may not be sufficiently buoyant to meet future spending demands. None the less, the agreement of 1977 was an important step towards providing the Community with a stable and reasonably fair basis for its budgetary resources.

BUDGETARY PROCEDURES

The formal procedure for adopting the Community budget is as follows:
  (i)   The Commission prepares a Preliminary Draft Budget for submission to the Council of Ministers before 1 September.
 (ii)   The Council adopts a Draft Budget, based on the Commission's Preliminary Draft, by 5 October by qualified majority (see Chapter 2), and sends it on to the European Parliament.
(iii)   Within 45 days of receiving the Draft Budget the European Parliament must complete its 'first reading'. The items of the budget are classified as either obligatory (or compulsory) expenditure or non-obligatory (non-compulsory) expenditure. Obligatory items are those, such as the Agricultural Fund, which derive directly from treaty obligations. On these the Parliament can suggest 'modifications' on a majority of votes cast. On non-obligatory items Parliament can make 'amendments' (on a majority of all members of the Parliament) and can even suggest increases in spending, unlike many national parliaments.
 (iv)   The Council then reconsiders the Draft as amended by the Parliament, and makes the final decision on the proposed 'modifications'. If it alters the 'amendments', however, the Draft must be resubmitted to the Parliament within 15 days.
  (v)   The Parliament then has a further 15 days to act on the Council's changes. It is then obliged to limit its amendments to a half of what is known as the 'maximum rate' of increase, calculated by the Commission and available to the Parliament and the Council for the budget as a whole.
If the Council and Parliament disagree during the process, an informal procedure, known as the conciliation procedure, comes into operation, by which the two bodies meet for direct discussions

to resolve the differences. If differences persist, the European Parliament has the power to reject the budget as a whole. Until 1979, it had never exercised the right. However, in 1979, having been directly elected for the first time, and fortified by what it saw as a popular mandate, the Parliament rejected the 1980 draft budget. It has also done so on a subsequent occasion in 1984 on the 1985 budget.

Supplementary budgets can be agreed during the year, and have often been required to take into account changes in the agricultural markets.

THE CONFLICTS

A foremost function of national budgets is the redistribution of income. In the original Community of the Six, because the economies of five of the member states (Italy was the exception) were close enough to make it unnecessary, the budget had a minimal role in redistributing resources between them. With the accession of the UK and Ireland, new pressures were created for a more prominent role for the budget. In the entry negotiations, the British argued that as the UK would receive relatively little from the CAP because of the relative size of British agriculture, it would have to carry 'an excessive burden' of contributions to the Community budget. The Community replied that the development of new policies would inevitably reduce this likelihood but they none the less recorded an undertaking in relation to Community finances that 'should unacceptable situations arise . . . the very survival of the Community would demand that the insitutions find equitable solutions'.

The most important of the new policies considered by the Community was the European Regional Development Fund (ERDF), which derived largely from the commitment to economic and monetary union undertaken at The Hague Summit of 1969 (see Chapter 13). This was particularly relevant to those 'regions' of the Community like Italy, the UK and Ireland which had lower growth and higher inflation than elsewhere. The emphasis on 'regional' rather than national development was important in reflecting a continuous effort by the Community to avoid discussion of national 'shares', and so discourage demands for a *juste retour*, that is, a balance between contribution to the budget and receipts from it. In the event, however, and in spite of reports such as that of Sir Donald MacDougall in 1977 on fiscal federalism, which concentrated on regional disparities, it became clear that neither the ERDF nor any of the other new policies being considered or implemented could solve the problem of what Britain saw as its overpayments to the budget. Moreover, as the economic recession deepened in the Community, other member states also began to be concerned about the budget. West Germany, for example, became increasingly alarmed at the scale of its net contribution. But all the member states began to regard the budget as a possible source of funds in the painful process of adjusting to new industrial competition, and in the fight against inflation and unemployment, as, of course, did the European Parliament.

By the end of the 1970s therefore, the budget itself had become a critical issue within the Community. The conflict over the 'British problem' was sometimes particularly bitter as well as being pro-tracted, not least because it meant that if Britain paid less others would have to pay more. The 1 per cent VAT ceiling provided a basic complication for if agricultural spending could not be contained, the ceiling meant that resources would not be available for new policies. Hence the growing emphasis on budgetary discipline. It was clear that the 'clawback mechanism' agreed to in Dublin in 1975 which concluded the Labour Government's renegotiation of the UK's terms of membership could not solve the problem of British contributions. For some time, however, only temporary solutions could be found. In the agreement reached on 30 May 1980, the UK received rebates for 1980 and 1981 paid in the form of additional Community expenditure in the UK which reduced its contribution by about two-thirds. These rebates formed part of a package determined by the Foreign Affairs Council which also included a review of the whole operation of the budget, and a permanent solution to the 'British problem' by the end of 1981, the so-called 30 May mandate.

The Community overshot its 1982 target by two years. The Commission produced its report on the future of the budget in June 1981. The subsequent discussion concentrated on the development of non-agricultural policies, reform of the CAP and 'budgetary imbalances', an intricately complex network of related issues. At the same time, Britain declared the refunds offered inadequate, but because a permanent solution could not be reached, additional temporary arrangements were agreed for 1982 and 1983. A final breakthrough occurred at the European Council in Stuttgart in June 1983, when negotiations began in earnest on improving controls over agriculture and other spending, on the problem of excessive net contributions to the budget, on the need to find resources for new policies and on the need to meet the costs of Spanish and Portuguese accession.

While Stuttgart might have provided a breakthrough, a sense of urgency was given to the negotiations by the fact that in 1984, the Community ran up against the 1 per cent ceiling – it did not have money to pay for the agricultural expenditure arising from the prices set by Agricultural Ministers. Finally in June 1984, the European Council at Fountainebleau reached agreement on all the areas of the negotiation.

In view of the significance of Fontainebleau, for the UK and the Community at large – it is unlikely that the Single European Act would have been negotiated without it – it is worth looking in greater detail at the agreement. The increase in own resources provided by VAT has already been mentioned. As far as the 'British problem' (or 'budgetary imbalances') was concerned, a new system was agreed beginning in 1985, whereby 'any member state sustaining a budgetary burden which is excessive in relation to its relative prosperity may benefit from a correction at the appropriate time' on the basis of the gap between its VAT payments and the share it receives of Community expenditure. The UK's refund for 1984 was set at 1000 million ECU (£600 million) and from 1985, the UK was to get back 66 per cent of the difference between its VAT share and Community expenditure, the refunds to be paid during the year following that in which the gap arose. Significantly, the rebate was to be paid through a reduction in the UK's VAT payments; that is on the revenue side, rather than by increased Community expenditure. Germany, too, obtained a rebate because of its large net contributions which was also to be achieved through adjustments in its VAT share. In a sense, the 'harmonised' VAT rate became even more fictitious; in 1986, for example, the UK paid a VAT rate of 0.82 per cent, Germany 1.33 per cent, and other member states 1.38 per cent. Of particular importance, however, was that the settlement of rebates was linked to the 1.4 per cent VAT ceiling. In an attempt to ensure that expenditure did not overrun receipts, Fontainebleau endorsed earlier decisions on the maximum level of expenditure and on agricultural spending which, on a three-year basis, was to grow less than the rate of growth in own resources. In addition, Fontainebleau agreed on a target date for the completion of negotiations with Spain and Portugal and established two *ad hoc* committees 'to respond to the expectations of the people of Europe by adopting measures to strengthen and promote its [the Community's] identity and its image both for its citizens and for the rest of the world' (the result of which were the Dooge and the Andonnino committees; see also Chapter 1).

As so often in the Community, implementation of the agreement was fraught with difficulty. In part, though part only, this was because of the European Parliament and its struggle with the Council over the budget. The Parliament has a considerable element of co-decision in relation to the budget even if budgetary powers are shared unequally. Before direct elections MEPs had been wary of using their powers. Once directly elected, however, they sought to exert what they saw as proper democratic control over the budgetary process. Most MEPS returned in the 1984 elections were determined to question the basis of the Fontaine-bleau agreement. They argued, for example, that they should have been consulted as part of the process of reaching the agreement. A majority thought that Britain should not have been allowed its rebate on the revenue side and that budgetary discipline seemed to be more important to the Council than the Community's obligations to farming or to new policies. Britain's opposition to the supplementary budget for 1984, made necessary because agricultural spending in particular had taken Community spending over the 1 per cent VAT limit exacerbated the conflict. While the UK eventually lifted its objection and the Parliament agreed to the UK's refunds for 1983 which it had blocked, it was not before the Commission had threatened to take the Council to the Court of Justice for not providing the money for the policies the Council itself had agreed to. Moreover, the Parliament also blocked the 1985 budget on the grounds that it was not large enough to finance the expected agricultural costs as well as the UK budget rebate.

In the absence of an agreed budget, the Community thus began 1985 operating on an *ad hoc* system of monthly 'twelfths' of the previous year's budget. By the end of June, however, the Council had approved a larger budget and Parliament had accepted the main lines of the Fountainebleau Agreement, including the system of budgetary discipline about which the Council had agreed that Parliament would be consulted. Harmony was merely temporary, for the Parliament then passed a budget for 1986 which was above the Council's limit (it argued that the limit did not take account of the accession of Spain and Portugal particularly in relation to social and regional spending). The Council thereupon took the Parliament to Court.

It is abundantly clear that the European Parliament will continue to make all possible use of its limited powers over the budget and extend them wherever it can. It was significant, however, that an extension of the Parliament's budgetary powers was not considered by the Inter-Governmental Conference. The Commission, too, is likely to continue to press for a significant role in the budgetary process, often with the support of the Parliament. The Commission, for example, has long sought to make its Preliminary Draft Budget a policy statement analogous to national budgets. The Council of Ministers has denied that the Commission has any right to propose policies in the guise of budget allocations and insists that no such allocations may be made before the Council has agreed to actual policy decisions. This view has even been applied when the Commission has rested its case for new or additional spending on earlier statements of the Council.

But the Council of Ministers itself is not well enough organised to determine overall policy on the budget. While the budget is finally determined by Finance Ministers sitting as the Budget Council, it is, in effect, a by-product of the individual decisions taken by the various Technical or Specialist Councils with little overall coordination. Member states attempted to improve co-ordination by instituting joint meetings of Foreign and Finance Ministers but to little avail; Agricultural Ministers persisted in taking decisions on policies that dominated the budget and squeezed out other expenditure. Even the increased involvement of Heads of Government in budgetary matters, largely brought about by the difficulty of solving the 'British problem', has not resolved the issue.

The fall in the value of the US dollar in 1985–6 inevitably increased the costs of the CAP. Although by the end of 1986, Agricultural Ministers had agreed on a new package of measures to cut costs, perhaps the most far-reaching to be introduced up to then, the continued preponderance of agricultural spending means that budgetary discipline will continue to be a highly relative term. It also means that the 1.4 per cent VAT ceiling is under threat very much sooner than anticipated so that the Community appears to face the possibility either of going bankrupt or perhaps being saved as in the past by national contributions; or it moves rather rapidly towards the 1.6 per cent VAT ceiling; or it agrees on new own resources. A move towards the new VAT ceiling calls into question the British budgetary settlement. In all these cases unanimity is required in decision-making. It was not easily achieved; indeed many predicted a major political crisis after the failure of successive European Council meetings to reach accord. It was not until the special European Council of February 1988 that a comprehensive agreement was reached which contained: a ceiling on overall agricultural spending; controls over spending on a number of individual crops; the rate of growth of the structural funds; the structure of the Community's own resources and the introduction of a fourth resource based on GNP; the UK's abatement; and the overall level of the Community's own resources (up to 1.2 per cent of Community GNP).

Annex I: European Investment Bank (EIB)

The EIB was set up in 1958 under Article 129 of the Treaty, with the member states of the Community as the shareholders. Its purpose is primarily to finance investment projects in member states. Since 1963 it has also financed projects in other states with whom the Community has cooperation agreements such as the African, Caribbean and Pacific states signatory to the Lomé Convention (see Chapter 16) and the Mediterranean Associates (see Chapter 15). Its capital, subscribed by member states, is 14 400 million ECU. The EIB raises funds by borrowing on the world capital markets. It is non-profit making. It has its own statute and is autonomous within the Community, with a Board of Governors, consisting of the Finance Ministers of the member states, and a Board of Directors appointed by the Governors (two from each member state). There is a Management Committee of five appointed by the Governors which is responsible for the day-to-day running of the bank; and an Audit Committee.

Annex II: The Court of Auditors

A Court of Auditors was set up under the 1975 Amending Treaty in Luxembourg in 1977. Although there had been an Audit Board under the Treaty of Rome (and an Auditor under the Treaty of Paris for the ECSC), it had inspired little confidence, especially after some well-publicised frauds within the CAP. With the introduction of own resources an improved, independent control mechanism was regarded as vital. The Court, with members nominated by the Council and endorsed by the Parliament, was based largely on the French Cour des Comptes, and functions in some ways similar also to the British National Accounts Office. Its purpose is to check on the legality, the operation and the management of budget revenues and expenditures. It draws up annual reports but also has the right to prepare special reports on its own initiative if it sees fit in the interests, especially, of 'sound financial management'.

SUGGESTIONS FOR FURTHER READING

D. Coombes, *The Power of the Purse in the European Communities* (Chatham House/PEP, 1972)
G. Denton et al., *The British Problem and the Future of the EEC Budget* TEPSA/Federal Trust, 1982)
D. Strasser, *The Finances of Europe* (EC Commission, 1981)
H. Wallace, *Budgetary Politics: the Finances of the European Community* (UACES/George Allen & Unwin, 1980)

For Treaty references see: Treaty of Rome, Part V, Title II, Articles 199–209 and Part III, Title IV, Articles 129–30.

13 Economic and Monetary Union and the European Monetary System

The signatories of the Treaty of Rome regarded the establishment of the European Community as the primary means of forging 'an ever-closer union'. That union was, and remains, largely undefined. But it was seen as involving the member states in progressively harmonising their economic policies. The objectives of the Treaty were, therefore, not limited to the establishment of a common market. Yet, as the preceding chapters show, it has been easier for member states to agree on the removal of barriers (sometimes termed 'negative integration') than on new common policies ('positive integration'). Economic relations with the United States have led to a cautious approach by the Community to monetary issues. Since the international monetary system was based on the US dollar (and to a lesser extent, sterling) as a reserve currency, it was difficult for the Community to conceive of an independent Community monetary system.

The situation had changed significantly by the end of the 1960s. During its first decade the Community enjoyed steady rates of growth, low inflation rates, near-full employment and stable exchange rates. But the gradual weakening of the dollar system and the parity changes of the French franc and the West German mark in 1969 ended the belief in the stability of Community exchange rates, and created a strong incentive to pursue monetary integration within the Community. Uncertainties derived from parity changes threatened to impede the free movement of goods, and the free movement of capital remained heavily circumscribed.

161

The operation of common policies, notably, of course, the Common Agricultural Policy, required stable exchange rates if common prices were to prevail throughout the Community. The pooling of reserves would, it was held, strengthen Community currencies in external relations, especially *vis-à-vis* the dollar. Resolutions in favour of the coordination of short and medium-term economic policies and monetary cooperation appeared no longer sufficient. Heads of Government, meeting in December 1969, declared themselves in favour of complete Economic and Monetary Union (EMU) by 1980.

A complete monetary union implies that national governments give up two major policy instruments, the exchange rate and independent monetary policy. The Community would operate a pool of foreign reserves, a common exchange rate policy towards third countries, and a common stand in international monetary negotiations. Issue of money credit and interest rate policies would be entrusted to a Community central bank, which would become the centre of a federal reserve system. Monetary union would require, in addition, common or highly coordinated policies in a wide range of economic matters: fiscal and budgetary policy; regional and incomes policies; and short and medium-term planning.

EMU implies, therefore, profoundly significant changes. It was, and remains, highly controversial. The methods and timing of moving towards EMU gave rise to innumerable debates both at the theoretical and the political levels. Immediately after 1969, the debate tended to revolve around the divisions between the so-called 'monetarists' and 'economists'. For the monetarists, monetary union was regarded as the primary goal, which would automatically entail the necessary coordination of economic policies. The economists, in contrast, held that unless economic policies and performance were harmonised first, monetary union would be unworkable. Substantial transfers from the richer to the poorer regions would be necessary to compensate for the loss of monetary flexibility. Despite their differences, the main economic logic used by both sides was similar, that incompatible and uncoordinated economic and monetary policies lay behind balance-of-payments deficits and surpluses. At a less abstract level, lay the fears, initially of Italy, and later of the UK and Ireland, that by abandoning control over the exchange rate as an instrument for adjusting the economy, governments of the weaker, peripheral countries would risk higher unemployment and lower prospects for growth. The stronger economies, on the other hand, were worried about the financial costs which they might be asked to meet in support of their weaker partners if there was a premature move towards monetary union.

Although the Council of Ministers were agreed on the establishment of EMU by 1980, there remained little consensus on how it should be achieved. The Werner report of 1970 (named after its chairman, the Luxembourg Prime Minister, Jean-Pierre Werner) attempted to reconcile the differences between the monetarists and economists by adopting the principle of parallelism. After prolonged debates in the Council, a decision based on the Werner proposals emerged. It was very much a compromise between French opposition to the supranational character of the Werner proposals and the German concern that they might be left to support weaker currencies, including the French franc. In order to ensure parallelism between the economic and monetary components of EMU, and time to allow a further consensus to be built up, a first stage of three years was agreed.

The monetary plan adopted was to narrow the margins of day-to-day exchange rate fluctuations among the currencies of member states by buying and selling US dollars on the commercial exchange markets. The narrower band, limiting fluctuations among the member states, became known as the 'snake', and the wider band of permissible fluctuations against the dollar, the 'tunnel'. Hence the policy became known as 'the snake in the tunnel'.

The monetary plan was almost immediately overtaken by events. The collapse of the international monetary system, based on the dollar, was signalled first by the floating of the German mark and the Dutch guilder in May 1971. In August the United States floated the dollar. In the face of this collapse, members of the Community proved unable to adopt a joint policy. After the conclusion of the new Smithsonian monetary agreement in December 1971 by the leading members (the 'Group of Ten') of the International Monetary Fund, the Community attempted to relaunch the first stage of the Werner Plan, in March 1972. The four applicant countries, the UK, Norway, Denmark and Ireland, also participated. But the UK withdrew after only six weeks, when it floated the pound in June 1972, and the Italian lira followed in January 1973, after special support arrangements had proved insufficient.

Nevertheless, at the Paris summit meeting of 1972, heads of government endorsed the objective of EMU in 1980 and decided to establish a European Monetary Cooperation Fund with the object, eventually, of running the Community exchange system. More immediately, it was to organise short-term credit facilities, taking over the functions of the Committee of Central Banks. In order to maintain parallelism between the components of EMU, and at the strong insistence of the UK, the summit also decided to launch discussions on a Community Regional Fund.

Monetary instability continued, however. In February, 1973, the dollar was devalued and a month later the Community 'snake' left the 'tunnel', so that all Community currencies floated against the dollar. In January 1974 the French franc also left the 'snake' to float, rejoined after six months, and later left again. In effect, therefore, after 1974 only five Community currencies were members of the 'snake' (together with the Norwegian kroner, and, until 1977, the Swedish krona); the UK and Irish pounds, the Italian lira and the French franc floated independently. The 'snake' in practice was limited to a 'Deutschemark zone'. Moreover, even within the 'snake' there was little exchange-rate stability. The smaller members of the 'snake' had to devalue against the German Mark several times as it was continuously pushed up against the dollar. On each occasion, however, they fixed a new peg for their exchange rate against the Mark, and continued to operate the rules of the 'snake'. Despite this, it was clear that, for the time being at least, EMU was impossible, and, at the Paris summit of 1974 further moves towards monetary integration were shelved.

Although the Paris meeting commissioned a report on European Union (undertaken by the Belgian Prime Minister, Leo Tindemans), the emphasis appeared to be on more limited practical economic measures. The Summit established the European Regional Development Fund – on an extremely modest scale. Other measures subsequently agreed to, included Community loans to finance balance of payments deficits to fend off competitive depreciations, and in April 1978 the Council of Ministers approved the doubling of the capital of the European Investment Bank, available for financing public and private investment. Economic coordination evolved largely as an attempt to persuade surplus countries, especially West Germany, to reflate their economies, to become the locomotives by which other economies could be pulled out of recession. It was an attempt not restricted only to Community members; West Germany came under strong pressure from the United States in the Western Economic Summits.

The subject of EMU, however, refused to disappear. Academic interest, for example, was intensified by the failure of flexible exchange rates to solve the problems of inflation and unemployment. The Commission itself instigated several studies such as that by Robert Marjolin in 1975 and by Sir Donald McDougall in 1977 (the latter on fiscal federalism). Some member states put forward proposals to reform the 'snake', including the French in 1975 (by M. Fourcade) and the Netherlands in 1976 (Mr Duisenberg). But in October 1977 the debate was revitalised by the lecture given by the President of the Commission, Roy Jenkins, at the European University Institute. Mr Jenkins suggested that EMU was necessary as a means of consolidating the customs union, the Common Agricultural Policy and other existing policies; that it could insulate the Community from continuing economic and monetary disturbances; that the Community and the world would benefit from having an international reserve currency alongside that of the US$; and that EMU could be more effective than national manipulation of exchange rates in overcoming balance-of-payments disequilibria, and the failure of national economic policies to combat inflation and unemployment. In the long term he envisaged the centralisation of monetary policy, the establishment of a European Bank, and a common currency. These ultimate goals were to be prepared in the shorter term by measures along the lines suggested in the MacDougall Report, of financial transfers and sectoral policies to reduce divergences within the Community.

While many were prepared to dismiss the Jenkins lecture as inopportune wishful thinking, others were not, most notably the West German Chancellor, Helmut Schmidt. There was a growing, general unease and dissatisfaction with floating exchange rates and they inspired neither long-term confidence nor investment. But, most importantly, they tended to encourage speculative and other movements out of dollars into Deutschemarks (and yen); between June 1977 and March 1978, the Deutschemark:dollar rate fell from DM2.35 to $1, to DM2.06 to $1. As a result the pressures on West Germany to reflate intensified. It was, in other words, largely to meet the challenge posed by the dollar that Schmidt took up the initiative to establish closer monetary cooperation in Europe and a zone of stability within an otherwise highly volatile international system. His initial ideas were conveyed to the French President, Valéry Giscard d'Estaing (like Schmidt, a former Finance Minister) who received them with considerable enthusiasm and together they appointed personal representatives to work out more detailed proposals. There was little further recourse either to their own national ministries or central banks, or to other member governments except to that of the UK. Unlike his two colleagues, however, the British Prime Minister, James Callaghan, appointed an official, from the Treasury. Whatever the political scepticism of the Prime Minister – the Labour Party continued to be hostile to the Community and elections could not be long delayed – it was reinforced by an institutional conservatism that meant that the proposals on a European Monetary System finally submitted to the European Council in Bremen in June 1978 were essentially Franco-German in inspiration and formulation.

Despite British reservations, the general response of the European Council to the proposals was favourable. Instructions were given to Economic and Finance Ministers and their officials to prepare a draft agreement on which heads of government could take a decision at the December 1978 European Council. The basis of the Agreement was the idea of a zone of monetary stability, a European Monetary System (EMS) which, in terms of its exchange rate mechanism was to be as strict as the 'snake' and at whose centre was to be the ECU as a means of settlement between monetary authorities. The details of the system were worked out, under the auspices of the ECOFIN Council, in the Monetary Committee, the Committee of Central Bank Governors and the Economic Committee, not always without considerable problems from sceptics and opponents, including at one point or another, the Bundesbank, which feared for its autonomy in the management of German monetary policy, and a wide swathe of French opinion which looked askance at the leadership and predominance exercised by Germany. And while difficulties had been expected from the British, the Italians and the Irish also found problems. As a result, the EMS was launched by the European Council in December 1978 with only six member states participating. However, the Irish, having had pause for reflection, and time to negotiate an improved package of grants and loans, agreed to sever the ties between the British and Irish pounds, and to join the EMS. The Italians, who had already been offered a wider margin of fluctuation, and who, during their period of reflection, received further assurances that they would not have to defend the lira regardless of the damage caused to Italian reserves, also agreed to join. After a short further delay caused by the sudden concern of France over the way in which the Common Agricultural Policy and monetary compensatory amounts (see Chapter 6) were to be integrated with the new system, the European Monetary System was finally established in March 1979 with only the British not full members.

The essential elements of the EMS are an exchange rate mechanism and a set of credit mechanisms together with a European Monetary Fund – the latter being of particular importance in a proposed second stage which has not yet been agreed. At the centre of the system is the ECU which is made up of a basket of member states' currencies, including the pound sterling, according to a prescribed ratio determined by shares of total GNP, shares of total trade, and country size. Shares in the ECU have been altered only to absorb new member states' currencies. The ECU has several crucial functions, including that of being the denominator or *numéraire* of the exchange rate mechanism, of being the indicator of divergence, the denominator of operation in both intervention and credit mechanisms, and a means of settlement between monetary authorities. On the establishment of the EMS the member states deposited 20 per cent of their gold and dollar reserves with the European Monetary Cooperation Fund which allowed them an equal amount of unconditional drawing rights denominated in ECU.

The exchange rate mechanism works as follows: a central rate is fixed for each currency in ECU and these rates form a grid which establishes bilateral exchange rates. The maximum margins of fluctuation around those central rates are set at 2.25 per cent, except for Italy which has a wider 6 per cent margin. If a currency moves across the so-called threshold of divergence, which equals 75 per cent of the maximum spread, then the monetary authorities are expected to adjust domestic policies, such as raising interest rates, and/or adjusting their foreign exchange rates. However, it is not simply a matter for the diverging currency's authorities; other monetary authorities are also expected to take action in support of stability. Moreover, any member state which considers that it is being adversely affected by another member's exchange rate fluctuations can call for consultations. Actual changes in the central rate of exchange are thus no longer the sole responsibility of each member state; decisions have to be taken on the basis of unanimity. There are now a number of cases where member governments have sought larger devaluations than were finally agreed: in 1982, for example, Belgium sought a 12 per cent devaluation and had to settle for 8.5 per cent; and in 1986, France sought an 8 per cent devaluation and had to settle for 5.8 per cent (although West Germany also revalued the DM by 3 per cent).

In all, by the end of 1986 there had been nine significant realignments of EMS currencies. To a considerable extent it remains a Deutschemark zone with other countries attached largely because of their close economic ties to West Germany, plus France. Relations between France and the other members have not always been smooth. The British, despite widespread support in financial and commercial circles (and in much of Whitehall) have remained aloof from the exchange rate mechanism. None the less, at least for much of its history, the EMS has proved remarkably successful in maintaining a semi-fixed exchange rate for its members. It has, however, been suggested that this success was the result of, rather than simply coincident with, a strong dollar. Certainly once the dollar had peaked in value in early 1985, the EMS came under increasing strain. The problem lay mainly in the fact that the Deutschemark (as well, of course, as the yen) came under particularly strong upward pressure, creating strains within the System. A concerted and effective policy *vis à vis* the dollar has been difficult to establish. It has also been suggested that the limits to the success of the system are indicated by the failure to move to the second stage envisaged under the agreement whereby credit mechanisms would be consolidated within the European Monetary Fund, which would begin to take on the character of a central Community bank.

Against these criticisms, defenders of the EMS have been quick to point out not only the relative stability in exchange rates, but to the contribution made by the EMS to economic convergence among the member states, especially in terms of inflation rates and balance of payments performance. By 1982, for example, nearly all governments, including those of France under M. Mitterrand, had adopted tighter fiscal policies to counter inflationary pressures. Perhaps even more spectacular has been the dynamic increase in the use of the ECU in the private sector.

By 1982 it was recognised as a currency by Italy, Belgium and France (although significantly not by West Germany) and by January 1983, the ECU was the third most widely-used currency in the Eurocurrency and Eurobond markets after the dollar and the Deutschemark. Its success was partly due to its attractiveness as a genuine alternative to the dollar and also because of its official use by Community institutions backed up by Community law.

So far, however, West Germany has refused to allow its citizens to use the ECU in private transactions. Several reasons have been put forward for this refusal by the German Bundesbank, which is the most independent of all the central banks in the Community, and for its general reluctance to develop the EMS significantly further. They include legal constraints (derived from anti-indexation legislation which was designed to prevent a recurrence of massive inflation which in the past so undermined political stability in Germany), the fact that other member states, including France and Italy have maintained restrictions on capital movements, and that still greater economic convergence is required before closer monetary unity can be established. The fact that the pound sterling is also not a full member has also sometimes been cited as a cause for further caution.

The British position, too, has depended on varying factors. If the initial rejection of membership was largely due to the hostility of the Labour Party, Conservative opposition to membership rested, to begin with, on the belief in the possible incompatibility of domestic monetary targets with the obligations of EMS membership. In the aftermath of the second oil-price shock of 1978–9, the pound also appeared to behave like a petro-currency which, it was held, would impose too many strains on the EMS – although by the mid 1980s it was clear that the 95 per cent of the British economy that was not linked to oil was probably more significant. The British Government has so far, however, remained unconvinced of the arguments in favour of membership, despite persistent invitations to join from the other member states, especially West Germany. British opposition to membership, especially on the part of the Prime Minister, Mrs Thatcher, and West Germany's reluctance to envisage the further development of the EMS derive essentially from the same cause, a fundamental concern over the loss of autonomy in decision-making. Together they were largely responsible for the limited references to the EMS in the Single European Act (it is mentioned in the Preamble and again, briefly, under a new Chapter of two short paragraphs on Monetary Capacity).

However, the private use of the ECU continues to grow, with, for example, the Bank of International Settlements in Basle agreeing to act as clearing house for such transactions. In addition France and Italy have indicated that they are prepared to lift restrictions on capital movements. Various other measures such as improved convertibility of ECUs and approval for non-member states to hold ECU reserves have also been agreed by the Council of Ministers. The major question marks that remain are those over joint policies towards the dollar, over British membership and over progress towards the long-delayed stage two of the EMS, the development of a European Monetary Fund.

SUGGESTIONS FOR FURTHER READING

J. Coffey, *The European Monetary System – Past, Present and Future* (Martinus Nijhoff, 1985)

M. de Cecco (ed.), *International Economic Adjustment: Small Countries and the European Monetary System* (Basil Blackwell/EUI, 1983)

D. Dosser, et al., *The Collaboration of Nations* (Martin Robertson, 1982)

A. M. El-Agraa, *The Economics of the European Community* (2nd edition, Philip Allen, 1985)

M. Hodges and W. Wallace (eds), *Economic Divergence in the European Community* (George Allen & Unwin, 1981)

S. Holland, *The Uncommon Market* (Macmillan, 1982)

Y.-S. Hu, *Europe Under Stress* (Butterworth/RIIA, 1981)

P. Ludlow, *The Making of the European Monetary System* (Butterworth, 1982)

G. Magnifico and J. Williamson, *European Monetary Unification* (Federal Trust, 1972)

T. Padoa-Schioppa, *Money, Economic Policy and Europe* (EC Commission, 1985)

L. Tsoukalis, *The Politics and Economics of European Monetary Integration* (George Allen & Unwin, 1977)

J. Van Ypersele and J.-C. Koeune, *The European Monetary System: Origins, Operation and Outlook* (EC Commission, 1985)

For Treaty references see: Treaty of Rome, Part III, Title II, Chapter 1, Article 103 and Chapter 2, Articles 104–109.

14 The Common Commercial Policy

The Community's external economic policy has often been re-garded as one of its major successes. It is second only to the Common Agricultural Policy in political importance, but has been far less divisive and contentious. The Community's ability to act as an equal partner with the United States became demon-strably clear when the Kennedy and Tokyo Rounds of the General Agreement on Tariffs and Trade (GATT) negotiations were completed in 1967 and 1979. A new relationship with a large part of the Third World, including the bulk of Africa, as well as a number of Caribbean and Pacific countries, was established with the conclusion of the Lomé Convention in 1975 (see Chapter 16). In between such great set-piece negotiations, moreover, the Com-munity has concluded a large number of trade or cooperation agreements with individual countries. It has also negotiated almost continuously on detailed issues in GATT, the United Nations Conference on Trade and Development (UNCTAD), and other international organisations. Well over 100 governments now have accredited diplomatic representatives to the Community in Brussels.

The strongest motive for integration, alongside Franco-German reconciliation and the belief in the benefits of the larger market, was the desire to redress the weakness of Western Europe in relation to the superpowers. The capacity to negotiate on level terms with the Americans in at least one major aspect of economic relations has been the Community's greatest achievement in this respect. The Community is indeed a formidable economic power. Its trade with the rest of the world (i.e., excluding trade between the member states) represented about 19 per cent of world trade by 1982, compared with 14 per cent for the United States and 8 per cent for Japan. In the same year Community imports and exports (again excluding trade between member states) represented an average of 12.6 per cent of GDP compared with 7.5 per cent for the US and 12.5 for Japan. The Community takes about 25 per cent of all world food products. It is a major source of technology and capital and the sum total of its aid to developing countries from member governments and the Community combined is considerably greater than that of the United States.

As with any nation state, the Community's policies have both internal and external aspects. The Community's Fisheries Policy, for example, not only involves fishing within the Community by member states but also by others in Community waters and by member states in others' waters. There have therefore to be contacts on fisheries between the Community and countries outside it. These external contacts derived from essentially 'internal' Community policies are dealt with where necessary in the relevant chapters. But the bulk of the Community's contacts with non-member countries stem from the Common Commercial Policy (CCP) which governs the Community's trading relationships with the rest of the world. To take fisheries again as an example, international negotiations on access to fishing grounds are governed by the Common Fisheries Policy, but international trade in fish by the CCP.

The CCP is based on the Community's adoption of the Common External Tariff (CET) which has been central to the conduct of international trade negotiations. It is principally the adoption of a CET which distinguishes a customs union from a free trade area; customs duties are abolished among the members of both, but in a free trade area member states are free to set their own tariffs towards countries outside. The Spaak Report (see Chapter 1), on which the Treaty of Rome was based, contended that a free trade area, in which member states were allowed to retain their own tariffs on imports from third countries, would be impracticable because of the distortions of trade that would result from the flow of imports into the higher-tariff members via the member countries with lower tariffs. The major political impetus towards the adoption of a CET came, however, from the French who, in 1957, were determined to give the Community a distinct political and economic identity in relation to the rest of the world.

Since tariffs have been the principal instrument of commercial policy, the logic of a CET led to a common commercial policy towards third countries. In the Treaty of Rome, the key Article is 113, which bases the CCP on uniform principles, especially in relation to tariff rates, the conclusion of trade and tariff agreements, measures to protect trade, export policy, and uniform liberalism of trade. The Commission is not only called upon to put forward proposals to implement the policy, as is normal, but is also called upon to conduct negotiations with third countries on the basis of a mandate from the Council of Ministers. It does so in consultation with the Article 113 Committee, composed of senior national officials. Member states also undertake (under Article 116) to coordinate their policies in international organisations of an 'economic character'.

Quite where, in international negotiations, the powers of the member states end, and those of the Community begin, has often been a divisive issue among the Commission and the member states. The doctrine that only the Community is competent in external relations for matters arising from common policies, or common rules, stems from a series of judgements and opinions delivered by the European Court of Justice. The best known is probably the case brought by the Commission against the Council on the European Road Transport Agreement (ERTA), Case 22/70. The agreement covered the work of crews of vehicles engaged in international road transport. The Court held that, since the Treaty provided for a common transport policy, member states no longer had the right to enter into international transport agreements themselves, but only the Community could do so (See also Chapter 5.) In the case of agreements which contain elements arising both from Community policies, and from those still within the competence of member states, negotiations are carried out and concluded by both the Commission and the member states (represented usually by the Presidency of the Council of Ministers). In practice, *ad hoc* working solutions to the problems of competence which have arisen between the Commission and the member states have been found (see Chapter 17). While the process of reaching agreement with third countries can be slow and difficult, this is less often because of disputes over competence than because of the substantial national interests members consider it necessary to defend.

In the same way as sovereign states, the Community conducts its external economic relations through multilateral and bilateral channels. The Community as such is a member of several multilateral organisations, of which the most important is the GATT. Although member states are all individual contracting parties to the GATT, the Commission speaks on their behalf, except in the Budget Committee. In other organisations, the Community is represented either by the Commission on its own or with member states, depending on the subject matter and the Community's status in the organisation. The same applies bilaterally, where the Community uses two main instruments of policy, preferential and non-preferential agreements. In the first, the Community grants and in some cases receives, special tariff and other trading concessions; examples include the Community's agreements with members of the European Free Trade Association (EFTA); the Mediterranean Association Agreements and the Lomé Convention. Bilateral non-preferential agreements, also known as trade or commercial cooperation agreements, involve no tariff concessions but aim at the encouragement of trade through joint consultations; examples include agreements with certain Latin American and South East Asian countries (see Chapter 16). This chapter covers the Community's external relations with developed countries and some of the international negotiations in which both developing and developed countries are involved.

RELATIONS WITH THE ADVANCED INDUSTRIALISED COUNTRIES

Although the Community's most important trading partners are the United States and Japan, it has no formal bilateral trading agreements with either. The history of its economic relations with both has largely been the history of international trade negotiations since the early 1960s. The Community has been a proponent of low average industrial tariffs, in keeping with the overall free trade philosophy of the Treaty of Rome. The absence of high Community tariffs originates in the averaging of the tariffs of Benelux, France, Italy and West Germany to form the common external tariff. In the process the highest tariffs of each were brought sharply down. The Community was active in the general liberalisation of international trade in the GATT Kennedy Round of the multilateral trade negotiations (MTNs), continued in the Tokyo Round. The Community's average weighted tariff, excluding zero tariffs, will as a result of the Tokyo Round negotiations, fall from its 1982 level of 9 per cent, one of the lowest in the world, to around 7.5 per cent by 1988. Although tariffs can still be contentious, as their levels have declined, trade negotiations have become far more concerned with non-tariff barriers (ntbs). This has been particularly the case as governments have turned to ntbs in one form or another for protection during the economic recession. It is principally over ntbs that the Community, the USA and Japan have been involved in some fierce trade disputes.

The United States Government, for political and stategic reasons, has generally supported European integration but not without some ambivalence. Many American farmers and commercial and manufacturing interests have been concerned about European Community competition. The CAP in particular has been a major cause of disagreement. As large exporters of food stuffs, American farmers have resented European export subsidies on agricultural produce (dairy products and grain in particular) which they claim have depressed world prices. The Community has argued that the Americans behave similarly but use different methods. Other disputes have arisen over Community exports of special steels to the United States and over US exports of synthetic textiles, chemicals and citrus fruit to the Community. The loss of US markets in Spain and Portugal as a result of their accession to the Community threatened to result in a 'trade war' at the end of 1986. In the early 1970s such trade problems several times threatened to spill over into more traditionally 'political' arenas – they were, of course, partly motivated by political considerations whether inspired by Gaullist perceptions of Europe or by Congressional pressure. Despite an attempt by Dr Kissinger in 1973 when Secretary of State, to link the political, economic and security aspects of these Atlantic relationships in the so-called 'Year of Europe' (see Chapter 17), they have tended to remain in fairly separate categories. There are signs in the 1980s, however, especially in view of American trade and monetary difficulties, that this separation is again being questioned.

Trade difficulties between the Community and Japan have also been a major topic for discussion. Competition from Japan and the semi-industrialised countries has sharply aggravated the troubles of industries such as shipbuilding, steel, man-made fibres, plastics, radio, television, cars, and many others. The Community, the United States, and some other importing countries have increasingly resorted to *ad hoc* measures for protection. Japan made some concessions during the Tokyo Round but Community countries continued, and continue, to find the greatest difficulty in penetrating the Japanese market. Japan, on the other hand, has been constantly increasing the level of its exports to the Community whose trade deficit with Japan stands now at well over 10 billion ECU. The fundamental problem for European exporters is how to break into the Japanese market, a problem made very much more difficult by Japanese non-tariff barriers, although Japanese tariffs are also relatively high on those goods from which they most fear competition.

Of the other developed countries with whom the Community has close trading relations, Australia and New Zealand have major interests in agriculture. Neither have formal trading agreements with the Community. But the agriculture exports of both countries, particularly those of New Zealand, were much affected by British entry into the Community. The main interest of both has been to improve access for their temperate agricultural produce and to counter the effect of Community exports on to the world market. Unlike Australia, New Zealand, when Britain entered the Community, obtained an undertaking that the UK could continue to import certain declining quantities of butter and cheese until the end of 1977 at a rate of levy lower than the Community's normal rate. The arrangements for butter were later extended annually on broadly the same lines until July 1985 when special arrangements were agreed for the years 1985–8, based on the level of imports for 1984. The arrangements for cheese, however, lapsed in accordance with the original agreement. The dispute in the Community over 'sheep meat' (the jargon for mutton and lamb but the regime also covers goat) was caused partly at least by the extent of New Zealand exports to the UK (see Chapter 6).

The Community's other main trade partners are the non-Community countries of Western Europe. With each of the members of the European Free Trade Association (EFTA) the Community has agreements for free trade in manufactured goods and certain processed food products. EFTA countries are bound by Community rules on fair competition (although they are liable to investigation under the Community's anti-dumping regulation, in the same way as other third countries) and have, in general, agreed to apply Community rules governing prices and transport costs. While all are eligible to join the Community, only Portugal has done so as yet. Norway rejected membership in a bitterly fought referendum in 1972. However, although its links, as with other EFTA members, are close on a wide range of issues (including monetary matters), by 1986 some sections of opinion in Norway had come to question whether such links were enough. While its close relations with the Community through its Free Trade Agreement allow Norway some opportunity to make its views known during the evolution of Community policies, its ability to influence decision-making directly either in the Community or European political cooperation remains limited. Moves were afoot therefore to reintroduce the question of Norway's membership on to the political agenda.

EASTERN EUROPE

It was only on 1 January 1975 that the Community assumed responsibility for trade relations with communist, or state trading countries, although, in principle, the application of the common commercial policy had been agreed in 1969. The delay was caused largely by the political importance of economic relations with the countries of Eastern Europe in the process of détente between East and West.

Trade between Eastern and Western Europe has been increasing rapidly since the beginning of the 1960s. Soviet and East European governments have placed considerable emphasis on increasing cooperation as an element of détente. Their aim has been both to eliminate the remaining Community obstacles to trade, and to secure more attractive credit facilities and industrial cooperation agreements for buying modern machinery and sophisticated technology. The importance of trade with the Community varies considerably among the state-trading countries. Soviet exports, as yet, are mainly in raw materials which encounter few Community trade barriers. Exports from other East European countries, however, are in agricultural goods and manufactures. Agricultural goods are of course, subject to the regulations of the Common

Agricultural Policy. The liberalisation of trading restrictions in manufactured goods has progressed until the Community has only a hard core of sensitive products subject to restrictions, including quotas. Several of these are, however, on goods produced by East European countries, in particular textiles and clothing.

Community relations with Eastern Europe have, therefore, been difficult, not least because the Soviet Union and East European states refuse to recognise the Community formally (see p. 179). That is not to say that a variety of issues, such as fisheries, have not been discussed between the Community and CMEA countries, including the Soviet Union. In addition, Romania has been accepted for treatment within the Community's Generalised Scheme of Preferences (see p. 200). Romania, Hungary, Poland and Czechoslovakia are members of GATT, and all the countries of Eastern as well as Western Europe are members of the United Nations Economic Commission for Europe, so there is a wide range of contacts in multilateral bodies. In spite of not recognising the Community formally, a number of East European countries were ready from 1976 to sign bilateral agreements with it. Romania, Hungary, Poland, Bulgaria and Czechoslovakia all have agreements with the Community on textiles and on trade in steel. Romania and the Community have a long-term agreement on industrial trade and an agreement setting up a joint committee. Negotiations for agreements to replace these started in 1987 (with Hungary and Romania) as part of a new attempt to put bilateral relations between the Community, individual east European countries and the CMEA on a more normal basis (see below).

The difficulties in establishing more comprehensive trading agreements between Eastern and Western Europe lie in the fundamental differences between the political and economic systems of the Community and its member states and the state trading countries. These were clearly revealed at the Conference on Security and Cooperation in Europe (CSCE). Neither the Community, nor its member states, have powers equal to those of communist countries to regulate and direct economic relations. This mismatch of economic powers and institutions has been revealed further in the protracted talks between the Community and the Council for Mutual Economic Assistance (CMEA, also known as COMECON). Preliminary contacts, despite no formal recognition, were made by the CMEA in 1973. In 1974 the Community proposed, in a series of letters to the members of the

CMEA, that the bilateral trade agreements between the nine Community members and CMEA members should be replaced by bilateral agreements between the Community as such and CMEA members. These proposals were not taken up. In their place, after a considerable interval, the CMEA proposed a complex series of agreements linking institutions and their members, and trade issues and other matters outside the common commercial policy. These proposals ran into the sand in the early 1980s because of two major problems. First, the CMEA wanted to include commercial matters for which the Community believed CMEA member states were responsible and not the organisation itself. Secondly, it looked as if the CMEA proposals would have given the CMEA rights in respect of the bilateral agreements between the Community and CMEA member states which the Community believed would have gone beyond the CMEA's rightful powers.

In 1984, however, there were signs that the CMEA was ready to renew contacts and, in 1985, Mr Gorbachev said in a speech at a dinner in Moscow in honour of the visiting Italian Prime Minister, Mr Craxi, that it was time to organise mutually advantageous relations in economic matters between the EC and the CMEA. The upshot was that negotiations started between the two organisations on a joint declaration which would result in the establishment of formal relations between the Community and the CMEA, and between the Community and individual East European countries. Negotiations were successfully concluded in 1988 and formal relations between the EC and CMEA established. Some but not all of the E. European states have as a result also established formal relations with the Community.

The section above deals only with the European states of the CMEA. There are no proposals at present for arrangements between the Community and the non-European members of the CMEA. As for other socialist countries, China has had diplomatic relations with the Community since 1975. The Community signed a framework trade agreement with the Chinese People's Republic in 1978 and also has long-term agreements on textile trade.

PROSPECTS

The main issues facing the Community and its trading partners in 1986–87 are those relating to the further round of multilateral trade negotiations, the Uruguay Round. The principal industrialised countries concerned, together with the Community indicated their agreement to such a round in a number of statements during 1985. For the Community, the Council of Ministers declared in March 1985 that they regarded a new round as 'of the utmost importance to a strengthening of the open multilateral trading system and to the expansion of international trade'. They also regarded it as an opportunity to press Japan 'to bring her import propensity into line with that of other partners'. The United States' primary aims are to challenge what it sees as the Community's agricultural protectionism and to reduce or remove barriers to trade in services. It is also seen by OECD countries in general as a chance to bring pressure on the Newly Industrialising Countries (the NICs) like Brazil, Korea and the ASEAN countries to follow the example of Mexico, accede to GATT and remove some of their own barriers to imports in return for others removing theirs. All countries are likely to face domestic pressures and difficulties in the new round, hence the caution with which it has been approached. The Community, for example, and particularly the French, have strong reservations about the importance attached by the US to agriculture. None the less, the meeting of GATT countries' Trade Ministers at Punta del Este in September 1986 opened the way for negotiations to begin.

SUGGESTIONS FOR FURTHER READING

P. Coffey, *The External Economic Relations of the EEC* (Macmillan, 1976)

J. Galtung, *The European Community: A Super-Power in the Making* (George Allen & Unwin, 1973)

R. C. Hine, *The Political Economy of European Trade* (Wheatsheaf, 1985)

J. Pearce & J. Sutton, *Protection and Industrial Policy in Europe* (Routledge & Kegan Paul/RIIA, 1985)

J. Pinder (ed.), *National Industrial Strategies and the World Economy* (Allanheld Osmun/Croom Helm, 1982)

A. Rothacher, *Economic Diplomacy between the European Community and Japan 1959–81* (Gower, 1983)

A. Schlaim et al., *The EEC and Eastern Europe* (Cambridge University Press, 1978).

M. Smith, *Western Europe and the United States* (George Allen & Unwin/UACES, 1984)

J. Steenbergen et al., *Change and Adjustment: External Relations and the Industrial Policy of the European Community* (Kluwer, 1983)

S. Strange and R. Tooze, *The International Politics of Surplus Capacity* (George Allen & Unwin, 1981)

P. Taylor, *When Europe Speaks with One Voice* (Aldwych Press, 1979)

L. Tsoukalis and M. White, *Japan and Western Europe* (Frances Pinter, 1982)

L. Tsoukalis (ed.), *Europe, America and the World Economy* (Basil Blackwell, 1986)

K. Twitchett (ed.), *Europe and the World* (Europa, 1976)

For Treaty references see: Treaty of Rome, Part III, Title II, Chapter 3, Articles 110–16; Treaty of Rome, Part VI, Article 238 and Declarations of Intention concerning the association with the Community of certain countries.

15 The Community and the Mediterranean

The countries of the Mediterranean have occupied the highest importance for the Community. The general tension in the Middle East caused by the Arab-Israeli dispute, the civil war in the Lebanon, the Iran–Iraq War and the growing problems of international terrorism to which these conflicts have contributed have inevitably had a strong influence on Community attitudes and policies. This is closely bound up with the fact that not only are certain Mediterranean countries producers of oil, but also a substantial part of Middle East oil is transported along its shipping routes. Morocco, Algeria and Tunisia (the Maghreb countries) have been traditional suppliers of the French market in a range of Mediterranean agricultural products – Algeria was after all still a part of Metropolitan France in 1957. The area as a whole is an important outlet for Community exports. This is coupled with strong investment interests on the part of the member states of the Community, particularly in Southern Europe and the Maghreb. Finally, much of the immigrant labour in the Community comes from Mediterranean countries.

In the period from 1961 to 1972, the Community concluded agreements with 12 out of the 17 countries of the area. Since it could not, during this period, agree to common guidelines, the agreements ranged from very comprehensive and complicated Association agreements to non-preferential arrangements based on the principle of 'most favoured nation' treatment by both sides. Their contents depended mainly on the country concerned and the time the agreement was concluded. It was only in 1972 that the first serious attempts were made to formulate an overall or 'global' Mediterranean policy.

Of the early agreements, the most far-reaching were the Association Agreements with Greece and Turkey (the Athens and Ankara Agreements). Greece applied for association under Article 238 of the Treaty of Rome in 1959. The Agreement came into effect in 1962. It aimed at a complete customs union between Greece and the Community after what was essentially a 22-year transitional period although Greece was to adapt itself fully to some Community requirements in a shorter time. The prospect of full Greek membership of the Community was mentioned in the Agreement but no date was given. During the Colonels' regime in Greece from 1967 to 1974, the Community 'froze' the Association Agreement. This meant that, while the tariff timetable continued, the Community gave no aid and there were no meetings of the Council of Association. The Agreement was adapted to take account of the enlargement of the Community in 1973, but lapsed when Greece joined the EC in 1981. The terms of Greece's membership included a five-year transitional period, apart from some sensitive agricultural products and free movement of Greek labour where the transitional period was seven years.

Turkey's Association Agreement with the Community came into effect in 1965 and is broadly the same as the original Greek agreement. The aim is to achieve a complete customs union although Turkey was given a longer period than Greece in which to eliminate its duties on imports from the Community. The Additional Protocol which came into force in 1973 laid down a 22-year transitional period for achieving full customs union. The complete elimination of tariffs is due therefore in 1995. Under the Agreement, there is a Council of Association which meets at ministerial level and, more frequently, at ambassadorial level. There is also a joint Parliamentary Committee. Turkey was given the possibility of membership although in somewhat qualified language; for example, 'when operation of the Agreement has made it possible to envisage the full acceptance by Turkey of the obligations arising out of the Treaty setting up the Community'.

However, relations between Turkey and the Community have not always been harmonious. The Community suspended the Council of Association in 1980 because of the military coup in Turkey. Several member states introduced a case against Turkey before the European Commission on Human Rights. Although the case was dropped in 1986, some governments have still expressed concern over, for example, the continuation of martial law in several Turkish provinces. None the less, the majority of Community governments (the Greek government being the exception) were satisfied that the situation justified a resumption of the Council of Association meetings, one being held in 1986. For its part, Turkey is suspicious of Greek influence in the Community both in general and over the question of Cyprus. Successive Turkish governments have declared their determination to join the Community, in part at least to counter what they see as this undue Greek influence. Although the Turkish Government submitted an application in early 1987, many member governments clearly signalled their unease over the prospect. Quite apart from the political problems Turkish membership could pose for the Community, it is doubtful whether the Turkish economy is yet advanced enough to face membership, even with a long transitional period. Turkey has not yet, for example, introduced the preferential tariff rates due under the Association Agreement.

In the period between 1963 and 1969 two limited trade agreements, with Israel and Lebanon, were signed. In 1969 the Community concluded Association Agreements with Morocco and Tunisia, although the term 'Association' was misleading since the agreements were basically only commercial cooperation agreements. The following year, a preferential trade agreement was signed with Spain, and a non-preferential agreement with Yugoslavia. In 1972 two further Association Agreements were signed with Malta and Cyprus. These were similar in principle and intention to those signed with Greece and Turkey but they envisage further negotiations before the start of a second stage which would lead to the establishment of a customs union. There is no mention of future membership of the Community, although this does not of itself exclude the possibility. Preferential agreements were signed in the same year with Egypt and Lebanon.

This multitude of differing agreements marked the first phase of the Community's Mediterranean policy. In September 1972 the Commission put forward proposals for a new 'global' Mediterranean policy. This reflected growing dissatisfaction with the existing agreements and was seen also as a necessary response to new factors. It was considered in Brussels that relations with

Mediterranean countries could no longer be determined by the type of piecemeal approach adopted so far; a jointly agreed set of rules and criteria was required to govern Community relations with the area. This was very much a French idea which reflected the worries of French, and Italian, producers of Mediterranean agricultural goods, that concessions were being made by the Community in each of its separate negotiations. The prospect of enlargement in 1973 also made it necessary to revise agreements or sign additional protocols in order to incorporate the new members into the old agreements. This was seen by the Commission as the opportunity to formulate a new, more coherent policy.

Two other factors played a part in the forming of the new policy. Firstly, there was growing American hostility to the proliferation of preferential agreements, particularly when these involved an element of reciprocity from the Mediterranean countries. Moreover, if the Community and the member states wanted to assert an independent political role in the world, strategic, political and economic considerations made the Mediterranean one of the first priorities.

The major objective of the Commission's proposals in September 1972 was the creation of a free trade area in industrial goods between the Community and each of the Mediterranean countries. Given the existence of the Common Agricultural Policy, free trade in agricultural goods was considered out of the question. Technical and industrial cooperation was envisaged between the two sides, with financial aid being given by the Community to the relatively less developed countries of the area. The Commission also proposed to try to find a common approach to the problem of immigrant labour. This principle of a 'global' policy was adopted by the Heads of Government at the Paris Summit of October 1972. The first agreement, with Israel, was signed in May 1975, rather later than the Community originally proposed, and those with the Maghreb countries not until April 1976. In January 1977, agreements were also signed with Egypt, Syria and Jordan, and a similar one with Lebanon, was initialled a month later. At the same time an additional protocol and a financial protocol were signed with Israel. The delay was due to three main factors: the difficulties of reconciling the very different interests of the members of the Community; the unacceptability of the Community's original proposals to Mediterranean countries; and the political and economic events stemming from the Yom Kippur War of 1973.

The two main issues which arose in the negotiations were the question of reciprocity in the dismantling of tariff barriers and the concessions to be made by the Community for Mediterranean agricultural exports. In the negotiations with the Maghreb countries, demands for reciprocity were finally abandoned by the Community, at least for the initial period of the agreements. The same arrangement was made later with the four countries of the Mashraq (Egypt, Syria, Jordan and Lebanon).

The agreements finally signed with the Maghreb and Mashraq countries envisaged free access to the Community for all industrial goods, with a few exceptions for 'sensitive' products, including refined petroleum products and cork products from the Maghreb, and phosphate fertilisers, textiles and aluminium from the Mashraq, to which ceilings on imports could apply for a limited period. A reduction in customs duties was offered for Mediterranean agricultural exports as well as quotas for wine products from the Maghreb, but only on condition that the rules applying to the organisation of the Community market were respected. All these concessions were subject to safeguard clauses. But no reciprocity was demanded, at least for an initial period of five years. In all the agreements particular attention was paid to industrial and technical cooperation. A specified amount of financial aid was also offered to each individual country. Separate clauses covered the treatment of immigrant workers from the Maghreb in the Community. All the agreements are of unlimited duration but subject to periodic re-examination by both sides.

The agreement signed with Israel in May 1975 was very much along the lines of the Commission's 1972 proposals. It centred on the creation of a free trade area in industrial goods by 1985, with Israeli tariffs being reduced more slowly than those of the Community. A reduction of Community customs duties on Israeli agricultural exports was granted, while similar concessions from the Israeli side were much more limited. Despite the fact that the global approach was intended to eliminate different levels of concessions, Israel was granted a reduction of Community duties on its export of citrus fruit of only 60 per cent, whereas the Maghreb had been offered an 80 per cent reduction. Limited financial aid was offered to Israel and provisions were made for technical and industrial cooperation in Protocols signed in 1977.

This was largely the result of the Community's desire to maintain some form of balance between the Israeli agreement and those signed with Arab countries.

Negotiations with Spain were particularly difficult and had got nowhere when the Spanish Government decided to apply for membership of the Community in July 1977. Portugal had already applied in March that year. The negotiations with both were long and difficult and became inevitably involved in the Community's internal negotiations over the budget and the CAP in particular. An indication of some of the problems involved in Greek, Spanish and Portuguese accession and the results of the negotiations in individual sectors has been given in earlier chapters. But enlargement to the south must affect the Community's relations with its Mediterranean partners and affects also the development of the Community's own Mediterranean regions.

The problem is similar in both cases. Improved access, especially for agricultural products of the new members, was seen as likely to cause considerable problems for existing Community producers and suppliers. There had indeed been concern for some time that it would become even harder to ensure that their products found a market in the Community once Spanish and Portuguese goods were added to those of the existing Mediterranean areas of the Community in Italy, Greece and France. The Council therefore agreed to negotiate adaptations of the Mediterranean Cooperation and Association Agreements to try to ensure that the countries concerned were not too badly affected by enlargement. Negotiations on most Adaptation Protocols were concluded in 1987, as were those on a new generation of Financial Protocols (that is, Community grants and loans).

The measures to be taken to help the Mediterranean regions of the Community cope with enlargement are known as the Integrated Mediterranean Programmes (IMPs) which involve Community expenditure of some 6600 million ECU over 7 years in Greece and certain parts of Italy and France. The countries concerned will contribute to the Programmes, but the bulk of the money will come from existing funds (Regional Development Fund, Social Fund and the EAGGF), from extra financing and from loans from the EIB and the new Community Instrument (see Chapter 12). The aim is that the Mediterranean regions present multi-annual programmes for regional development (rather than applications for individual projects) using the various Community instruments available (see also Chapter 10). The IMPs were very largely the result of pressure from the Greek government which sought 'compensation for enlargement'. The Programme sought by the Greek government was considered excessive by the northern member states who would bear the brunt of the financing and who were not keen to pay for large funds additional to those provided by existing Community instruments. The negotiations came to a head during the Budget negotiations in 1985 when Greece blocked progress on own resources and threatened to veto Portuguese and Spanish accession.

The Community is thus embarking on a new phase of its relations with its Mediterranean partners and its activities in its own Mediterranean regions. The concepts which lie behind the Community's policy may be logical but it will be difficult to ensure the continuation of coherence in action as well as coherence in conception when so many different interests are engaged. The incipient division within the Community between north and south, on what some have referred to as 'the olive tree line', will become increasingly clear over a wide range of issues, whether in terms of agricultural support, other budgetary expenditures or transfers of technology. At the same time, at both the political as well as the economic level, the interest in and concern over Middle East and North African issues will increase.

SUGGESTIONS FOR FURTHER READING

B. Kohler, *Political Forces in Spain, Greece and Portugal* (Butterworth, 1982)
G. Luciani, *The Mediterranean Region* (Croom Helm, 1984)
P. Preston and D. Smith, *Spain, the EEC & NATO* (Chatham House/RKP, 1984)
G. Rosenthal, *The Mediterranean Basin* (Butterworth, 1982)
A. Schlaim and G. Yannopoulos, *The EEC and the Mediterranean* (CUP, 1976)
D. Seers and C. Vaitsos, *The Second Enlargement of the European Economic Community* (Macmillan, 1982)
L. Tsoukalis (ed.), *Greece and the EEC* (Saxon House, 1979)
L. Tsoukalis, *The European Community and its Mediterranean Enlargement* (George Allen & Unwin, 1981)

A. Williams (ed.), *Southern Europe Transformed: Political and Economic Change in Greece, Italy, Portugal, and Spain* (Harper & Row, 1984)

For Treaty references see: Treaty of Rome, Article 238 and Declarations of Intention concerning the Association of the Community with certain countries.

16 The Community and the Third World

The delicate and complex relationship between developed and developing countries makes it unavoidable that the Community should have an agreed policy towards the Third World. But at the time when the Treaty of Rome was drawn up, such a policy did not seem to be an essential ingredient for the creation of a common market. The Spaak Report (see Chapter 1) made no mention of relations with developing countries. However, the French were insistent that the Community should take account of the effects of the establishment of the common market on the colonial empires of its members, and the effects of those empires on the working of the common market. One of the objectives of the Treaty of Rome, therefore, was the 'association' of overseas countries and territories in order to 'increase trade and promote jointly economic and social development'. It was a policy centred on France's African territories.

The reasons for the inclusion of the overseas countries and territories (OCTs) stem from the nature of the customs union and the common commercial policy. It would have been contrary to the principles of the common commercial policy if members of the Community had maintained different tariff levels on imports from the OCTs. But it was unacceptable to France if members could no longer give preferential treatment to their colonies. As a compromise, the latter gained preferential access to all member states. This had the added advantage for the OCTs themselves that it opened up a much larger market, not only in raw materials, but also in manufactured goods, so helping them to alleviate their over-dependence on exports of raw materials. In return for offering preferential treatment, Community members without colonies demanded access to the OCTs for their products no less favourable than that of the colonial powers. This in turn led the colonial powers to insist that all members of the Community should provide aid, so that the former alone did not have to bear the burden of developing the economies of the OCTs when this would benefit all Community members.

Part Four of the Treaty of Rome, and the Convention attached to it, therefore, spelled out the measures to be taken by the Six (for themselves and on behalf of their colonies) to bring the OCTs into association with the Community. Association was based on trade concessions from both sides (although the OCTs were allowed to modify this principle of reciprocity by maintaining some duties) and on aid from the Community granted through the European Development Fund, to which all member states contributed. Algeria and France's other overseas *départements*, that is, those overseas territories which formed part of metropolitan France, benefited from the Development Fund in addition to French colonies.

By 1963 a large number of the countries listed in Part Four of the Treaty had become independent. Largely because of their continuing close relations with France, the Community concluded with them the first Yaoundé Convention (Yaoundé I), and on its expiry in 1968, Yaoundé II. Both Conventions followed the pattern of the 1957 arrangements. But both were negotiated and signed, on the one hand by the Community and its members, and on the other by the associated countries themselves. Those remaining dependent territories were given broadly the same terms by the Community which had been negotiated with the independent associates.

At the same time these close relations with mainly African countries led the Community towards adopting a more comprehensive African policy to include at least some of the ex-British colonies as well as the ex-French colonies. The Community offered associated status and broadly similar (if not quite so good) terms as those agreed with the Yaoundé associates. Since the Community's economic weight in international negotiations was being increasingly felt, several countries took advantage of the Community's approach. The first to do so was Nigeria, but the agreement signed was not ratified because of the Nigerian civil war. Kenya, Uganda and Tanzania concluded the Arusha Agreement with the Community in 1969.

British accession to the Community resulted in a number of changes in the scope of the Community's relations with less developed countries, if not to their general pattern. The most important result was the conclusion in 1975 of the Lomé Convention, which extended a special relationship with the Community, on similar lines to the earlier Yaoundé Conventions, to the less developed, independent Commonwealth countries of Africa, the Caribbean and the Pacific. Under Protocol 22 of the Treaty of Accession, three choices were offered by the Community: participation in the successor to Yaoundé II; special association under Article 238 of the Treaty of Rome; or a series of non-preferential trade agreements. The Commonwealth countries chose, in concert with the Yaoundé signatories, to negotiate a new type of agreement, similar to Yaoundé II, but with significant differences. The developing countries that signed the Lomé Convention (collectively known as the ACPs since they are all in Africa, the Caribbean and the Pacific) originally number 46, and now number more than 66 (see Table 16.1). Since many of the ACPs considered the term 'associates' to have colonialist connotations, the term is no longer used (although in Community jargon those developing countries which are not ACPs are often referred to as 'non-associates'). In addition to replacing the earlier association agreements, the Lomé Convention replaced many of the economic arrangements which previously linked Britain with the Commonwealth – particularly Commonwealth trade preferences and the Commonwealth Sugar Agreement.

The Lomé signatories pledged themselves to create a 'new model for relations between developed and developing countries, compatible with the aspirations of the international community towards a more just and more balanced economic order'. To this end they agreed to promote trade relations, to attempt to stabilise the ACPs' export revenues, to encourage industrial cooperation, to further the ACPs' economic development through Community-financed aid, and to consult each other through a range of institutions resting on parity between the two groups of partners. The Convention was signed on 28 February 1975. Its trade provisions came into force on 1 July 1975 and the full Convention on 1 April 1976. The duration of the convention was for four years.

Table 16.1   The signatories of Lomé III

*Angola	Gambia	*St Lucia
*Antigua and Barbuda	Ghana	*St Vincent and the
Bahamas	Grenada	Grenadine
Barbados	Guinea	*São Tomé and
*Belize	Guinea-Bissau	Principe
*Benin	Guyana	Senegal
Botswana	Ivory Coast	*Seychelles
Burundi	Jamaica	Sierra Leone
Burkina Faso	*Kiribati	*Solomon Islands
(formerly Upper	Kenya	Somalia
Volta)	Lesotho	Sudan
Cameroon	Liberia	Surinam
*Cape Verde	Madagascar	Swaziland
Central African	Malawi	Tanzania
Republic	Mali	Togo
Chad	Mauritania	Tonga
*Comoros	Mauritius	Trinidad and Tobago
Congo	*Mozambique	*Tuvalu
*Djibouti	Niger	Uganda
*Dominica	Nigeria	*Vanuatu
Ethiopia	*Papua New Guinea	Western Samoa
Equatorial Guinea	Rwanda	Zaire
Fiji	*St Christopher and	Zambia
Gabon	Nevis	*Zimbabwe

*Countries which have acceded to the Conventions since 1975

The second Convention (Lomé II) was signed on October 1979, came into force on 1 March 1980 and was intended to last for five years, ending on 28 February 1985. Because of delays in the negotiations on Lomé III, it was not signed until December 1984 and came into effect on 1 May 1986. In the meantime, the provisions of Lomé II were simply carried forward.

Cooperation under Lomé III goes wider than under its predecessors. the areas covered include: agriculture (and rural development and conservation of natural resources); fisheries; industrial development; mining and energy; transport and communications; trade and services; regional cooperation; and cultural and social cooperation. The fundamental instruments used in the Convention are trade cooperation (that is, Community treatment of ACP products); financial and technical cooperation (Community aid to ACP countries); and investments, capital movements, establishment and services. The most important area is probably trade cooperation and the most important instrument, financial cooperation (through which commodity cooperation works).

The trading arrangements in the Convention give the ACPs more or less open access to Community markets. Almost all ACP industrial exports to the Community have duty-free entry (textiles have been an exception and quotas have been introduced on, for example, some Mauritian imports to the Community) and the great majority of their agricultural exports also enter freely. The ACP countries, unlike the Yaoundé signatories, were not obliged to give reciprocal preferences to Community exports. With two major exceptions the Community does not, however, give free access to products which fall within the Common Agricultural Policy, although it undertook to grant ACP exports more favourable treatment than that available to any other third country (in practice, not of great importance to the ACPs, who have few temperate agricultural products). The two exceptions have been beef and veal, where arrangements were introduced in 1975 to allow Botswana and others to export their beef to the Community almost entirely free of Community levies and sugar.

The ACPs made the conclusion of satisfactory arrangements for sugar a major precondition for signing the Lomé Convention. This was largely at the insistence of the Commonwealth sugar producers, who were particularly concerned that they would be adversely affected by the ending of the Commonwealth Sugar Agreement. The result was a protocol to the Convention under which the Community agreed to import some 1 321 500 tonnes of cane sugar at guaranteed prices for an unlimited period. In return the ACP countries agreed to guarantee deliveries. The sugar protocols have been negotiated separately from the main convention (for further details, see Chapter 6). Separate protocols also cover arrangements for the import of rum and bananas into the Community; the import of beef and veal are covered by an exchange of letters.

The Trade Cooperation Section commits the Community to help the ACPs' export efforts. This was regarded as particularly important by the ACP countries, who were concerned that their preferential treatment under the Conventions was being whittled away by general tariff reductions under the GATT and by the Community's Generalised Scheme of Preferences (see below). Certainly the Community's share of the exports from many of the larger ACP countries fell marginally over the period of the first two Conventions. Under Lomé III, the Community has, for example, agreed to extend cooperation into the field of services, especially tourism, and has simplified the rules of origin to make it easier for the ACPs' processing industries to export to the Community. And while the Community remained unwilling to increase the range of agricultural products for which it would give free entry (largely because of the position taken by the Mediterranean producers), it agreed to speed up its procedures for dealing with requests for ACP countries for improved access for particular agricultural products.

STABEX AND SYSMIN

Stabex – the export revenue stabilisation scheme – was an entirely new instrument in relations between developed and developing countries when introduced into Lomé I. It is intended to compensate ACP countries for their loss of earnings from exports. It originally covered twenty-nine primary products (listed in the annex to the Convention) and others have since been added (in Lomé III, for example, dried bananas, mangoes and shea nuts or karite oil). All are products which are subject to considerable price fluctuations in world markets.

Under the system the Community compensates any ACP country whose revenue, in any one year, from the export to the Community of the product concerned drops below a level based on the revenue from the export of the same product during the previous four years. The amount by which receipts must fall below this reference level varies between different groups of ACP states, based on the classification of developing states used by the UN – although the lists are not identical.

Lomé II and Lomé III both improve the system for the ACPs. For the least developed, landlocked or island countries, revenues must fall by at least 1.5 per cent, while for other states they have to drop by at least 6 per cent. Stabex transfers have, in principle, to be repaid by all except the least developed recipients. They are restricted to those products where normal export receipts amount to a minimum share (called the 'dependence threshold') of a country's exports to all destinations. For the least developed, landlocked or island states, Lomé III brought this dependence threshold to 1.5 per cent (that is the product must account for at least 1.5 per cent of all export earnings) and for the remaining ACPs it is now 6 per cent. Balancing these concessions in Lomé III, the Community insisted on the tightening-up of a number of procedures to be followed by the ACPs, in particular those designed to ensure that ACP states give full information on how they use the transfers which are designed to help the sector in which the export losses occur. Stabex, for which a set sum is provided annually from the EDF, was twice unable to meet all the claims on it at the end of the year. Some extra money was found from elsewhere in the EDF and from extra payments by member states but it was not enough for all claimants. There were criticisms, too, that the larger, better-off ACP countries were benefiting disproportionately. None the less, Stabex was an important innovation in relations between the developed and developing worlds and remains of use to countries still over-whelmingly dependent on the export of commodities.

Sysmin was introduced under Lomé II and extends the Stabex principle to ACP mineral exports which, with the exception of iron ore, were not included in Stabex. The products covered by Sysmin are principally bauxite, cobalt, copper, iron ore (trans-ferred from Stabex), manganese, phosphate and tin. The depen-dence threshold is 15 per cent (unchanged from Lomé II) and there must be a production drop for export earnings loss of at least 10 per cent. The system originally concentrated on the mainten-ance of production capacity. Under Lomé III, the emphasis has shifted to restoring the viability of mining industries (rehabilitation, maintenance and rationalisation). There are also new provisions aimed at speeding up procedures.

INSTITUTIONS

There is a joint EC/ACP Ministerial Council which must meet once a year and which is presided over alternatively by Com-munity and ACP representatives. The work of the Council is prepared by a Committee of Ambassadors. Improved mechanisms have been introduced for consultation between the Community and the ACP countries and for interpreting the Convention. The so-called Article 193 Committee (acting under Article 193 of Lomé III; formerly it was known as the Article 108 Committee), for example, meets at least four times a year, including once at ministerial level, with representatives from the member states of the Community, an equal number of representatives from the ACPs, together with the Commission, the European Investment Bank (the EIB), the Centre for the Development of Industry (CDI) and the Technical Centre for Agricultural and Rural Cooperation (the CTA). The former parliamentary bodies, the Consultative Assembly and its preparatory body, the Joint Committee, have been replaced, for reasons of efficiency, by one parliamentary body, the Joint Assembly. This is composed of an equal number of parliamentarians from the European Parliament and ACP states' parliaments or 'failing this, representatives designated by the ACP states'. It meets twice a year. It has consultative status only.

FINANCIAL AND TECHNICAL COOPERATION (AID)

Lomé III established a sixth European Development Fund (EDF VI)). The first EDF was set up under the original Part IV arrangements, the second and third under the two Yaoundé and the fourth and fifth under Lomés I and II. EDF VI has a capital of 7400 million ECU. To this can be added 1100 million ECU to be made available for loans by the EIB. The tables below show the divisions of aid. Most of it is in the form of grants with some special provisions; EDF loans carry nominal interest rates with repayments up to 40 years and no repayment of capital in the first ten years. European Investment Bank loans are available at the prevailing market rate but ACP countries can take advantage of EDF-financed interest rebates of up to 3 per cent. In addition to grants and concessional loans, the Development Fund can also finance a limited number of risk-capital undertakings.

The negotiations on the size of the Fund were particularly difficult, especially within the Community. The position of the ACP group was clear; they wanted a fund in the region of 10 billion ECU (excluding EIB loans) which, they argued, represented the maintenance of the value of EDF V in real terms plus compensation for increases in their populations. The Community, however, was divided. The Commission favoured a fund of around 8.5 billion ECU. They were supported by France and Italy in particular, who preferred to pay more in cash than make trade concessions which would be mainly at the expense of their Mediterranean producers. Britain and Germany, on the other hand, favoured a smaller amount, a result both of their political disposition, being generally more concerned with increasing trade opportunities than aid flows, and of more straightforward budgetary considerations. The impasse was eventually resolved by Italy making a special contribution, which in effect increased its share of the fund, as shown in Table 16.3, and by anticipating the contributions that Spain and Portugal would make when they joined the Community. It is anticipated that Spain and Portugal will accede to the Convention in 1987.

Table 16.2 Aid to the ACP states under EDF VI (in million ECU)

EDF VI	*7400*
Of which	
projects (grants and special loans)	5770
Stabex	925
Sysmin	415
Exceptional Aid	290
EIB	1100
	8500

Table 16.3 The member states' contributions to EDF VI (in %)

Belgium	3.96	Ireland	0.55
France	23.58	Luxembourg	0.19
Denmark	2.08	Netherlands	5.64
Germany	26.06	Portugal	0.88
Greece	1.24	Spain	6.66
Italy	12.58	United Kingdom	16.58

The essence of the new Convention for the Community is its emphasis on making aid more effective. Twenty years or so after independence and after received considerable sums in aid, the economies of many ACP states still face formidable difficulties, especially in Africa. In keeping with policies developed by the World Bank among others, the Community's objective has been to release funds only on the basis of agreement between the Community and the recipient state on how they can be most effectively used, a process usually termed 'policy dialogue'. Carried to its limits, it would mean that the Community would not give any money to a country with whose policies it disagreed. The ACPs successfully resisted any explicit expression of this degree of 'conditionality' in the Convention. There was also resistance from the Commission and some member states to anything which appeared to run counter to the contractual nature of the Convention. Nevertheless, as the President of the ACP Council of Ministers, Mr Rabbie el Namaliu said in his speech at the signature of Lomé III in Togo, on 8 December 1984, 'in the end, a *modus vivendi* was found by which the desiderata of consultation, efficiency and accountability were accommodated without any excessive notion of conditionality and Community intervention'. Reference to the policy dialogue is in Part I of the Convention, entitled 'The General Provisions of ACP/EEC Cooperation'.

The Community had also sought to include in the Convention the right to halt aid or other assistance to countries whose governments violated fundamental human rights. The ACP states in reply pointed to violations of human rights in Community and other developed countries also, particularly through racial discrimination. The result of the negotiation was that the Preamble to the Convention contains a reaffirmation by both sides to respect human rights, reinforced by a joint declaration reiterating their attachment to human dignity, and their commitment to the elimination of all forms of discrimination.

Among the other changes, perhaps the most important is the change of emphasis from capital projects to 'programme aid', that is, aid to sectors of the economy where rehabilitation and maintenance are necessary (for example, money to import tractor spares). There is also increased emphasis on agriculture and food production. There are entirely new chapters on cultural and social cooperation and the section on the encouragement of investment in ACP countries has been considerably increased. Lastly, shipping has been added to the chapter on Transport and Communication.

THE COMMUNITY'S AID PROGRAMME AND RELATIONS WITH
NON-LOMÉ DEVELOPING COUNTRIES

The Treaty of Rome does not give the Community overall competence in aid in the same way as it does in commercial relations (see Chapter 14). Member states continue to operate their own bilateral aid policies, with the Community's policy running in parallel or in addition to them. This applies both to Lomé and non-Lomé developing states, for the Community does not confine its aid or its commercial concessions to the ACP countries.

The principal instrument used by the Community for non-Lomé countries is the Generalised Scheme of Preferences (GSP), operated by the Community under the Common Commercial Policy. The GSP is a UN-sponsored scheme introduced in 1971, under which developed countries have agreed to give tariff concessions to all developing countries and to seek to make continuous improvements to them. As they are improved, so the preferences granted under Lomé are reduced, which has caused problems for ACP countries. The present Community GSP arrangements came into effect in December 1980 and were designed to last for ten years, with annual reviews and a major review in the fifth year. The main thrust of the new arrangements was to concentrate the benefits on the poorest and less competitive developing countries.

The need to continue to give a margin of preference to the ACPs complicates the Community's relations with other developing countries. Britain, for example, would have liked to see the Commonwealth countries of Southern Asia included in any successor to the Yaoundé Conventions and receive aid and preferential access. But it became clear in the earlier negotiations on British entry that this was unacceptable to the Six, who feared that a country as large and as powerful as India would dominate any association and take up a disproportionate amount of aid. The most the Six would agree to was the Joint Declaration of Intent. This set out the Community's intention to do all it could to extend and strengthen trade relations with Ceylon (later Sri Lanka), India, Pakistan (Bangladesh was later added), Malaysia and Singapore. All benefit from the Community's GSP. The Community has concluded non-preferential trade agreements, known as commercial cooperation agreements, with all except Malaysia and Singapore. These two countries at first saw little advantage in such agreements, but in 1980 joined the rest of the Association of South East Asian Nations (ASEAN Indonesia, the Philippines, and Thailand), in signing an economic and commercial cooperation agreement with the Community which does not involve any preferential treatment for ASEAN exports to the Community (although ASEAN countries receive GSP concessions). The agreement also has a political aspect in that Community Foreign Ministers, acting in the framework of European Political Cooperation, discuss foreign policy issues with their ASEAN counterparts.

In 1983 the Community signed an agreement similar to that signed with ASEAN with the countries of the ANDEAN Pact (Bolivia, Colombia, Ecuador, Peru and Venezuela) although Ecuador delayed ratification. There is also an agreement with the five Central American countries (Nicaragua, Costa Rica, Honduras, El Salvador and Guatemala) who are parties to the General Treaty on South America, an agreement that had an additional political dimension given the conflict in the area. Discussions with the countries of the Gulf Cooperation Council (GCC – Bahrain, Kuwait, Oman, Saudi Arabia and the United Arab Emirates) continue. There have been strong pressures from the GCC for a preferential or free trade agreement, although the Community prefers a normal commercial cooperation agreement. The Community has commercial cooperation agreements with other non-Lomé countries (still sometimes referred to as 'Non-associates') such as Mexico, Brazil, Uruguay and China. The agreement with Argentina was abrogated by the Argentinians, before the Falkland Islands conflict, on the grounds that they received little benefit from it.

During the early 1980s, largely because of the world economic recession, there was a general movement away from the search for global solutions for economic problems which had characterised the 1960s and 1970s together with demands for a New International Economic Order (NIEO). While many of the most heavily indebted countries still looked for global solutions to cover their own debt problems, in fact, negotiations have been conducted between individual debtor countries and their creditors. In the same way, attention has turned more to the solution of the problems of individual developing countries or regions, particularly sub-Saharan Africa. In 1984, the Community's as well as much of the world's attention became focused on the famine which resulted from a tragic combination of economic and political mismanagement, drought and harvest failures. The disaster underlined the need for close cooperation between aid donors and recipients in directing aid efficiently both in the long and the short term.

The immediate need of many African countries in these conditions has been for food aid. The Community has had a food aid policy for many years. It is a member of the Food Aid Convention and has undertaken to provide 1 670 000 tonnes of wheat or wheat equivalent per annum. The British national share is 110 700 tonnes. The Community share is 927 700 tonnes, to which all the member states contribute through the Community Budget. Food aid has played a major role in providing famine relief in Africa, particularly Ethiopia and the Sudan. In addition to its regular food aid programme, the Community provides emergency aid. Following a commitment made by the European Council in Dublin on 3/4 December 1984, for example, the Community and member states provided emergency relief in the form of almost 1.2 million tonnes of grain to countries in Africa severely affected by famine. The 1986 Budget also included provision for a reserve within the food aid programme for use, if and when required.

The Community's food aid policy has generally had as much to do with reducing European food surpluses as with helping those with food deficits. This is commendable in many instances, but food aid can be a double-edged instrument. Most of the Community's food products stockpiled under the CAP are unsuitable for famine relief or have much cheaper substitutes which can provide equivalent levels of nutrition. Moreover, in the longer term, food aid provided for general developmental purposes rather than for emergency relief can be dangerous: it can, for example, depress the prices of local produce and therefore production; it can introduce damaging dietary habits; and it can increase dependence on imports. The British, among others, have therefore argued that food aid should be concentrated on emergencies. As this has not been generally accepted, the Community will continue to provide a significant quantity of food aid, and concern over its effectiveness will persist.

All aid donors, and not just the Community, are under pressure to increase their aid to developing countries and to improve its effectiveness. But aid cannot have maximum impact over the longer term unless developing countries have easy or easier access to wider markets, especially those of the developed world. A halt to protectionism is obviously of vital importance. The Uruguay Round of the GATT is thus a crucial negotiation for developing countries alongside negotiations on aid and technical assistance.

SUGGESTED FURTHER READING

F. A. M. Alting von Geusau, *The Lomé Convention and a New Economic Order* (Sijthoff, 1977)

S. Harris and B. Bridges, *European Interests in ASEAN* (Routledge & Kegan Paul/LIIA, 1983)

F. Long (ed.), *The Political Economy of EC Relations with African, Caribbean and Pacific States* (Pergamon, 1980)

J. Ravenhill, *Collective Clientelism: The Lomé Conventions and North-South Relations* (Columbia University Press, 1985)

C. Stevens (ed.), *EEC and the Third World: A Survey – Vol I, 1981, Vol. II, 1982* annually (Hodder & Stoughton/ODI/IDS)

C. Cosgrove Twitchett, *Europe and Africa: A Framework for Development* (George Allen & Unwin, 1981)

For Treaty references, see: Treaty of Rome, Part IV, Articles 131–6 and Annex IV.

17 Political Cooperation

Cooperation among the twelve member states of the Community on foreign policy became regarded as a major achievement of the later 1970s. In part this was because in contrast to the seemingly endless wrangles within the Community, cooperation on foreign policy appeared to be developing particularly smoothly. The beginnings of what is known as European Political Cooperation (EPC) were extremely modest; it was designed as a tentative first step towards political unification and was based on inter-governmental cooperation outside the formal Community structure. As a result it was viewed with considerable suspicion by many federalists and other supporters of Community orthodoxy. However, the distinction between the inter-governmental political cooperation machinery and the Community, as such, became increasingly blurred. The Community and the twelve member states were obliged to respond to too many issues that could not clearly be categorised Community as such and this was formally recognised by Foreign Ministers in the London Report of the Ten in 1981. The Single European Act of 1986 went further, both by declaring that the European Commission should be fully associated with EPC and demanding that Community and EPC policies should be consistent. None the less, if the issue of Community–EPC relations has been settled, there remains a major question mark over the extent to which foreign policy and security and defence policies can be or should be separated.

The Treaty of Rome limits the external role of the Community largely to trade and some aid. The Commission negotiates on behalf of the Community with third countries or in international organisations on a mandate agreed by the member states in the Council of Ministers. Questions related, in the broadest sense, to issues of security (sometimes described as 'high politics', as distinct from 'low politics' or economic issues) remained the prerogative of the member states. None the less, countries, especially in the Third World, where matters such as aid and cooperation are 'high' rather than 'low' politics, tended increasingly to view the Community as the relevant body in external relations. Among the member states, however, the traditional prerogative of the state has been particularly guarded by the French. The Commission's formal diplomatic style, as much as the content of its policy, was one issue which aggravated the tension between General de Gaulle and the Commission. Although de Gaulle had himself proposed closer cooperation on foreign policy issues in the early 1960s (p. 8), based very firmly on the principle of inter-governmental cooperation, it was seen to a considerable extent as a means of bolstering France's own foreign policy, independent of that of the United States and the UK. To that extent, therefore, it had been unacceptable to the other members of the Community.

The Hague Summit of 1969, after de Gaulle's retirement, returned to the subject of political union and closer political cooperation. It did so as a response to growing international pressures as much as from the political desire for greater integration. The stature and weight of the Community in economic terms was in no way complemented by its political influence, or that of its individual members. The increasing number of multilateral negotiations, on issues that went beyond those designated the responsibility of the Community, complicated the ability of the Community and the member states to negotiate effectively. The United States also appeared increasingly frustrated by a situation in which on some issues it had to speak to the Commission, and on others to the Six individually. Under Dr Kissinger, US foreign policy clearly favoured the recognition by the Six of the interrelationship between economic and political issues and, indeed, defence issues.

The Hague Summit, avoiding details itself, called for a study of possible steps towards political unification. Compared to the ambitiousness of the Werner Plan to bring about Economic and

Monetary Union (see Chapter 13), the proposals of the so-called Davignon Committee (named after the then Belgian Political Director, Vicomte Davignon) were modest and cautious. The objectives set out in his report were 'to ensure, through regular exchanges of information and consultations, a better mutual understanding on the great international problems; to strengthen their [that is, the member states'] solidarity by promoting the harmonisation of their views, the coordination of their positions and, where possible and desirable, common actions'. The machinery proposed was also modest. Foreign Ministers, meeting as a Conference of Ministers, rather than as the Council of Ministers within the Community framework, were to meet at least twice a year in the capital of the country holding the Presidency of the Council of Ministers. Below the ministerial level, a Political Committee was created of Political Directors (in the UK a senior Under-Secretary in the FCO) which mirrored the Community's Committee of Permanent Representatives, and which was to meet at least four times a year. Provision was also made for the establishment of working groups to deal with specific issues. The machinery is organised and coordinated by the country holding the Presidency of the Council, a solution which overcame past problems, largely caused by the French insistence that any permanent Political Committee should be located in Paris, rather than in Brussels. It was only in 1986 that agreement was reached on a small permanent secretariat to service the Presidency. The country holding the Presidency was also given the responsibility of reporting on the work of the political cooperation machinery to the European Parliament.

The establishment of the political cooperation procedure in 1970 was an important landmark in the continuous debate on the character of Western European integration. Political cooperation was based, not on the Treaty of Rome, but on the mandate of the Heads of Government of the Six and was, therefore, separate from, if related to, the Community proper. It gave rise to some considerable concern, especially within the Commission which was initially formally excluded from the new machinery. The fear was that a new flexible machinery based solely on unanimity would threaten the established position of the Community in favour of Gaullist intergovernmentalism. Certainly, the first few years of political cooperation saw long discussions on procedures and legal issues, particularly over the respective authority or competence of the member states and the Commission. The French, and later to some extent the British and the Danes, favoured a clear demarcation between political cooperation and Community business. The division between the two reached its most extreme form in a midday flight from Copenhagen, where Foreign Ministers had met to discuss political cooperation, to Brussels, where they met in the afternoon as the Council of Ministers.

However, such a rigid distinction gradually became untenable. In part this was in response to external demands on the Community and the member states. One of the first tests of the new procedure was the Conference on Security and Cooperation in Europe (CSCE), in which the 35 European and North American participants discussed, not only security and human rights issues, but also economic cooperation (in the so-called 'Basket II' of the Conference's Final Act). In many respects the CSCE welded political cooperation into a flexible and efficient procedure through which the member states could maintain a united front. The CSCE also laid the basis for a reasonable solution to the question of the relationship between Community coordination and political cooperation, since the Commission claimed, successfully, that the member states were not authorised to take decisions on their own in matters which fell within the scope of the Treaties, i.e. within Basket II, nor negotiate on them. Thus the Commission was included in the Nine's discussions and in the Conference itself (despite the non-recognition of the Community by the Soviet Union and many of its Warsaw Pact allies). A similar pattern was followed at the various follow-up meetings of the CSCE in Belgrade (1977–78) and Madrid (1980–83). The latter meeting, which saw considerable debate over the establishment of a subordinate Conference on Confidence and Security – Building Measures (otherwise known as the Conference on Disarmament in Europe which met in Stockholm 1984–86), revealed clearly the difficulties of separating out security issues from those of foreign and foreign economic policies.

Other issues, too, demanded the establishment of a *modus operandi* between the Community and European Political Cooperation. The Dialogue with members of the Arab League after the oil boycotts which followed the 1973 Arab-Israeli War, was begun in political cooperation. However, it was primarily seen to be a Dialogue on relatively low technical cooperation matters, which would necessarily include the Community as such. It was seen as necessary, though, for political cooperation to continue to be involved because the Dialogue was essentially concerned with highly political issues, including the recognition of the Palestine Liberation Organisation. While EPC remains quite distinct from the Community, the member states are now much more at ease with the distinction. Foreign Ministers often transact EPC business when they meet for Foreign Affairs Councils. The act of liaising between those involved in EPC and those on the Community side, while still respecting their different competences, appears to be well-developed.

While international problems frequently involve both EPC and the Community, their distinctiveness has sometimes been regarded as of considerable use. In Europe's relations with the United States, for example, the degree to which economic, political and strategic issues have been kept in separate compartments by both European and US governments in order not to affect the common underlying security interest adversely has sometimes been remarkable. That is not to say that periodic efforts have not been made to bring about a more comprehensive or 'ball-of-wax' approach, particularly on the part of the United States both at governmental and Congressional levels. At governmental level, the most notable attempt was that of Dr Henry Kissinger in 1973, in the so-called 'Year of Europe', when he suggested a new Atlantic Charter covering economic, political and defence issues. The proposal brought to the fore the differing attitudes of the members, particularly between France and the Eight. The immediate result was agreement among the Nine on a 'European Identity Paper', which was adopted by the Heads of Government at their meeting in Copenhagen in December 1973. To a certain extent, the Paper proposed a European identity that was unified only in contradistinction to an Atlantic identity. But it also suggested the existence of serious divisions between Europe and America that have not been far below the surface during the past decade. These can be seen over a wide range of issues: in East–West relations, for example, over sanctions against the Soviet Union and Poland after the imposition of martial law in December 1980; or over the Middle East issues, with American hostility to the Ten's Declaration of Venice, also of 1980, which called for the inclusion of the PLO in the search for peace, and widespread European opposition to the American military strike against

Colonel Qaddafi in 1986. At the same time, increasing differences over trade issues, especially steel and agriculture, led many in Congress to question the political and military value of the Atlantic Alliance – or at least the cost of America's commitment to it, in terms of US troops stationed in Europe. However, both European and American governments have continued to emphasise the importance of the Atlantic Alliance, even while recognising the stresses to which it has been subjected.

Such an emphasis on 'European' differences with the United States should not, of course obscure the range and the depth of the links between individual European governments and the US. These bilateral ties often remain crucial. None the less, as a result of the concern aroused by the Year of Europe over Euro-American relations a procedure known as the 'Gymnich formula' was introduced in order to encourage a better understanding of each other's viewpoint. This was agreed on by Foreign Ministers meeting at the Schloss Gymnich in Germany in 1974. It entails the Presidency of the Council (acting as the chairman of political cooperation) informing the US of the discussions held by Foreign Ministers and discussing the broad outlines of the issues beforehand.

The initially modest political cooperation procedure has now extended to a wide network of contacts. The 1972 Summit agreed that political cooperation should include consideration of medium and long-term common positions. The 1973 Summit increased the number of Ministerial meetings to four a year, and formally recognised the creation of a new group, European Correspondents, below that of Political Directors, to provide closer liaison among Foreign Ministries. Their role is almost exclusively geared to making the political cooperation machinery work. Preparation for the Political Directors' meetings, now usually monthly, is largely carried out in various working groups, attended by experts from member states' Foreign Ministries. Increased cooperation among embassies in third countries was also encouraged, and closer contact with community institutions were held to be necessary. A telex network, COREU, was also created so that Foreign Ministries could be in touch immediately and continuously.

The outcome has been a growing collective involvement of diplomats from the member states in most major – and many minor – international issues. These range from the conflicts in the Middle East and the Eastern Mediterranean, including Cyprus, to Southern Africa, South East Asia, and Central America. Consultations at the United Nations have become particularly firmly established even if the result has not always been common voting on the part of member governments. International terrorism has also featured prominently on the EPC agenda with, for example, the establishment of the so-called Trevi group. Common voting at the UN or the increasing number of common declarations have sometimes marked an important change in national foreign policies. However, the instruments available to underpin such declarations have frequently been beyond the control of EPC. Action in the field of aid and trade, for example, is within the competence of the Community. It is here that close interaction between the two bodies is vital. In the Falkland Islands conflict between the UK and Argentina in 1982, for example, the condemnation of the Argentine invasion and the possibility of a trade embargo were first discussed in EPC (by the Political Directors who happened to be meeting on another issue), and then in the EC. The issue and the response demanded inevitably straddled both EPC and EC concerns – although the actual details of the embargo were of course worked out in the EC framework, particularly, at official level, by COREPER.

The successful interaction between EPC and the EC over the Falklands (even if the sanctions agreement lasted for only a month) reflected the gradual integration of the two systems that has characterised the 1970s. The involvement of the European Commission in EPC, initially often barred, later accepted only on sufferance, was finally accepted as a necessity in the London Report of 1981, and as a legal fact in 1986 in the Single European Act which dealt with EPC and the EC together. But if the 1970s marked the closer integration of foreign policy and external economic relations, there was less success in allowing for consultation on wider security and defence issues. There were strong pressures for such discussions as they related to foreign policy, partly arising from the very success of Foreign Ministers in reaching agreement on a growing number of issues in EPC. In part too it was seen as a logical development that built on discussions within the CSCE framework. It was also regarded as of increasing necessity in view of the growing strains to which the Atlantic Alliance appeared to be subject.

But there was also considerable reluctance on the part of some member governments to allow for the greater discussion of security issues, notably on the part of Ireland, which as a neutral state was not, of course, party to NATO discussions, Denmark, which has sometimes appeared a reluctant member of the Atlantic Alliance and opposed to further moves which might complicate relations with its Nordic partners, and, after 1980, Greece. In view of the need for unanimity, the result was a heavily qualified statement in the London Report of Foreign Ministers issued in 1981 that the political aspects of security might be discussed within the EPC framework – a lack of any more precise definition appeared to reflect the view that vagueness was synonymous with flexibility. However, the limitations imposed upon the consideration of security issues led the seven members of EPC who were also members of Western European Union (established in 1948 under the Brussels Treaty and extended in 1954 to include Italy and West Germany) to try to revitalise the latter body. In 1984 a number of changes were introduced in WEU with the aim of re-establishing it as the major forum for the discussion of defence and security issues. However, a number of doubts remain as to its effectiveness, its membership (several other states immediately applied for membership including Portugal) and its relationship with NATO and with EPC. Under the SEA, defence issues remain firmly within the province of NATO and WEU. However, it declares that the Twelve 'are ready to coordinate their positions more closely on the economic and political aspects of security' (Article 30, para. 6). Where more precisely the distinction lies between these aspects of security and defence issues is likely to remain little more than a rule of thumb, but there are likely to be pressures for the widest interpretation of 'the economic and political aspects of security'.

The procedural and political limitations of EPC remain significant. The latter have perhaps been most clearly revealed in the somewhat maverick behaviour of the Greek Government under Mr Papandreou which has caused a number of declarations on the Middle East, for example, to be issued by the Nine (later the Eleven) with Greece publicly dissenting. EPC remains, in other words, an inter-governmental procedure subject, among other things, to the consequences of democratic change. Procedurally too, despite the various Reports refining and enlarging on the scope and depth of consultations, it retains a number of weaknesses. The machinery remains in the hands of the Presidency of the Council – without, that is, a permanent home – and is susceptible, therefore, to breaks in continuity. An attempt to offset this was made with the introduction of the 'troika' principle, whereby the Presidency was assisted by the immediately preceding and the immediately succeeding Presidencies. The Single European Act has now created a small permanent secretariat in Brussels to assist the Presidency and so again reduce the problems of discontinuity, although its precise role has yet to be determined.

While there has been a steady development of the range of common foreign policy positions adopted by the member states this does not mean that the Twelve have yet evolved a common foreign policy. In terms of procedure, cooperation among the Twelve has developed extensively, as can be seen in the range of consultations that take place at the level of national capitals, embassies in third countries and in Brussels. However, even after such extensive consultations and when common positions have been agreed, the Twelve still tend to speak in harmony rather than in unison, so allowing for the nuances created by different traditions and approaches and, indeed, interests. EPC continues above all to be a procedure. It has, partially as a result, often been criticised for providing only a means by which member states can react to events rather than take more positive action. It has also been held to encourage declarations rather than action. Both criticisms are to some extent valid, yet both also perhaps miss the point: much of diplomacy is inevitably reactive, without the additional difficulty of getting 12 member states to react together; a great deal of diplomacy is also 'verbal' or declaratory – few states even of middle size have the ability or the inclination to take either economic or military action unless obliged to do so. Thus even if EPC does not yet add up to a common foreign policy, the habit of cooperation has taken root firmly. Even if a country in the end decides to take a step unilaterally, it now has to weigh up the advantages of doing so against the disadvantages of having to provide lengthy explanations to its partners.

SUGGESTIONS FOR FURTHER READING

D. Allen, R. Rummel and W. Wessels, *European Political Co-operation* (Butterworth, 1981)

D. Allen and A. Pijpers (eds), *European Foreign Policy-Making and the Arab–Israeli Conflict* (Martinus Nijhoff, 1984)

Sir B. Burrows and G. Edwards, *The Defence of Western Europe* (Butterworth, 1982)

C. Hill (ed.), *National Foreign Policies and European Political Cooperation* (George Allen & Unwin/RIIA, 1983)

W. Paterson and W. Wallace (eds), *Foreign Policy-Making in Western Europe* (Saxon House,1978)

P. de Schouteete, *La Cooperation Politique Europeene* (Libor, Brussels, Second edition, 1986).

T. Taylor, *European Defence Cooperation* (Routledge & Kegan Paul/RIIA, 1985)

Abbreviations Commonly Used in the Community

AASMM	Associated African States, Madagascar and Mauritius (Associated under the Yaoundé Agreements)
ACP	African, Caribbean and Pacific States (signatories of the Lomé Convention)
ASEAN	Association of South East Asian Nations
BLEU	Belgian–Luxembourg Economic Union
BRITE	Basic Research in Industrial Technologies for Europe
CAP	Common Agricultural Policy
CARICOM	Caribbean Community and Common Market
CBI	Confederation of British Industry
CCAs	Common Commercial Agreements
CCP	Common Commercial Policy
CDI	Centre for the Development of Industry (Lomé)
CERD	European Research and Development Committee
CERN	European Organisation for Nuclear Research
CET	Common External Tariff
CFP	Common Fisheries Policy

CID	Centre for Industrial Development
CIEC	Conference on International Economic Cooperation
CMEA (or Comecon)	Council for Mutual Economic Assistance
COMITEXTIL	Coordination Committee for the Textile Industries of the European Community
COPA	Committee of Agricultural Organisations in the European Community
COREPER	Committee of Permanent Representatives
CREST	Scientific and Technical Research Committee
CSA	Commonwealth Sugar Agreement
CSCE	Conference on Security and Cooperation in Europe
CTI	Technical Centre for Agricultural and Rural Cooperation (Lomé)
DG	Directorate-General of the European Commission
EAGGF/FEOGA	European Agricultural Guidance and Guarantee Fund
ECE	United Nations Economic Commission for Europe
ECSC	European Coal and Steel Community
ECMT	European Conference of Ministers of Transport
ECOFIN	Council of Ministers – Economic and Finance Ministers
ECU	European Currency Unit
EDC	European Defence Community
EDF	European Development Fund
EEC	European Economic Community
EFTA	European Free Trade Association
EIB	European Investment Bank
EMCF	European Monetary Cooperation Fund
EMS	European Monetary System
EMU	Economic and Monetary Union
EP	European Parliament
EPC	(originally) European Political Community, (more commonly) European

	Political Cooperation
ERDF	European Regional Development Fund
ESC	Economic and Social Committee of the European Community
ESF	European Social Fund
ESPRIT	European Strategic Programme for Research and Development in Information Technology
ETUC	European Trades Union Confederation
EUA	European Unit of Account
EUROFER	European Confederation of the Iron and Steel Industry
Euratom	European Atomic Energy Community
FAST	Forecasting and Assessment in Science and Technology
GATT	General Agreement on Tariffs and Trade
GCC	Gulf Cooperation Council
GSP	Generalised Scheme of Preferences
ICAO	International Civil Aviation Organisation
IEA	International Energy Agency (OECD)
IMF	International Monetary Fund
IMPs	Integrated Mediterranean Programmes
JET	Joint European Torus
JRC	Joint Research Centre
LDC	Less developed country
MCA	Monetary Compensatory Amount
NATO	North Atlantic Treaty Organisation
NGOs	Non-governmental Organisations
OAU	Organisation of African Unity
OCT	Overseas Countries and Territories
OECD	Organisation for Economic Cooperation and Development

OECC	Organisation for European Economic Cooperation
PREST	Scientific and Technical Research Policy Committee
RACE	Research and Development in Advanced Communication Technology in Europe
SDI	Strategic Defense Initiative
SEA	Single European Act
SME	Small and Medium-sized Enterprises
STABEX	Export Revenue Stabilisation Scheme
SYSMIN	System for Safeguarding and Developing Mineral Production
TACs	Total Allowable Catches
ua	unit of account
UNCTAD	United Nations Conference on Trade and Development
UNICE	Confederation of Industries of the European Community
VAT	Value Added Tax
WEU	Western European Union

Major Sources of Information on the Community and its Policies

General information on Community policies

The Commission of the European Communities Information Offices
8 Storey's Gate
London SW1P 3AT   01-222 8122

4 Cathedral Road
Cardiff CF1 9SG   0222-37 1631

7 Alva Street
Edinburgh EH2 4PH   031-225 2058

Windsor House 9/15 Bedford Street
Belfast BT2 7EG   0232-40708

European Parliament Office
2 Queen Anne's Gate
London SW1H 9AA   01-222 0411

The best detailed sources of information on current Community politics are:

Agence Europe (daily)
European Report (fortnightly)

Journals and other sources include:

International Affairs

Journal of Common Market Studies

West European Politics

World Today

and Reports of the Select Committees on the European Communities of the House of Lords and the House of Commons.

Index

220